The Clinician's Guide to

SUICIDE MANAGEMENT

A Proactive, Compassionate Approach to Manage Risk, Navigate Crises, and Minimize Hospitalization

PAUL BRASLER, LCSW, CAIMHP

THE CLINICIAN'S GUIDE TO SUICIDE MANAGEMENT
Copyright © 2025 by Paul Brasler

Published by
PESI Publishing, Inc.
3839 White Ave
Eau Claire, WI 54703

Cover and interior design by Emily Dyer
Editing by Jenessa Jackson, PhD

ISBN 9781683738466 (print)
ISBN 9781683738473 (ePUB)
ISBN 9781683738480 (ePDF)

All rights reserved.
Printed in the United States of America.

It is difficult to dedicate a book about suicide to anyone, given its serious and difficult-to-discuss content. I am reminded of friends who died by suicide and clients I worked with who died by suicide (or unknown circumstances). The content of this work is dedicated to people who struggle with suicidal ideation, people touched by the suicide death of a loved one, and the many awesome people who dedicate their lives and their work to bring hope to this world.

The book itself, especially the time and energy spent writing it, I dedicate to my three sons:
Samuel (Sam) | Benjamin (Ben) | Elijah (Eli)

You are the absolute best sons a father could ever want. Your mother and I are so proud of the men you are becoming. I love you guys.

TABLE OF CONTENTS

Introduction 1

1. Suicide Defined 13
    Defining Suicide 14
    Language and the Stigma of Suicide 16
    Myths About Suicide 18
    Theoretical Basis of Suicide 24

2. Professional Self-Care, Part 1 29
    Establishing Safe Practices 29
    The Challenges of Working in Demanding Situations 31
    Countertransference 37
    The Importance of Informed Consent to Treatment 40
    Dealing with the Death of a Patient by Suicide 42
    Patients Who Conceal Their Suicidal Ideation 46

3. Suicide Risk and Protective Factors 49
    Suicide Risk Factors 49
    Additional Risk Factors 65
    The Swiss Cheese Model 66
    Protective Factors Against Suicide 73

4. Suicide Ideation to Action 79
    Suicidal Ideation 79
    Suicide Warning Signs 81
    Suicide Ideation-to-Action Theories 82
    Suicide Intent (Planning) 84
    Suicide Methods 85
    Relationship Between Method and Intent 86

  Suicide Attempts and Death by Suicide 90
  Non-Suicidal Self-Injury 92
  Malingering Patients 94

5. Suicide Screening and Assessment 97
  Making the Connection: The Importance of Set and Setting 97
  Screening Tools 99
  Suicide Assessment 102
  Sample Suicide Assessment 111

6. Additional Mental Health Emergencies 117
  Assessing Clients Who May Be Psychotic 117
  Preparing for Potentially Violent Clients 128
  Murder-Suicides 133
  Duty to Protect 137

7. Disposition 143
  Psychiatric Hospitalization 144
  Why No-Harm Contracts Are an Incredibly Bad Idea 150
  Safety Planning 151
  Collaborative Assessment for Management of Suicidality (CAMS) 156
  Sample Safety Plan 160

8. Treatment of the Suicidal Client, Part 1 163
  Cognitive Behavioral Therapy 164
  Brief Cognitive Behavioral Therapy for Suicide Prevention 177
  Dialectical Behavioral Therapy 179

9. Treatment of the Suicidal Client, Part 2 183
  Psychopharmacology of Suicide Treatment 183
  Ketamine and Psychedelic-Assisted Psychotherapy 184
  Spirituality and Suicide 190
  Case Management 193

10. Special Populations 195
Children and Adolescents.. 195
Active-Duty Military Personnel, Veterans, and First Responders 201
Older Adults.. 205
Supporting Loved Ones Affected by Suicide 207

11. Ethical and Legal Issues 209
A Client's Right to Self-Determination Versus Our Legal Responsibilities.. 209
Managing Liability 215
Decision-Making Trees 220

12. Professional Self-Care, Part 2 223
Ambivalent Endings... 224
How Do We Take Care of Ourselves? 228

References 231
Acknowledgments... 239
About the Author 241

INTRODUCTION

I wasn't sure what to do next.

I had passed my board exams about a year earlier, achieving my long-sought goal of becoming a licensed clinical social worker. During and immediately after my years of study in graduate school, I had accrued seven years of experience working in a residential treatment program for abused and traumatized adolescents (we called them "emotionally disturbed" back then) and had changed to a community-based outpatient counseling center for adolescents about a year and a half earlier. To supplement my income, I joined a moderate-sized outpatient therapy practice near my home to see clients in the evenings a few days a week.

This was my second session with Jason, a young man in his late 20s. He came to counseling to address his depressive symptoms, which appeared to be greatly impacted by his stressful job and problematic marriage.

"I sometimes wonder if it is all worth it," he said quietly, not looking at me.

"If what is worth it?" I asked.

"Getting up every day. Going to a job I hate. Trying to make my marriage work despite my wife's disinterest. I can't tell you how many times I've woken up in the morning and been disappointed that I didn't die in my sleep."

I suddenly felt slightly anxious. I sat up straight in my chair and leaned forward slightly.

"How long have you felt this way?" I asked.

"Several weeks, maybe a month," Jason replied. "It seems to be getting worse." Still no eye contact.

"Sounds kind of hopeless," I replied, without really thinking.

That seemed to grab Jason's attention, as he looked at me for the first time in several minutes. "It is," he said.

I paused, afraid to ask the question I knew I needed to ask—and fearful of what Jason might say.

I took a breath. "Jason, are you thinking about killing yourself?"

"Yeah. I am."

I took another breath. "Have you thought about how you might try to kill yourself?"

Jason paused, breaking eye contact with me. I could tell he was thinking hard, probably deciding how he was going to respond and how I might react.

"I've been thinking about a couple of things. I don't want it to hurt."

That stopped me in my tracks. My mind raced. What did I need to do? It was early evening, and a few other counselors were around, seeing patients, but I did not know who to ask for guidance. In the residential treatment program where I had worked, there were protocols and a lot of other staff in place when we were confronted with people who were suicidal. At my full-time job at the counseling center, we had a whole crisis team on standby for situations like this. But at the private practice, I was alone and in somewhat uncharted territory. I was unsure what to do. I was afraid to say the wrong thing, but there was Jason, looking at me and wondering what my next move would be.

As is true for many clinicians, my formal education, field placements, internships, supervision, and initial clinical experiences had lacked exposure to people experiencing suicidal ideation or behaviors. What I had learned about suicide was often confusing and even contradictory. For example, I remembered a field supervisor assuring me that clients who signed a "no-harm contract" rarely died by suicide—but then I also remembered a peer who was quick to call the police and have clients assessed for suicide by the local community-based crisis team any time a person mentioned suicide. I considered what I could and could not do in an outpatient setting. What if Jason decided to walk out? What if he wound up killing himself? How would my actions impact my license? What would my employer say? I thought about the fact that I had another client scheduled after Jason—what would I do with that person if I was still trying to solve this situation?

I took a deep breath and asked Jason to explain more about what he was feeling. He said that he felt trapped and disconnected from others. While he had some vague thoughts of how he might try to kill himself, he admitted to being ambivalent about wanting to die. I thanked him for being honest with me. As we talked, he identified several people, including his father, who were supportive and understanding of him. We then created a plan that included calling his father and arranging for Jason to "take a break" and spend some time with his father before

Introduction

he decided what to do about his marriage and job. Jason and I agreed to speak by phone daily over the next few days, and we scheduled our next session for the following week. I left my practice that night greatly relieved but also cognizant of my lack of experience and understanding of working with people who were suicidal. That realization led me to want to learn more about suicide.

That was 20 years ago. Since that time, I've spent 10 years working in emergency departments in my community, and I later ran a behavioral health clinic as part of an integrated federally qualified health center in Richmond, Virginia. In those settings, nearly every day, I encountered people experiencing suicidal ideation, people with suicide plans and intent, people who had attempted suicide, and occasionally, people who would later die by suicide. I also engaged with people who were violent, some of whom expressed homicidal ideations. In addition, I regularly interacted with people living with psychotic disorders, including people experiencing substance-induced psychosis and people living with schizophrenia.

It was in the emergency department that I honed my skills working with clients in crisis, particularly people experiencing a mental health emergency—most often suicidal ideation or behaviors. I had the awesome pleasure of working alongside medical and mental health professionals who taught me a lot. Soon, I had the opportunity to supervise students working in their field placements. That, in turn, led to me teaching at the graduate level at Virginia Commonwealth University, my alma mater for my master of social work. In 2016, I started teaching a class for PESI—Mental Health Emergencies—which later evolved into High-Risk Clients. I was lucky enough to publish a book based on this course in 2019. In many ways, this text is an expansion of what I tried to do in that book.

I continue to see clinicians and other professionals struggle when working with people who are suicidal (or psychotic or potentially violent). They struggle because they lack the same education and practical tools I did when faced with clients in crisis like Jason. I decided to undertake the endeavor of writing this book because I want people who help others in crisis to feel more confident in their responses to those in need.

Reflecting on my early clinical experiences, I can identify four major knowledge and practice gaps in our field. First, a lot of what I *thought* I knew about suicide as a new clinician ended up being outdated, a myth, or plain wrong. For example:

- "If I ask someone about suicide, it might make them want to kill themselves."
- "No-harm contracts work."
- "More suicides occur during the winter holidays than any other time."
- "People who cut themselves are rarely, if ever, actually suicidal."
- "If I send the client to the hospital, it will destroy our therapeutic relationship."
- "If I don't immediately send the client to the hospital, I could lose my license or get sued for malpractice."
- "If a client dies by suicide, it will be my fault."

As is the case for many clinicians, my coursework, supervision, and clinical experiences included little information on suicide and (more importantly) how to work with a person sitting across from me saying, "I want to die!" In fact, while conducting research for this book, I came across the following quote that summarized what I saw as a huge need in our profession:

> [Most] mental health professionals receive little to no skills-based training in suicide-focused treatments and interventions. This happens in part because most of the instructors and supervisors affiliated with mental health professional training programs did not receive this training themselves. As a result, status quo knowledge and expertise are passed down to their students, some of whom will eventually become instructors and supervisors themselves and pass down status quo knowledge and expertise again. Even more alarming, however, is how many mental health professionals—up to one in three, according to one study—continue to endorse older, less effective procedures like contracting for safety even *after* they have received training in suicide-focused treatments. (Bryan, 2022, p. 145)

Introduction

In this book, I will delve into this complex topic and examine evidence-based and up-to-date information, including tools you can use to help your clients in crisis.

Second, on many occasions when I worked in the emergency department, I assessed clients who had been sent there for mentioning suicidal ideation to their counselor. Most of these individuals had no plan to harm themselves, let alone any intention to die—they had simply expressed how they were thinking and feeling. Repeatedly, I heard clients tell me, "I was just saying how I felt. I wish my therapist had heard me out instead of jumping to conclusions." The reason many clinicians automatically send their clients straight to the emergency room whenever they hear the word *suicide* is because they believe that to do otherwise will endanger their careers or put them at risk of a lawsuit. They are also worried about their clients and unsure of what to do. We jump to conclusions when we feel afraid or unprepared. We jump to conclusions when we do not know what else to do. This book can change that.

Third, I quickly realized that experienced crisis clinicians (often with years of service), used a variety of factors to determine whether a person was at imminent risk of suicide or homicide—or was experiencing psychosis—but there was little consistency in their decision-making. Many clinicians used their "gut" to make decisions or used outdated (or inappropriate) tools to make decisions that radically impacted another person's life. While we cannot, with absolute certainty, predict a person's behaviors, there are ways we can accurately measure risk and communicate a plan to patients (and their families) that provides appropriate care and keeps everyone safe.

Lastly, I found that clients who wound up being hospitalized needed quick and appropriate follow-up by their outpatient providers *and* other members of their community. A growing body of research suggests that a psychiatric hospitalization can contribute to client suicide within a year of hospitalization (Baldessarini et al., 2019; Fehling & Selby, 2021; Hughes et al., 2023), possibly because the treatment provided in psychiatric hospitalization does not directly address the client's suicidal behaviors and the experience of hospitalization is more traumatic than helpful. A key to changing this is to explore options other than hospitalization when possible, as well as providing prompt, appropriate, and sometimes intensive follow-up once the client is discharged. Many clinicians believe their job ends when their client is admitted, but the opposite is true—their job has just begun. This book will provide you with tools to help your clients during this extremely tough time.

Who Is This Book For?

Given the correlation between mental illness and suicide, you might assume this book is only for mental health professionals, such as psychiatrists, psychologists, clinical social workers, or professional counselors. While mental illnesses can be a factor in suicidal behavior, any person can be at risk of suicide, so this book is intended to benefit anyone working in a human-service capacity, including the following:

- Marriage and family therapists
- Substance use treatment providers
- Case managers
- Pharmacists
- Medical physicians
- Physician assistants
- Nurse practitioners
- Registered nurses
- Probation and parole officers
- Judges
- Police officers
- Paramedics and other first responders
- Clergy
- Chaplains
- Military religious affairs specialists
- Teachers
- School administrators
- Concerned parents

While this book is intended for a variety of helping professionals, I expect that most readers will be behavioral health clinicians or medical providers. Because of this, I will use the word *client* to describe any person we are trying to help. At times, when discussing clients who are in a hospital setting, I will use the word *patient*. Remember that regardless of your practice setting, you should strive to treat people as unique individuals who deserve the best from you.

In addition, while I hope this book will provide health professionals with readily accessible information on working with clients who are suicidal or experiencing another type of mental health emergency, I want to make it clear that this book is not just for people working in crisis environments. I left the

Introduction

emergency department after 10 years and returned to a community-based outpatient practice, where I saw firsthand how quickly clients were sent to the emergency room after expressing suicidal ideation. I spent much of my first year in this new position working with my teammates to unlearn a lot of what they had been told about the necessity of immediately sending clients to the hospital. I also saw how much anxiety my peers exhibited when they had to reengage with clients who had been admitted for psychiatric care, as my colleagues were afraid they wouldn't know what to do. Therefore, this book is also designed to help you work with your clients after the immediate crisis is over.

What Is in This Book?

This book is organized into the following 12 chapters:

Chapter 1: Suicide Defined

While society appears to be more willing to talk openly about suicide, myths about suicide continue to confuse people and further stigmatize those struggling with suicidal thinking or behaviors. In this chapter, I will attempt to define suicide in a way that decreases stigma. I will also examine some of the theoretical bases of suicide.

Chapter 2: Professional Self-Care, Part 1

In this chapter, I examine the challenges of working in demanding situations, including burnout, compassion fatigue, and vicarious trauma, and review the importance of establishing safe practices regardless of setting, including informed consent to treatment. I also discuss how to navigate countertransference, deal with the death of a patient by suicide, and work with patients who conceal their suicidal ideation.

Chapter 3: Suicide Risk and Protective Factors

People rarely engage in suicidal behaviors because of a single risk factor (or even a few risk factors). Therefore, this chapter introduces the many risk factors that clinicians need to be aware of, particularly the role of trauma, when assessing clients for suicidality. It also examines the importance of protective factors when responding to clients struggling with suicidal ideation.

Chapter 4: Suicide Ideation to Action

Thinking about suicide and attempting suicide are two different phenomena. This chapter will answer questions such as: How does a person move (or not move) from thinking about suicide to acting on their thoughts? How can we engage people at different points along this continuum? What are the means that people use to attempt (and die by) suicide? How are non-suicidal self-injurious behaviors connected (and not connected) with suicide?

Chapter 5: Suicide Screening and Assessment

As you will learn, suicide is relatively rare, so identifying clients at greater risk of suicide can be difficult. In this chapter, you will learn about the more commonly used screening tools for depression and suicide, including how to best utilize them in practice. I will then introduce a comprehensive suicide assessment and discuss effective ways to conduct the assessment.

Chapter 6: Additional Mental Health Emergencies

Even more than working with people who are suicidal, clinical education and supervision often overlook how to work with potentially violent clients. This chapter answers questions such as: How do we prepare for potential violence? What are the risk factors for potential violence? What responsibility do we have for people who may be the targets of a client's threatened violence? It will also examine psychosis, the ways it can manifest, and how to respond appropriately.

Chapter 7: Disposition

When you have a client who expresses a desire to kill themselves, are there alternatives to automatically sending them to a hospital? In this chapter, I discuss how to conduct safety planning with clients who are not in imminent danger of suicide and highlight why no-harm contracts are an incredibly bad idea. I also provide an overview of a very effective safety planning tool—the Collaborative Assessment for Management of Suicidality (CAMS)—and explain how this can be an alternative to psychiatric hospitalization in some situations.

Chapter 8: Treatment of the Suicidal Client, Part 1

This chapter centers on the use of cognitive behavioral therapy (CBT) for treating clients who are suicidal or have experienced a suicide attempt. I also examine a specific CBT approach—brief CBT (BCBT) for suicide prevention—and close the chapter by discussing dialectical behavioral therapy (DBT) and its use in treating chronically suicidal clients.

Chapter 9: Treatment of the Suicidal Client, Part 2

This chapter examines the role of pharmacotherapy in suicidal ideation and behaviors, including emerging trends such as psychedelic-assisted therapy. I also examine the role of spirituality in suicidal ideation and treatment, as for many people, their spirituality relates to their existential question of "to be or not to be." The chapter concludes with a discussion of case management and the importance of linking clients to additional services.

Chapter 10: Special Populations

This chapter explores interventions and assessments designed to help specific populations, including children, adolescents, and young adults, as well as military personnel and first responders, as these groups have unique challenges related to suicide. I also discuss suicide in older adults (one of the groups with the highest suicide rates) and how to help people in this age group. I conclude the chapter by examining how we can support individuals, families, and communities who have experienced a loss from suicide.

Chapter 11: Ethical and Legal Issues

The biggest concern for professionals working with suicidal clients, apart from the client's well-being, is the concern for their own legal liability. This chapter answers questions such as: How do we manage liability while providing the best possible care? How do we balance a client's right to self-determination with our societal and legal obligations? I present case studies and a decision-making tree to help navigate these issues.

Chapter 12: Professional Self-Care, Part 2

This closing chapter links to the second chapter by focusing on the emotional impact of working with people who are suicidal or experiencing another type of mental health emergency. I examine the difficulties of ambivalent endings when working in high-stress situations and discuss ways we can take care of ourselves (and our peers) when doing this demanding work.

Words of Warning and Hope

I don't know your story, and you'll find only a little of my story in these pages. However, our experiences shape how we think about and see the world, and some of our experiences can be traumatic, especially when it comes to suicide. As you delve into this material, I suggest you do so with an eye toward caring for yourself. If something is difficult to read and think about, then I invite you to step away and care for yourself. Only by taking care of yourself can you help others.

I also want to leave you with some words of hope as you begin reading these pages. In 2024, I was asked to give a brief commencement talk to a group of physician assistant students I had given half a dozen lectures to over the previous two years. As I tried to come up with something brief, and not a complete waste of everyone's time, I thought of some of the best advice I had been given. Here are some parts of the speech that I'd like you to keep in mind as you explore ways to help people.

Introduction

"Be Humble"

All the other things that will make you an exceptional clinician, partner, parent, or child, stem from this one way of living—being humble. What do I mean by this?

For starters, humility is the opposite of arrogance.

Arrogance leads to unnecessary mistakes. It ruins relationships. It causes unnecessary pain. Arrogance closes our minds to learning. Arrogance is also the opposite of wisdom. When you are humble, you listen. When you are arrogant, you hear only your voice. When you are humble, you can learn. Your best teachers will be your peers and your patients.

When you are humble, you realize that you are not what you do. So have a life outside of your job. Work hard and go home. Have interests and relationships outside of your work.

When you are humble, you can work as part of a team. You remember that nurses, technicians, physicians, pharmacists, registrars, administrators, custodians, chaplains, cooks, and (especially) social workers are just as important as you, and they know things you don't, and they can do things that you can't do—just as you know things and do things that they can't.

When you are humble, you know that you are not God. So don't act like God! Instead, be humble and believe in something that is greater than you!

When you are humble, you set boundaries with others. Being humble does not mean you let people abuse you or treat you poorly. It does not mean that you let people walk over you. Humble people kindly, but firmly, set limits with others.

Being humble means you don't gossip or treat others badly. Humble people are kind. You are secure in who you are and have no need to put yourself above others or pull people down to make yourself feel better.

Being humble means you take care of yourself, physically, emotionally, mentally, socially, and spiritually. You acknowledge that our time on Earth is limited, and you strive to make the most of every day.

Being humble means you can admit that things get under your skin—things can bother or hurt you. Treating a child you realize was abused, talking with a person who has been trafficked, trying to get through to a person you just revived after they overdosed, or having to tell a family that their loved one has died. This is difficult work. And when we are humble, we can admit to others and ourselves that the work is hard.

Being humble means we take time and space to think and feel what we need to think and feel. Being humble also means we accept that we may need help sometimes in navigating the difficulties of work and life.

CHAPTER 1

Suicide Defined

It comes as no surprise that a clinician's number one fear is that their client will kill themselves (Knapp, 2020). Sometimes, this fear can be overwhelming to the point that we as clinicians become paralyzed when faced with a client saying they are having serious thoughts of suicide or have a plan to die by suicide. We must acknowledge this fear and admit to ourselves that we may feel unequipped to help the person in front of us.

Anytime I teach a course, I start with two assumptions, which I call my "no duh!" statements. The first is that, as a helping professional, you must care about people in general. This may seem obvious, but one of the first things that happens when a provider becomes burnt out or experiences compassion fatigue is that they stop caring about people. A few years ago, one of my clinical supervisees noticed he was experiencing this, and he brought the matter to our group supervision. Before I could reply, he stated, "But that's on me, not my clients. I am responsible for whether I burn out or not." He used this insight to find a job in a healthier environment and he continues to excel in working with people in challenging situations.

The second assumption is that you must have the willingness and ability to connect with the person in front of you, whether it is a client, student, parishioner, or patient. The assumption is that you possess the basic skills needed to listen to others, hear (and observe) what they are trying to say, and then respond in an empathetic and professional manner. Does this mean you will like everyone you meet? Of course not. You do not need to like everyone you work with, and they do not have to like you, but you must be willing to work with that individual.

I include these assumptions because if you cannot agree with them, then most of what I say in this book will not be helpful. This work is based on these foundational assumptions. Furthermore, I cannot teach anyone how to care about people and how to connect with individuals in need. I believe that a person's education and life experiences create these values. Caring for people comes from your beliefs, specifically how you see the world and your role(s) in helping others. If you are unsure about this in your life, this could be a good time to reflect before reading any further.

Defining Suicide

Ronald Maris (2019), in his excellent book on suicide, *Suicidology: A Comprehensive Biopsychosocial Perspective*, quotes philosopher David Mayo (1992), who stated that suicide has four basic elements:

1. A death has occurred.
2. The death must be of one's own doing.
3. The ending of life was intentional.
4. The agency of death was active (occasionally passive).

Edwin Shneidman (1985) wrote an entire book defining suicide. He defines suicide as "a conscious act of self-induced annihilation, best understood as a multidimensional malaise in a needful individual who denies an issue for which suicide is perceived as the best solution" (p. 186).

For our purposes, I will define suicide as a person acting on their desire to die and taking an active (or sometimes passive) role in making their death occur. As you will see in the chapters ahead, there are many reasons why people consider, plan, desire, act upon, and succeed in killing themselves. While suicide is a broad concept, there are two types of "suicides" that I will not address in this book.

The first is altruistic suicide, or sacrificing one's life to save others. One example that comes to mind is a soldier or marine throwing themselves on a live hand grenade to absorb the blast and shrapnel to save their fellow soldiers or civilians. This is a definitive act—the person doing this likely knows they will not survive the event, but they sacrifice themselves to save others at the expense of their own life. Sometimes, heroes wind up losing their lives to save others, but we are unsure if they expected to die like someone throwing themselves on a bomb. A great example of this is Arland D. Williams Jr., a passenger on Air Florida flight 90 in 1982. Flight 90 took off from Washington National Airport outside of Washington, DC, and crashed shortly thereafter due to ice buildup on its wings. Williams was on the flight, and he survived the initial crash into the icy waters of the Potomac River. As rescue teams passed a rope to him in the water from a hovering helicopter, Williams, on five separate occasions, passed the line to other survivors and helped secure them so they could be taken ashore to safety. When the helicopter returned to Williams for the sixth time, some of the plane wreckage had shifted, pulling him underwater where he drowned. Did Williams know he was going to die? That remains a mystery. However, his altruistic act saved others. I will not consider altruistic or heroic sacrifices as suicide in this work.

Likewise, I will not consider the act of killing oneself (and others) as suicide if that takes place as part of a terror attack. The men who hijacked civilian airliners on September 11, 2001, planned to end their lives by crashing their planes into buildings. Their motivations were political and religious, and their actions were evil. I will not consider this as suicide in this book. Likewise, people who jumped to their deaths from the World Trade Center to avoid burning to death clearly took their lives, but it stands to reason they would not have had to make this choice had others not chosen to fly planes into the buildings. Incidentally, medical examiners later classified people who jumped to their deaths from the Twin Towers as homicide victims (Maris, 2019).

While I touch on physician-assisted suicide in a later chapter, I do not intend to look closely at this complex and ever-changing issue. In most situations where medically assisted suicide is considered, the person seeking death typically has a terminal illness, is competent to make decisions for themselves, and wants to avoid prolonged pain and suffering. This type of suicide is therefore different from the types of suicide I will examine throughout this book.

Language and the Stigma of Suicide

Despite increasing public awareness of suicide, the subject remains highly stigmatized. I believe that part of this is due to our society's general discomfort regarding death, but it is also because there are usually many unanswered questions when a person dies by suicide. Furthermore, we automatically equate suicide to mental illness, which itself remains stigmatized.

Many years ago, one of my friend's sons died by suicide. This was understandably devastating to all who knew the young man, especially his mother. She was wracked with guilt. How could this happen? Had she failed as a parent? Why hadn't she (or someone else) seen that her son was hurting?

The initial police report made things even more confusing when the investigating detective indicated that my friend's son's death was an accident. He had been drinking and was upset with his estranged girlfriend, and the detective thought he had not intended to die by suicide. Since he did not leave a suicide note, the detective said it was an accidental death. This action initially lightened the emotional load for my friend. Yes, her son was dead, but it was an accident, not a suicide. There was less shame. Talking about his death became easier for her and others.

A month or so later, the coroner labeled the death a suicide. My friend was confused, so she met with the detective again. He admitted that he had wanted to save my friend additional anguish, and while he had suspected that the death was a suicide, he labeled it accidental. This threw my friend back into self-blame and self-doubt and caused her to question whether she could go on with life herself. I also wondered how other people saw her. Did they say to themselves: *She must not have been a good mother,* or *I wonder what happened that he killed himself?*

Through the passage of time, a lot of hard work in counseling and support groups, and by leaning on her friends and family, my friend shed her feelings of shame and self-doubt. She still talks about her son and honors his life. I wonder, however, if her path to healing could have been easier if there were less stigma connected to families who experience a death by suicide.

Language plays an important role in maintaining and discouraging stigma, so how we talk about suicide is important. Knapp (2020) notes, "The phrase 'committed suicide' implies that the suicide [death] was a crime akin to committing robbery or committing murder. Instead, suicide almost always occurs when an individual's judgment is compromised by extreme negative emotions" (p. 13). We should also avoid terminology such as "successful suicide attempt" or "completed suicide" because it sounds as if the person accomplished something. As Knapp adds, the real accomplishment comes from remaining alive.

For our purposes, I will use the phrase "died by suicide" in this book. Some of the sources I quote may use older terminology, which is now considered outdated. Examples of this are suicidal "gestures," suicide threat, and parasuicide (a vague term used to address the full spectrum of violence directed against oneself). Two other terms I will use are:

- "Suicide attempt: A nonfatal, self-directed, potentially injurious behavior with any intent to die because of the behavior. A suicide attempt may or may not result in injury" (Bryan & Rudd, 2018, p. 34).

- "Non-suicidal self-injury: Behavior that is self-directed and deliberately results in injury or the potential for injury to oneself. There is no evidence, whether implicit or explicit, of suicidal intent" (Bryan & Rudd, 2018, p. 34).

Some people may ask: If we agree that suicide is to be discouraged (and I completely agree with this), then what is the problem with stigma being attached to it? As you will see when I examine the myriad risks and protective factors associated with suicide, fear of stigma is rarely a reason that a person thinking about suicide dissuades themself from acting on their thoughts. Rather, the stigma rests on the family, friends, and community connected to the person who dies by suicide (or makes a suicide attempt).

We have a tendency in our society to seek blame and find simple explanations for complex events. If something goes wrong, then someone *must* have done something wrong. There must be a reason. In the absence of clear answers, we seek blame, even if there really is no one to blame. People who have had a loved one die by suicide know this—they feel it deeply. At the time in their lives when they need the most support, they often find themselves alone, even outcasts. This is the stigma I hope we can begin to break down by learning more about why people die by suicide. To better understand suicide, we need to dispense with the myths that have been created about it.

Myths About Suicide

Part of what makes working with people who are suicidal so difficult is that we cannot predict which clients who express suicidal ideation may go on to attempt suicide (Knapp, 2020). Another factor that makes working in these clinical situations challenging is that there are still many myths about suicide that permeate clinical practice and society in general. As I pointed out in the introduction, many clinicians do not receive adequate training in working with people who are suicidal, largely because the people teaching them have limited experience in working with suicidal clients themselves.

The following are some of the myths associated with suicide, specifically in the United States.

1. Suicide is common.

We can agree that losing a single person to suicide is a tragedy. The reality, however, is that suicide is rare—which is one of the many reasons why studying it is so difficult (Maris, 2019). In 2022, the Centers for Disease Control and Prevention reported that just under 50,000 United States citizens died by suicide. This represented a 2.6 percent increase in suicide deaths from 2021, and suicide remained the 11th leading cause of death (CDC Newsroom, 2023). As you will see, the overall suicide death rate is likely higher than reported due to some suicide deaths being misclassified as accidents. However, when we consider that the US population was 333,300,000 in 2022, even if we double the suicide death rate to 100,000 people, the ratio of suicide death comes to 0.03 percent of the total population. Again, I am not minimizing the loss of any person, but I want to caution readers not to succumb to panic and see suicide everywhere. While each person likely carries varying degrees of risk, most people—including those with major depressive disorder, bipolar disorder, schizophrenia, substance use disorders, and a host of other risk factors and illnesses—will not die by suicide.

2. Suicide is predictable.

If suicide was predictable, then this book would be unnecessary. While we can identify risk factors, limit the methods that people use to kill themselves, treat underlying conditions that may increase suicide risk, and educate the public about risks of suicide, we cannot predict which individuals will attempt to kill themselves. Screening tools can help us identify risk and assessments can help us engage clients, but no single measure has been shown to be predictive (Bjureberg et al., 2022; Nock et al., 2022). When we acknowledge the difficult fact that suicide is unpredictable, perhaps we will stop looking for simple, easy-to-understand reasons as to why people kill themselves and instead embrace the larger complexity of the problem.

3. People who attempt suicide, or who die by suicide, have a mental illness.

Mental illnesses, particularly affective disorders such as depressive disorders and bipolar disorders, are more common among people who attempt and die by suicide, but mental illness itself is not a causative factor. I have heard friends and colleagues opine, "If they killed themselves, they must have been depressed." But this is simply not true in every suicide death. As you will see in the chapters ahead, mental illness is only part of the picture. Maris (2019) notes that some people who die by suicide never have a diagnosable mental illness.

4. People who attempt suicide, or who die by suicide, leave clues about their suicidal actions.

This is a multifaceted myth. Some believe that most people who die by suicide leave notes, but only around 15 to 20 percent of people who attempt or die by suicide leave any message (Maris, 2019). Many of us have also been taught that people who plan on killing themselves will give away prized possessions. While this may be true in some situations, most people who attempt or die by suicide do not leave any clues or messages.

5. The suicide rate is highest among adolescents and young adults.

Children, adolescents, and young adults who die by suicide may garner more attention than older adults who die by suicide, but the number of young people who die by suicide pales in comparison to middle-aged and elderly adults. Suicide rates typically increase as individuals age (Joiner, 2007; Maris, 2019). In 2022, the highest rates of suicide were people aged 85 and older (CDC, 2025). You will learn more about why this is the case in the coming chapters.

6. Suicide "runs" in families.

There is statistical evidence that having a relative die by suicide can be a risk factor for clients (Wasserman et al., 2021). There are a few reasons why this may be so, including broad genetic factors and learned behaviors, but there is no definitive causality between an individual's suicide and a family member's suicide. In other words, there does not appear to be a "suicide gene." Rather, suicide may occur more in some families than others due to many other variables that happen to be present in one family system versus another.

7. Suicide is typically due to one or two stressors.

Just as an attempted suicide or death by suicide is not necessarily due to a severe mental illness, there are usually many reasons that come together at the right time to lead to suicidal behavior. Trying to distill this complexity into something simplistic runs the risk of missing some of the factors that could contribute to suicide. As you will see when I examine suicide risk factors, many stressors or situations must come together at a specific moment that could lead to a suicide attempt.

8. Suicide is an impulsive act.

I noted earlier that suicide is not predictable, but that does not mean that suicide is necessarily impulsive. This can be difficult to accept when it appears that a suicide attempt or a death by suicide was impulsive. However, most suicide attempts and deaths are not impulsive (Joiner, 2007). Rather, people who attempt suicide have usually thought about killing themselves for some time. As you will see when I look at suicide risk factors, there are often "windows" during which suicide is higher than usual, and these windows usually involve many risk factors that come together at the same time, *plus* the presence of means, *plus* an initiating event (Jobes, 2023). Recognizing this can be a key to intervening.

9. People who are suicidal really want to die.

While some people who are suicidal wish to end their life, the majority do not typically want to die. They simply feel hopeless about their current situation and wish to end the unbearable emotional pain they are feeling. Knapp (2020) adds that people who want to die often feel this way due to clouded judgment and an unclear and inconsistent emotional state. We know from discussions with people who have attempted suicide and then stopped, or who were otherwise unsuccessful in their attempts (e.g., survived jumping off a bridge), that they were ambivalent about dying (Maris, 2019). Many people who survive a suicide attempt later regret their attempt and find reasons to live.

10. If someone is determined to die, they will find a way to kill themselves and there is nothing anyone can do.

Sometimes people say, "If someone really wants to die, there is nothing you can do about it." I will admit that I have said this in the past when I was frustrated or feeling helpless about a client's situation. However, the danger in accepting this fatalistic attitude is that we may give up on trying to help others or believe that any assistance we provide will be useless. In addition, this statement is simply not true. For example, research has shown that if one form of suicide is removed (e.g., removing access to firearms from a person who is planning on shooting themselves), the person will *not* do something else to kill themselves (Knapp, 2020). This means that if we can determine the expected means of suicide and block the person from accessing those means, we can decrease suicide risk.

At the same time, we should recognize our limitations in helping people who may be struggling with suicidal intent. Should we hospitalize our clients who express suicidal ideation with a plan and intent? We know this may be effective in stopping some individuals, but in other cases, could doing so add to suicide risk? Whether we hospitalize a client or not, we must accept that, to some degree, suicide involves a choice on the part of the client. We may not agree with the choices a client makes, and we should acknowledge the impact that these choices—particularly those that lead to their deaths—can have on others, including clinicians. This is not to absolve clinicians or other helpers of all responsibility but to remind each of us that, ultimately, our clients are responsible for keeping themselves alive.

11. Asking people about suicide may give them the idea about killing themselves.

This is an older myth, like the outdated adage: "People who talk about killing themselves really do not want to kill themselves." Both statements are wrong. Consider the following unlikely exchange:

> THERAPIST: Are you having thoughts of killing yourself?
>
> CLIENT: Well, I wasn't, but now that you bring it up . . .

Research has strongly concluded that asking about suicide does not lead clients to attempt suicide when they otherwise would not have done so (Bender et al., 2019). The bigger risk is that clinicians (in particular) may not ask about suicide. Knapp (2020) states that 30 percent of clinicians do not routinely ask about suicidal thoughts and behaviors.

12. Self-harming behaviors are unrelated to suicide.

This is an interesting one. When I was in graduate school, we were taught that people who engaged in self-harming behaviors (e.g., cutting) were suicidal and needed to be hospitalized. I facilitated several hospitalizations of adolescents from the residential program I worked in who had cut themselves, as we assumed they were suicidal even though they denied being so. However, when clinicians and researchers got around to asking clients about the reasons for their behaviors, they were surprised to learn that many people (and nearly all adolescents and young adults) denied wanting to die. Their reasons for cutting included wanting to feel physical pain to mask (or manifest) their emotional pain. Others self-harmed to either stop themselves from dissociating or to facilitate dissociation, but most denied actual suicidal intent. At the same time, we must remember that ambivalence often accompanies suicidal ideation, meaning that some people who harmed themselves may not have cared if they lived or died.

Regardless, our increased knowledge about self-harm has unfortunately led to an overriding view that people who cut themselves are *never* suicidal. I remember several of my peers saying, "People who cut themselves are rarely suicidal" or "Cutting is a protection *from* suicide." In some cases, these statements may have validity, but I tend to agree with Joiner (2007) that many people who attempt or die by suicide have engaged in previous self-injurious behaviors (including substance use disorders and eating disorders) to work themselves toward an eventual attempt.

This myth highlights a prevailing trend in our society. Our view of things has become "either/or" instead of "both/and." People are complex, as are their motivations, thoughts, beliefs, and actions. To distill something as complex and multifaceted as suicide into something simplistic is extremely arrogant and dangerous, as such beliefs can undoubtably lead to practices that miss identifying suicidal risk. Regarding this specific myth, the current practice is to ask about self-injurious behaviors when conducting a suicide assessment and to see self-injurious behaviors as a suicide risk.

13. No-harm contracts are an effective clinical response in working with a client who expresses suicidal ideation.

When I was in graduate school, a professor told the class that having a client sign a piece of paper stating that they would not kill themselves was 98 percent effective in preventing suicide. Being students, we accepted this. Later, while working in residential treatment with adolescents, I was told the same thing several times, but I noticed that the percentages seemed to change—anywhere from 99 percent to 85 percent. But I accepted this, and later even repeated it to newer staff. This is a good example of our willingness to accept "common knowledge" as actual truth. However, the reality is that no-harm contracts do not work, and they have never worked. As you will see in chapter 7, this practice is dangerous for both client and clinician. Use of these contracts does not limit suicide in any way. They also do not protect clinicians or other helpers from liability.

14. Suicide rates increase over the year-end holiday season.

Another example of common knowledge (e.g., "Everybody knows that!") is that the suicide death rate increases over the Christmas holiday. I remember hearing this as a child, around the time I first learned that some people killed themselves and this was called suicide. Like most people, I accepted this. But it is wrong. Most years, the month with the highest suicide rate is in the spring. In 2022, it was May (CDC, 2025). Why this is so? We honestly do not know, and it is likely due to several factors that remain in flux.

I will reexamine some of these myths in chapter 3 when we look at suicide risk factors, but before putting this knowledge into practice, we need to examine some of the theories related to suicide to understand the complexity of this issue.

Theoretical Basis of Suicide

While no one theory can explain all human behaviors, the theories I will examine here have (historically and currently) attempted to bring an understanding of why some people attempt or die by suicide. The study of suicide, which is a nascent area of research, is called suicidology. The following theories are some of the more prominent. I believe that each of them has merit in attempting to understand suicide.

Émile Durkheim, a French sociologist, could arguably be called the first suicidologist. His 1897 text, *On Suicide* (*Le Suicide* in French), examines suicidal behavior as a reaction to societal stressors. In particular, he established the concept of "anomie"—a breakdown of "normalcy," or the norms and values previously held—in a community and how this could impact individuals. Durkheim examined suicide from a sociological perspective as opposed to a psychological one, and even though some of his concepts have not held up well to the passage of time, viewing an individual's suicide as a reaction to external factors was decidedly different from the emerging field of psychoanalysis championed by Durkheim's contemporary, Sigmund Freud. The following are the four types of suicide Durkheim described in his work (Mueller et al., 2021):

- Egotistic suicide is due to excessive individualization or isolation, such as we might see as indicative of a mental health problem.

- Anomic suicide is due to changes in external stabilizing factors, such as social norms (e.g., sudden loss of job or money), that caused the individual to feel estranged from society. Durkheim was especially concerned about how industrialization could cause this in individuals.

Chapter 1 • Suicide Defined

- Altruistic suicide is due to too little individualization, as is the case in which someone's planned death helps the greater whole (e.g., a soldier who throws themselves on a grenade).

- Fatalistic suicides are caused by too much regulation and loss of control, such as we might we see with people in prison. (There is a high rate of suicide among incarcerated individuals.)

While some of Durkheim's conclusions are now dated, his efforts to understand why people kill themselves were some of the first to try to ameliorate suicide.

Another prominent researcher on suicide was Karl Menninger, a psychiatrist in the United States whose seminal work, *Man Against Himself* (1938), provided a psychodynamic examination of the reasons people kill themselves or act in self-destructive ways. A disciple of Freud, Menninger's analytic-heavy case studies may appear outdated to some, but his examination of the reasons people work hard to overcome our innate desire to survive and instead hurt ourselves is thorough and fascinating. Menninger also spent a lot of time on the many ways that people kill themselves slowly (e.g., his belief that alcoholism can be a form of "slow" suicide) and illustrated ways that people engage in self-harming behaviors. Like Durkheim, Menninger delved into the complexity of *why* people try to take their own lives but from a psychiatric instead of sociological perspective.

Historically, Edwin Shneidman is considered the father of suicidology. In 1968, he suggested that all suicides can be categorized as being egotic, dyadic, or ageneratic. Egotic suicides are "essentially psychological in their nature" (Shneidman, 1985, p. 23), meaning they involve an internal struggle, as in the case of a person struggling with a mental illness such as major depressive disorder or schizophrenia. Dyadic suicides are social in nature and involve self-imposed death as part of an interpersonal relationship. This can include examples such as a person killing themselves as a result of a failed relationship. Finally, ageneratic suicides occur because the person loses a sense of connection with their community (or a loss of connection with humanity as a whole). An example might be an elderly person who feels isolated and alone. Shneidman later collapsed his different categories into a single category—egotic.

Shneidman's work in trying to understand *why* individuals die by suicide, and his focus on the complexities of individuals (as opposed to Durkheim's sociological viewpoints and Menninger's strict psychodynamic approach), created the foundation of suicidology. Shneidman (1985) later suggested ten commonalities of suicide (Maris, 2019, p. 27):

1. The common purpose of suicide is to seek a solution to a life problem.
2. The common goal is cessation of consciousness.
3. The common stimulus is intolerable psychological pain.
4. The common stressor is frustrated psychological needs.
5. The common emotion is hopelessness–helplessness.
6. The common cognitive state is ambivalence.
7. The common perceptual state is constriction.
8. The common action is egression.
9. The common interpersonal act is communication of intent.
10. The common consistency is lifelong coping patterns.

While these aspects of suicidal behavior do not apply to every person who may be suicidal, Shneidman's work was instrumental in changing the view of suicide as simply a symptom of mental illness or a reaction to the vicissitudes of society, to a varied, complex situation that changes over time and is unique to everyone. Every subsequent theory of suicide is heavily indebted to Shneidman's work.

Perhaps the best book to start with when learning about suicide is Thomas Joiner's (2007) *Why People Die by Suicide*. This accessible work was instrumental for me as I began my learning journey about suicide. Joiner's theory, now called the interpersonal theory of suicide (IPTS), is centered on the belief that people develop suicidal ideation because they are not connected with others (what he called "thwarted belongingness") and their belief that they have become a burden to others (what he called "perceived burdensomeness"). Joiner also states that over time, people gradually acquire the ability to engage in suicidal behavior by repeatedly engaging in experiences that both reduce their fear of death *and* increase their tolerance for physical pain. Essentially, they habituate to the fearsome and painful aspects of self-harm, making lethal self-injury more likely.

Second only to *Why People Die by Suicide* in terms of my learning about suicide is Ronald Maris's (2019) apt-named text on the subject, *Suicidology*. Maris's work is probably the most comprehensive that I have come across in learning about suicide. His primary theoretical contribution is the stress-diathesis theory of suicide: Individuals have varying traits and genetic predispositions that they are born with, along with early life environments in which they are raised. These factors, known as diatheses, alone do not necessarily lead to suicidal behaviors, but when an individual is placed under enough stress, the combination of those factors can increase suicidal thinking and behaviors (Maris, 2019). Maris's work has done a lot to challenge what were once assumed to be facts regarding suicide. His work is also reflected in the many suicide risk factors we will examine in chapter 3.

When considering theories of suicide, the inevitable question arises as to which theory to use. In my own experience, I have—and I think this is reflected in this book—relied on parts of all these theories when working with individuals who were suicidal. I invite you to examine these theories, and others, on your own as you learn about suicide. Keep in mind that there are more theories about suicide than the few I have listed. In addition, these theories (and others) are not mutually exclusive. For our purposes here, I will rely heavily, but not exclusively, on Maris's stress-diathesis theory, especially as I examine suicidal risk factors. But before delving into a client's potential risk, it's important to examine how well prepared we are as professionals to engage in this work, which is the focus of the next chapter.

CHAPTER 2

Professional Self-Care, Part I

Before we begin examining suicide risk factors and assessing suicide, we need to ensure that our practice settings are appropriately established to work with people who are experiencing suicidal ideation or engaged in suicidal behaviors. We also need to look at ourselves as professionals and human beings and consider how we prepare to work with people experiencing challenging situations.

Establishing Safe Practices

When we step into our role of working with people, especially people who are hurting, we must acknowledge the limits of how we can help. That means we must remember that we can do everything possible to keep our clients safe, yet a client could still die by suicide. If this happens, are you automatically at fault? The answer to this depends on what you have done *before* working with the client and how you conduct the work you do.

Many clinicians, ministers, medical professionals, and the like are reluctant to work with higher-risk clients, assuming that if a client dies by suicide they may lose their professional license or be sued by surviving family members. This belief is held by many members of the mental health and medical fields who are new to the field, as well as their experienced counterparts (Bryan, 2022). The fact is, however, that being sued for a client's suicide is rare. In most situations, unless there has been gross negligence or malpractice, the chances of a mental health provider losing their license or being sued are unlikely (Maris, 2019). Major reasons for this include:

1. Suicide itself is a rare occurrence.
2. We cannot predict suicide; therefore, we cannot completely anticipate another person's actions to be able to divert their suicide.

In cases where clinicians are sued, the court must find that the clinician was "grossly negligent" in discharging services. This may include engaging in outdated or inappropriate services, such as not conducting a suicide assessment, believing that people who engage in self-harming behaviors are not suicidal, or not treating the client's suicidality. It may also include a failure to assess potential suicide risk or take prudent action once suicide risk is identified. Perhaps the biggest risk lies with clinicians who fail to assess for suicide at all (Knapp, 2020). In addition, failure to completely document a suicide assessment would pose a risk of litigation. As I noted in the previous chapter, many of these failures lie not just with the experience and training of clinicians, but with their character and dedication to their work (i.e., giving a damn). It is difficult to do our best work when we are burned out, traumatized (vicariously or otherwise), or chronically fatigued. Creating a safe environment for our clients, therefore, lies with us as professionals taking care of ourselves.

Over the years, as I have developed training courses and written my own books, I've read a lot of other authors' books. One of the things I've noticed is that when it comes to self-care, most authors talk about clinician self-care at the very end of the book. Indeed, I am guilty of this myself with my first two books. I essentially say: "Oh and by the way, since we are engaged in difficult work with people who are really hurting, here are a few thoughts on how you might want to take care of yourself." I'm embarrassed by some of the things I have written in this area because I see now it was not enough.

My plan with this book is to put this important material here—right in the front. If we don't take care of ourselves, how can we ever be ready to take care of anyone?

Chapter 2 • Professional Self-Care, Part I

The Challenges of Working in Demanding Situations

It is a paradoxical skill—learning how to be emotionally involved yet emotionally distant, united but separate. The demand to be attuned, to be interested, to be energetic for the other person—a person who is often in misery, anger, defiance, or hopelessness—and to continue to do it over and over again with client after client is taxing, as well as deeply rewarding, work. (Skovholt & Trotter-Mathison, 2016, p. 27)

I love this quote because it encapsulates what we do as helpers. In this section, I want to focus on some of the ways that working with people can impact us as helpers, specifically burnout, compassion fatigue, and vicarious trauma.

Burnout

People experience burnout after working in a high-stress situation for a prolonged period until they become overwhelmed with physical and mental exhaustion. When people are overworked, lack a sense control over their environment, feel they were hired into the wrong role, and lack sufficient rewards for their work, they are more likely to experience burnout (VandenBos, 2013). Burnout can happen in any profession.

Perhaps the largest cause of burnout that I have seen (and experienced) in the human services field is poor agency leadership. Just because a person is a good clinician does not necessarily mean that they will be a good leader. In addition, people tend to conflate management and leadership. Managers help people accomplish tasks and get things done. Leaders cast a vision and equip others to be the best that they can be. Leaders must also be honest, humble, and have integrity. In an organization with leaders who lack these traits, I have found that burnout becomes common. Therefore, a good way to limit burnout is to either have good leaders in your organization or to do your best to work in organizations that foster good leaders.

Vicarious Trauma

After decades of viewing mental health issues as largely due to genetic and biochemical processes, at the turn of the century, researchers began to consider a person's lived experiences—particularly traumatic experiences—as causative factors for mental health symptoms. These can include experiences such as directly witnessing a traumatic event (e.g., being present when a client dies or is injured) or hearing about others' traumatic experiences (e.g., speaking with a military veteran). However, not every bad thing that happens to a person is a traumatic event. Everyone experiences bad things, but not everyone experiences trauma. Rather, trauma is an exceptional situation that creates a reaction in an individual that exceeds their typical abilities to cope and that causes distressing symptoms (sleep problems, hyperarousal, anxiety, and so on) for more than 30 days. Between 3.5 to 8.7 percent of people in the US will experience a traumatic event in their lives that results in post-traumatic stress disorder (PTSD; American Psychiatric Association, 2013).

If you work with people who are experiencing (or have experienced) trauma, it is possible to develop your own traumatic reactions to what you hear from clients. For example, a first responder might see their coworker killed in the line of duty, or a child protective services worker might be regularly exposed to situations in which children are abused or trafficked. Vicarious (or secondary) trauma often comes on quickly and can overwhelm you, leading to lasting traumatic symptoms, including hypervigilance, avoidance behaviors, mood and anxiety disorders, exhaustion, somatic symptoms, and dissociative episodes. Therefore, when working in high-risk situations such as these, it is imperative that you take care of yourself, especially outside of work. We will examine this further in chapter 12.

Compassion Fatigue

The terms *burnout* and *compassion fatigue* are often used interchangeably, even though they are different. I view compassion fatigue as the intersection of burnout and vicarious trauma. Whereas burnout can occur in any job or profession and can even be caused by things outside of work, compassion fatigue occurs primarily among those who work in helping professions. Figley (2002) describes compassion fatigue as "a state of tension and preoccupation with traumatized patients by re-experiencing the traumatic events, avoidance/numbing of bearing witness to the suffering of others" (cited in Skovholt & Trotter-Mathison, 2016, p. 110). Newell and MacNeil (2010) add that "The experience of compassion fatigue tends to occur cumulatively over time; whereas vicarious trauma and secondary traumatic stress have more immediate onset" (cited in Skovholt & Trotter-Mathison, 2016, p. 111).

Laura van Dernoot Lipsky (2009), in her excellent book *Trauma Stewardship*, identified many different responses that clinicians can have when they are exposed to trauma. These are all warning signs that you might be experiencing vicarious trauma:

1. **Feelings of helplessness and hopelessness.** I am not referring to the occasional questioning that we might experience as clinicians ("Why am I trying to help?" or "What difference am I making?"). Rather, when we feel this way nearly all the time, it can denote a vicarious trauma response. We may even believe that the trauma will never end, so we wind up stuck in our own flight-fight-freeze cycle.

2. **A sense that you can never do enough.** A person experiencing this trauma reaction places blame for the traumatic event on themselves and their perceived lack of intelligence, competence, or hard work. They often compensate for these feelings by working longer and more difficult hours, resulting in increased fatigue and secondary traumatic stress.

3. **Hypervigilance.** One of the hallmark symptoms of a trauma response is the feeling of being "on edge" or being constantly attuned to everything going on around us. Clinicians experiencing secondary or vicarious trauma experience this same hyperawareness to everything in their environment.

4. **Diminished creativity.** Trauma exposure often limits our desire or ability to exercise our creativity—both in our jobs and in our personal lives. This can lead to problems with chronic boredom or attention difficulties.

5. **Inability to embrace complexity.** Life is rarely simple, but when we have faced prolonged trauma exposure, we can see the world

(or individuals) in simplistic ways: all good or all bad. Nuance and complexity go out the window, and we often assume the worst about others or situations.

6. **Minimizing.** We witness so much trauma that we begin to downplay anything that doesn't meet the extreme levels of trauma we've seen ("You think that car accident was bad; it was nothing compared to the accident we worked last year!"). This is where we lose our compassion and ability to empathize with others, which can create a negative work culture where only the most extreme situations are deemed worthy of attention.

7. **Chronic exhaustion and physical ailments.** It is common knowledge that emotional trauma causes physical symptoms, including fatigue, pain, high blood pressure, and a host of other physical problems and illnesses.

8. **Inability to listen and deliberate avoidance.** These behaviors can occur at work or in our personal lives. We choose to do less and may go out of our way to avoid interacting with others.

9. **Dissociative moments.** We are physically present but mentally and emotionally absent. We lose sense of who we are, what we're doing, or where we are, or we may find ourselves experiencing another person's trauma experiences or reliving our own experiences.

10. **Sense of persecution.** At a minimum, people who are traumatized, or who are exposed to others' trauma, may come to believe that they lack power in their own lives. In more severe situations, people may develop paranoid thinking.

11. **Guilt.** When experiencing positive emotions, we may be overcome with guilt for feeling good when we remember that others are suffering. We may feel that we do not deserve to feel good. Or we may feel guilty for something that happened that was completely out of our control.

12. **Fear.** While fear is a natural and healthy response, in the context of compassion fatigue, we may become overwhelmed by fear to the point of feeling paralyzed.

13. **Anger and cynicism.** Like fear, anger itself is not bad, but when we cannot express it in healthy ways, anger can lead to cynicism. We need to recognize when we are angry and find ways to express it that do not hurt others.

14. **Inability to empathize or numbing.** When this occurs, we become unaware of our own feelings, and we are unable to care about what others are experiencing.

15. **Addictions.** Drugs (including alcohol) or behavioral addictions (such as gambling) can help us "check out" and not care about anything. We know this because the relationship between trauma and substance use disorder (addiction) is very strong.

16. **Grandiosity.** In response to trauma, some clinicians develop an inflated sense of importance related to their work. They may believe, *Who else will do this if I'm not here?*—and in doing so work harder and not take time for themselves outside of work.

Do you see yourself (either currently or in the past) expressing any of these responses? I invite you to take some time to reflect on the following questions about your experiences with burnout, vicarious trauma, and compassion fatigue. You may have experiences with none, one, or many of them—that is okay. As you will see shortly when we examine countertransference, you need to be aware of these reactions in yourself so you don't lose focus on the purpose of the clinical interaction—your client's needs, not yours.

1. What are some ways that you have experienced (or are experiencing) burnout?

_____

_____

_____

_____

_____

2. What are some ways that you have experienced (or are experiencing) vicarious trauma or compassion fatigue?

   _____
   _____
   _____
   _____
   _____

3. Which of the 16 trauma stewardship responses have you experienced?

   _____
   _____
   _____
   _____
   _____

4. Of these, which one is the most severe?

   _____
   _____
   _____
   _____
   _____

5. What steps can you take (or have you taken in the past, or are you taking now) to address your trauma responses?

   _____
   _____
   _____
   _____
   _____

Chapter 2 • Professional Self-Care, Part I

Countertransference

Each of us is going to die. This is a fact that we cognitively acknowledge but often emotionally ignore—we can admit to it without fully understanding its true meaning. When working with people who have attempted suicide or are contemplating suicide, we come face-to-face with death. Whether we realize it or not, our clients' deaths (or attempts at death), or their stated desires to die, remind us of our own mortality. It is therefore extremely important that we ask ourselves the following questions. These are not simple questions that can be answered with brief answers; they are questions we spend our whole lives considering.

1. What does it mean to die?

   _____
   _____
   _____
   _____
   _____

2. What, if anything, happens to us when we die?

   _____
   _____
   _____
   _____
   _____

3. Do you wonder *why* we have to die?

   _____
   _____
   _____
   _____
   _____

4. Why are we so afraid of death? Relatedly, is it a *good* thing that we are afraid of death?

_____

_____

_____

_____

_____

As a middle-aged man living in the United States, I have come to believe that part of life is coming to terms with our own mortality. For some of us, this can be a key part of our spirituality or faith. For others, we can look to those we share our lives with to find meaning both in how we handle life or our impending deaths.

The first time I saw a dead person was early in my time working in the emergency department. The gentleman who had died (not by suicide) did not look asleep—he looked dead; there is no other way to describe it. Empty. A shell. This was a stranger who had died alone. I remember one of my friends, a nurse, weeping quietly as the hospital chaplain said a brief prayer for our patient before I helped put him into a body bag.

More recently, I watched as my mother died from cancer. She was a hospital chaplain and was all too familiar with death, as she had sat with thousands of patients in their final moments. She was an incredibly wise and kind person. Mom chose to die in the hospital where she had served others for over 20 years. When she knew that death was near, she elected to enter hospice care. I remember one of my last conversations with her, when I asked her if she was afraid of dying.

"No, I'm not," she said matter-of-factly. "I've seen so many people die. I am at peace. I have had the opportunity to say my goodbyes and not leave anything out. But what I am afraid of is pain—the pain that I've been in for these past few months. I wouldn't wish that pain on the worst person in the world. I'm afraid of that pain coming back. I'm not afraid of dying."

A little more than a week later, Mom died peacefully.

I share the stories of the first dead person I saw and my mother's death because they impact how I view death. They are a part of "my stuff." Since suicide and death are synonymous, how I reacted to these deaths could impact how I deal with a client's suicidal ideation. In other words: countertransference.

Countertransference occurs when we put our "stuff" on our clients—and this includes our personal reactions to how our clients behave. Countertransference cannot be completely avoided—it is part of the interchange between provider and client (Michaud et al., 2023). Although we may kid ourselves that we are immune to countertransference, this simply makes us less aware of it and leads to arrogance on our part as helpers. For example, after the death of my friend's wife from cancer, I remember getting angry my first day back at work in the emergency department when I was asked to speak with a suicidal client. I remember saying to a nurse that my friend's wife would have given anything for more time to live, and here was this person who wanted to throw away their life. The wise and compassionate nurse gently reminded me that these were different people and that I needed to remain professional.

Wise providers acknowledge countertransference. They make a mental note when they feel themselves reacting to clients—or in my case, they have a wise person nearby to correct them. Hopefully, they pause, take a breath, and proceed cautiously or try a different direction. Humble providers admit countertransference to themselves and seek appropriate consultation or supervision from peers and, if need be, their own psychotherapy. There is nothing wrong with this. Helpers seeking help should be encouraged.

The issue of countertransference can bring with it the strategy of self-disclosure. I believe that self-disclosure, when used appropriately, can be an effective part of the helping process, but not in situations where there is countertransference. For example, when I had to talk with the suicidal client shortly after attending the funeral for my friend's wife, it would not have been appropriate for me to go into the room and tell the patient about my friend's loss. Not only would that have nothing to do with their situation, but sharing this information would have put the focus on me and not on the client.

I think that self-disclosure can be useful in counseling when used sparingly and appropriately. If you choose to utilize self-disclosure in treatment, please consider the following questions for reflection before you do so. Remember that therapeutic self-disclosure should always benefit the client and not be utilized to meet your own needs (Danzer, 2019).

1. What are positive ways your self-disclosure could impact a client?

   _____
   _____
   _____
   _____

2. What are negative ways your self-disclosure could impact a client?

   _____
   _____
   _____
   _____

3. Are you certain your disclosure is about the client and not you? (Think this over carefully.)

   _____
   _____
   _____
   _____

The Importance of Informed Consent to Treatment

I cannot emphasize enough the importance of informed consent when providing clinical services in any setting. It is imperative that your clients understand what is expected in treatment, the limitations to your work together, and the responsibilities you both have for each other. You should have your clients read the informed consent agreement at the beginning of treatment before signing it and verbally review what is in the agreement. Some of the basic parts of an informed consent to treatment agreement should include:

1. A definition of the services to be provided, including potential benefits and risks
2. Information about psychiatric services or medication
3. Information on telehealth services
4. Patient responsibilities:
    a. Payment
    b. Use of insurance providers
    c. Scheduling
    d. Late and no-show policies and fees
5. Professional relationships and conflicts of interest
6. Statement on recording of sessions
7. Communication (how the client would prefer to be contacted and how the client can contact you)
8. Emergency or after-hours access
9. Termination of services
10. A statement about weapons allowed (or not allowed) on the property
11. Arbitration of disputes (optional)
12. Disclosures

Given that the first 11 items on this list are all basic elements of informed consent that I would expect all clinicians to know, I will not review them here. Rather, it is the final item on this list—disclosures—that is the most important when it comes to the issue of suicide. It is imperative that you explain to clients the situations in which confidentiality must be broken, specifically: when the client is a danger to themselves, is a danger to others, or is unable to care for themselves. I acknowledge that these situations may differ among localities, so be mindful of the laws and regulations of your locality. I also explain to clients that reporting feelings or thoughts related to suicide does not mean that I will automatically contact emergency services; instead, we will need to talk about what the client is going through. However, in the event that the client is unable or unwilling to keep themselves or others safe, I must act and disclose the situation to the appropriate authorities.

You'll also want to include specific statements on your informed consent agreement that discuss disclosures and, in particular, explicitly mention exceptions to confidentiality, such as:

- "Patient consents to disclosure of specific patient information to a specific recipient."
- "Emergency medical services personnel will be notified in the event of a medical emergency."
- "Law enforcement or crisis personnel may be notified in situations where a patient is deemed to be an imminent threat to their own safety or the safety of others."

I also strongly suggest you consult with an attorney and review the laws and statutes of your state and locality as you develop a consent to treat for your practice.

Dealing with the Death of a Patient by Suicide

If you are a behavioral health provider, it is possible that you will have a client die by suicide at some point in your career, even if the client is no longer under your care. In fact, one study found that 23 percent of counselors had a client die by suicide (McAdams & Foster, 2000). This was my experience many years ago, when I was a part of a juvenile drug court program in a county south of Richmond. I really loved my job. I was part of an extraordinary team of professionals that included two prosecuting attorneys, a defense attorney, a probation officer, a police officer, another clinician (besides me), an administrator, and most importantly, our judge. The adolescents in our program had been found guilty of one or more nonviolent felony convictions related to their drug use. As an alternative to lengthy incarceration and a permanent felony on their criminal record, clients could enter our program. They were required to remain in school (or work), attend therapy, pass regular (and random) drug screens, abide by a curfew, and not get any additional charges. If they completed the program, which took an average of 18 months, their record was expunged.

Aaron was a young man in our program, and when I interviewed him in juvenile detention before he entered our program, he assured me he would complete our program in 12 months. In the end, it took him more than twice that time, but he did it. He also completed his general equivalency diploma (GED) and started working full-time while in our program.

About a year and a half after Aaron left the program, I received a phone call from our administrator, who informed me that Aaron had died while working at a construction jobsite. Details were limited at first, but it was later determined that Aaron had taken a fatal overdose of several prescription medications. I had heard that he had returned to using, but I had not been in contact with him. I was also aware that he had a significant trauma history, and he struggled with depression. Was this an accidental overdose, or was it a death by suicide?

We must acknowledge the ambiguity that often occurs when a person dies by suicide. It is often difficult to determine whether the death was intentional or accidental. Regardless, there are essential steps we can take when this occurs.

The first is to notify your teammates. If you work in an organization, this includes notifying your supervisor immediately. In the case of Aaron, the drug court administrator (who was my supervisor) notified each member of the team about his death—an unenviable task that she handled with extraordinary grace and concern that I will never forget.

The second thing to do is to notify your liability insurance provider. As I will later discuss, clinicians are often anxious about liability issues regarding client suicide. This is understandable, even though clinicians are rarely sued for client suicide. However, your liability insurance provider needs to know what happened. They can then provide you with further directions on how to proceed.

The next step is to secure the client's records. In our age of electronic medical records, this is easier than it used to be. Document that you have been informed of the patient's suicide and your following actions.

Once this has taken place, you need to take care of yourself. This may mean canceling previously scheduled appointments—honestly, how could anyone give a client their undivided attention with the knowledge of another client's death on their minds? I cannot overemphasize the importance of taking care of yourself. This could mean seeking additional supervision and therapy for yourself. I availed myself of both when dealing with Aaron's death.

One of the individuals who helped me care for myself following Aaron's death was our drug court judge. He was one of a handful of people in my life who I can say made me the person I am today—not just as a social worker, but as a father and a human being. Judge H. treated people in his court with grace and compassion, while adhering to the laws he had sworn to uphold. We met as a team every Thursday afternoon prior to our drug court docket. During our first meeting after Aaron's death, as we were moving to the courtroom at the end of our meeting, the judge pulled me aside.

"How're you doing?" he asked.

"I don't know, Judge," I said. "Sad, angry, confused . . ."

"Are you wondering if there was anything else we could have done?" he asked, getting right to the point.

I didn't say anything.

"Well, I'm wondering that myself, and here's what I am going to do. I've asked my clerk to clear space on my schedule for next week and to pull Aaron's criminal file. It is quite substantial. I plan on reading the whole record in my chambers. I suggest you do the same with his treatment record. Then let's touch base next week and see if we found anything."

I nodded in agreement, and then we walked into court. The judge did an amazing job of informing our clients and their families about Aaron's death. His approach was more pastoral than judicial. I don't think there was a dry eye in the courtroom, even among the tough, seasoned bailiffs.

The following Tuesday, I sat down with Aaron's lengthy treatment record. This was before the agency transitioned to electronic medical records, and Aaron's record was at least four inches thick. In examining just my portion of the record (as he had worked with therapists in our agency prior to me), I found that I had provided 100 group therapy sessions (about a third of which included his mother in a multifamily group format), about 60 individual sessions, and 12 family sessions.

I arrived early to our next drug court meeting and was not surprised to see Judge H. enter the conference room early as well.

"Did you get a chance to read Aaron's record?" he asked.

"I did, sir."

"What did you find?"

"I was reminded of the many challenges that Aaron faced, but also his incredible resiliency, in addition to his stubbornness and wicked sense of humor," I replied.

The judge smiled. "My records were legal, so they were drier, to say the least. But I can honestly say we did everything we could do. We worked hard, as he did. We did what we needed to do."

"We did our job, sir."

"Yes, we did our jobs—and then some." He smiled.

While Judge H. was not my direct supervisor, he was in a position of leadership and mentorship, and that mattered immensely to me. My actual supervisors were incredible in helping me process Aaron's death and allowing me the time I needed to deal with the situation. The agency I worked for, in conducting a review of the incident, was also supportive and sought only to ensure that best practices had been followed, rather than looking to assign blame.

Once you've processed your client's death and taken some steps to care for yourself with the help of a therapist or supervisor, the final step depends on the specifics of your client. Do you contact next of kin? Do you offer your condolences? Do you attend the funeral? What if family members blame you for their loved one's death? These are excellent questions, and it is up to you to decide what you will do. My preference is to send a letter or card to the client's family, emergency contact person, or both, saying that I am sorry for their loss. This is not admitting responsibility for the client's death—it is a human gesture of concern and care. I sent a short letter to Aaron's mother, expressing my sorrow for her loss. I never heard anything from her. Since that time, I have wondered if she blamed me in some way for her son's death. I am now a parent of adolescents, with one of my sons nearly the same age as Aaron when he died, and I can understand Aaron's mother's feelings. Regardless, I think this is the best way to approach the death of a client by suicide: with compassion for the people who loved them—and for ourselves.

Patients Who Conceal Their Suicidal Ideation

There is a common misconception that people who are suicidal will usually admit that they are thinking of or planning their death. However, the reality is that people who die by suicide are more likely than not to deny suicidal ideation (Maris, 2019), which raises the question: Why ask about suicide if people are likely to be less than honest if they are actually suicidal?

As I noted in the first chapter, people make their own decisions, even if their judgment is clouded by mental illness, substance use, or emotional distress. That means we cannot control other people's behaviors. Our role as mental health providers is to assess the potential risk of suicide based on a clinical interview, screening tools, our clinical observations, our knowledge of the client's history, and our training and clinical judgment. Our job is to ask the questions, and the biggest way that we can fail in this area is to not ask questions about suicide. Let me repeat that: The largest mistake we can make as providers is to not assess for suicide *and* then fail to act on our conclusions.

We also need to consider *why* people do not admit to suicidal ideation when asked. As I noted in chapter 1, people who are suicidal are often ambiguous about wanting to die. Therefore, it is possible that they are not necessarily concealing their desire to die as much as they are unsure about it. Clients may also not disclose their ideation because they are afraid it will lead to an involuntary psychiatric hospitalization, even if they are not at imminent risk of harm. Indeed, most people who have suicidal ideation will never formulate an actual suicide plan or attempt suicide. Finally, clients may not disclose their ideation because their therapist simply doesn't ask about it, or they may explicitly conceal it if it seems like their therapist doesn't care enough about their well-being (Blanchard & Farber, 2018). Regardless of what our clients bring to us, we must remain open, empathetic, and professional in our responses to their issues. As one client put it, "Promise to listen to everything I say and take into consideration my emotional state at this time [. . .] Then see admitting me to a hospital as a LAST resort" (Blanchard & Farber, 2018, p. 8).

Now that I have discussed some things that you need to have in place to be ready to assess and work with people who may be at risk of suicide, you need to understand the many risk factors for suicide. As you will read many times in this book, suicide is not predictable, but by understanding and identifying risk factors, you can better intervene to limit the possibility of suicide. You also need to be knowledgeable about protective factors that can limit the likelihood of suicidal thinking and behaviors.

CHAPTER 3

Suicide Risk and Protective Factors

Although we cannot predict suicide, it nonetheless imperative that we conduct a solid suicide assessment and formulate a detailed treatment plan that includes a consideration of the major risk factors. While this chapter describes many suicide risk factors, it is not a complete list—the risk factors I discuss here are the more widely recognized ones. I also want to emphasize that people rarely attempt suicide due to a single risk factor. Rather, people develop suicidal intent due to many factors, and this also occurs within a specific time frame for that individual. After we examine the more common risk factors, I will describe a method of conceptualizing risk factors and their possible relationships with one another. I then conclude this chapter by examining the prominent suicide protective factors.

Suicide Risk Factors

Maris (2019) notes that the typical person who dies by suicide in the United States is a middle-aged or older White male who is depressed, has alcohol use disorder (or opioid use disorder, or both), is lonely or socially isolated, and uses a highly lethal method of suicide (most often a gunshot to the head, hanging, or falling from a great height). Of course, there are millions of individuals in the US who are middle-aged, identify as male, feel isolated, and use substances—and most of them don't die by suicide or ever consider taking their own lives. Therefore, it is not just the risk factors themselves, but *how* the risk factors align for an individual at a specific time.

While recognizing and identifying risk factors is important when working with people in any capacity, identifying risk factors alone is not enough. As Bryan (2022) notes, "If we assume that suicidal behaviors result from linear cause and effect relationships, we can mistakenly assume that suicidal warning signs are always apparent before the occurrence of suicidal behavior when in reality that may not always be the case" (p. 63). Risk factors are actions, thoughts, and beliefs that are more common among people who have died by suicide, but they are not universal, and they do not appear to work in a linear manner. Despite this caveat, let's look at the traits previously identified by Maris and examine additional risk factors so we can begin to get a better understanding of what we need to be aware of when assessing clients for suicide.

Sex: Males

As I write this book, 2023 is the year with the most recent suicide data. In 2023, the Centers for Disease Control and Prevention (CDC, 2025) reported 49,316 suicide deaths in the United States. For comparison, the CDC reported 49,476 suicide deaths in 2022. Suicide rates are often explained by ratios of number of deaths per 100,000 people, so the suicide death ratio for 2023 was 14.12 per 100,000 people, and the suicide death ratio for 2022 was 14.21 per 100,000 people.

The CDC reported consistently increasing suicide rates from 1999 to 2018, then a decrease in suicides in 2019 and 2020. As of 2022, we have essentially "caught up" to the increasing suicide rate that had been underway for 20 years before the slight decreases in 2019 and 2020. There are no firm answers to explain the decrease in suicide deaths in 2019 and 2020, especially in 2020, given the COVID-19 pandemic and resulting shutdowns and economic impact. Maris (2019) notes a historical trend of suicide rates dropping suddenly in response to national emergencies,* but this does not explain the decrease in suicides in 2019— the year before the COVID-19 pandemic.

---

* Maris (2019) notes a near lack of suicide deaths recorded in the week following the assassination of President Kennedy in November 1963, and he noted a decrease by more than half of calls into suicide hotlines in the weeks following the terrorist attacks of September 11, 2001. He suggests that communities may foster a greater sense of connection in times of emergencies.

Male suicide deaths outnumber female suicide deaths by a factor of four to one (3.85 to 1 in 2022 and 2023), and this ratio has been consistent for many years (CDC, 2024). The primary reason for this difference is that males tend to use more lethal means overall (e.g., a firearm). Over the past 20 years, there has been a slight change in the ratio of male versus female suicide deaths, with a slight increase in female deaths and a decrease in male deaths. However, females historically attempt suicide far more often than males yet die by suicide at a significantly lower rate compared to males (Maris, 2019).

Race and Ethnicity: White/Caucasian

White males accounted for over two-thirds of all suicide deaths in the US in 2022 and 2023 (CDC, 2025), continuing a pattern from previous years of White adults comprising most suicide deaths. However, we also need to consider the ratio of suicide deaths within each ethnic group. For example, the suicide ratio in 2023 among Native Americans and Alaskan Natives was 23.8 per 100,000, compared to 17.6 per 100,000 for White Americans (CDC, 2025; AFSP, 2025). Maris (2019) notes that while variability exists between tribal groups and communities, the overall suicide ratio remains highest among Native Americans compared to any other ethnic group in the US.

Lower rates were reported among Black Americans (9.1 per 100,000), as well as Latino (8.2 per 100,000) and Asian and Pacific Islander Americans (6.5 per 100,000), and these rates have also been historically lower compared to White Americans and Native Americans (AFSP, 2025). However, the suicide rate for Black Americans and Asian and Pacific Islander Americans increased by 30 percent and 16 percent, respectively, between 2014 and 2019 (Ramchand et al. 2021). This underscores the fact that a person's racial and ethnic background does not in and of itself increase the risk for suicide. Rather, it is the discrimination and racism that certain racial and ethnic groups face that increases this risk (Knapp, 2020).

Age: Middle-Aged and Older Adults

Suicide rates generally increase as a person ages (Joiner, 2007; Maris, 2019), likely due to major life changes that come with aging. For example, elderly adults who experience the death of a lifelong partner may see little reason to continue living without their partner. They may also struggle to face being able to do less for themselves. In addition, older individuals are more likely to attempt suicide using methods of greater lethality, such as firearms (Maris, 2019). Indeed, according to the American Foundation for Suicide Prevention (AFSP, 2025) and the CDC (2025), in 2023, the highest rate of suicide (22.7 per 100,000 people) was among people 85 and older—this group has had the highest rate since 2019. In addition, the higher suicide risk among those 85 and older is primarily in the male population (Shah et al., 2016). In 2023, the second-highest rate was among adults 75 to 84 years old (19.4 per 100,000 people), followed by adults aged 35–44 (19.2 per 100,000 people; CDC, 2025). From 2013 to 2018, the highest suicide rate was among adults 45 to 54 years old. These results are consistent with longitudinal data noted by Maris (2019) and Joiner (2007).

Most people in society at large (and perhaps some human-services providers) are surprised to learn that the highest suicide rates are among middle-aged and older adults, as opposed to adolescents or young adults. While death by suicide is horrible at any age, we appear to notice the suicide deaths of younger people more (Wasserman et al., 2021). Perhaps this is because of more media attention (social and traditional media alike), or maybe there is greater connection among people who are younger.

Regardless, what is alarming is that one in six teenagers in the US have seriously considered attempting suicide in the past year (Moutier et al., 2021). We are also more likely to see "suicide clusters" among adolescents and young adults, since suicide contagion is much more likely among youth (Fehling & Selby, 2021; Maris, 2019). Adolescents may also be more susceptible to certain external factors that could increase their suicide risk, including family violence, physical abuse, sexual abuse, rejection related to sexual orientation or gender identity, bullying, or experiences with loss or humiliation (Moutier et al., 2021). I will examine adolescent and young adult suicide in a later chapter.

Previous Suicide Attempts

People who attempt suicide but survive are almost 40 times more likely to reattempt and die by suicide than those who have never attempted before (Moutier et al., 2021). Therefore, past suicide attempts are a major risk factor—some would argue the biggest risk factor—for further suicidal behavior (Fehling

& Selby, 2021). When I assess someone for suicide, and they state that they have made a suicide attempt, I ask for details:

- What was going on when you attempted suicide?
- What was the attempt (i.e., what did you do)?
- When did this happen?
- What happened as a result?

While examining past suicide attempts is important in determining current risk, Maris (2019) points out a sobering fact: "Among [people who die by suicide], about 70 percent make one attempt, 13.8 percent make two attempts, 4.8 percent make three, 3.9 percent make four, and 3.3 percent make five or more attempts before dying by suicide" (p. 68). In other words, most people who die by suicide make a single attempt—and die as a result.

Mental Illness

As I stated in the introduction, society equates suicide as a symptom of mental illness, specifically depression. While 7 percent of the US adult population experiences a major depressive episode each year, Maris (2019) notes that about 90 percent of people with severe major depressive disorder will die a natural death—not by suicide. While suicide can be an outcome of depression, most people who have depression do not attempt, let alone die, by suicide. Therefore, can we say that a person who attempts (or dies by) suicide is not depressed?

The easiest answer, and perhaps the most accurate, is—we do not know. Note that many people who experience the death of a loved one by suicide are surprised or shocked that the person ended their own life. I have heard people say: "I didn't know they were depressed." The fact is that we do not know, and we likely will never be able to find out if the person was depressed, so automatically assuming a depressive disorder or other mental health disorder is a mistake. In fact, many people who die by suicide have never sought out mental health services or been diagnosed with a mental illness (De Leo, 2022). While depression is a major risk factor for suicide, it often appears to be assumed as the major (or only) risk factor. Feelings of sadness, disappointment, and loneliness can be present for a person, and can be contributing factors to suicidal behaviors, but in and of themselves, they do not mean that the person is depressed. Bryan (2022) supports this assertion, noting that "because the majority of individuals who die by suicide did not pursue mental health treatment prior to their deaths, there isn't always clear or direct evidence to support the diagnosis of a mental illness" (p. 30).

At the same time, we know that people living with a mental illness are at greater risk of suicide. Maris (2019) argues that the presence of a mental illness is the most important risk factor. However, some mental illnesses have a higher rate of suicide than others, so in this next section, I examine them in greater detail. I recommend readers familiarize themselves with the *Diagnostic and Statistical Manual of Mental Disorders, Fifth Edition, Text Revision* (*DSM-5-TR*). I also recommend Allen Frances's (2013) *Essentials of Psychiatric Diagnosis* as a companion to the *DSM* to better understand the nuances of mental health diagnoses.

Depression. Major depressive disorder is one of two mental health disorders where suicidal ideation is one of the diagnostic criteria. (Borderline personality disorder is the other one.) As previously noted, most people with depression, even severe depression, do not attempt or die by suicide, but about 60 percent of all suicides in the United States occur among those with major depressive disorder (Maris, 2019). Co-occurring substance use disorders, anxiety disorders (especially panic attacks), agitation, and insomnia increase suicide risk among clients with major depressive disorder.

Despite improvements in treating depression, the overall suicide rate has increased. While there is a connection between depression and suicide, this connection is not as clear-cut as many people believe. Although depression is a predictor of suicidal ideation, it does not predict suicidal behavior, nor do most people with depression attempt suicide. In addition, treatments for depression do not necessarily reduce suicidal behavior (Fehling & Selby, 2021).

Bipolar Disorders. The *DSM-5-TR* recognizes two types of bipolar disorder. To be diagnosed with bipolar I disorder, a person must have experienced a manic episode, which involves a heightened period of mood and energy that lasts at least one week (see the *DSM-5-TR* for specific diagnostic criteria for a manic episode). About 90 percent of people who experience a manic episode go on to experience a major depressive episode, but a depressive episode is not required for a diagnosis of bipolar I disorder. (I know, it is confusing.) A diagnosis of bipolar II—which is much less understood than bipolar I (see Frances, 2013)—requires a hypomanic episode *and* a major depressive episode. As I mentioned in my last book (Brasler, 2022), clients are often misdiagnosed with bipolar disorder when the actual problem is a trauma-related disorder, a substance use disorder, or a personality disorder, so it is imperative that these issues are ruled out prior to a diagnosis (and subsequent treatment) of bipolar I or II.

Clients with bipolar disorders have some of the highest rates of suicide, with rates 28 times that of the general population (Maris, 2019). This risk is further elevated when clients have mixed features or agitation, or if they have a co-occurring substance use disorder (Baldessarini et al., 2019). Not only is the death-by-suicide rate higher among clients with bipolar disorder, but suicidal ideation is common as well. In particular, the lifetime risk of suicidal ideation is higher among those with bipolar disorder (29.2 percent) compared to major depressive disorder (17.3 percent), and especially higher among those with bipolar II (35 percent) versus bipolar I (25.2 percent). Suicide risk appears to increase during times of transition between manic or hypomanic episodes and depressive episodes. In addition, the depressive episodes that are a part of bipolar disorders are usually more severe than the depressive episodes that occur with major depressive disorder.

Schizophrenia. About 1 percent of the US population has schizophrenia (American Psychiatric Association, 2013). Like bipolar disorder, schizophrenia can be misdiagnosed in clients with trauma-related disorders and substance use disorders. Also like bipolar disorder, individuals with schizophrenia are at an increased risk for suicide, with the rate of death by suicide being 4.5 times higher than the general population (Olfson et al., 2021). Clients with schizophrenia who die by suicide often kill themselves in bizarre ways, such as self-immolation (Maris, 2019). One reason that their suicide risk is higher may be due to their symptoms—for example, a voice or voices telling the person to kill themselves because they are evil, or delusions that the person is impervious to harm. We need to remember that schizophrenia symptoms cycle in severity and that clients can experience major shifts in their awareness and insight about their illness. Clients coming out of a severe psychotic state might see suicide as an option that would keep them from returning to being psychotic.

We also need to consider the medications used to treat schizophrenia, many of which have severe and sometimes permanent side effects. When I was working in the emergency department, I remember a police officer bringing in a patient who had schizophrenia and who was well known to us.

"Why can't he just stay on his meds?" the exasperated officer asked.

Having some familiarity with this officer, I responded, "Would you want to take something that made you lethargic, bloated, restless, unable to concentrate, thirsty all the time, and gave you erectile dysfunction?"

"You mean that's what the meds can do?" he asked.

"Yeah," I responded.

"I get it," he replied. "No thanks!"

Given the choice between living with the symptoms of schizophrenia and the side effects of the medications used to treat them, it is not a mystery why people choose not to stay on their medications. We also need to consider that schizophrenia often disrupts a person's sleep cycle and causes insomnia—which is itself a suicide risk factor.

Eating Disorders. Eating disorders share many characteristics of anxiety, mood, obsessive-compulsive, and substance use disorders (and often co-occur with these disorders as well). Two of the better-studied eating disorders are anorexia nervosa and bulimia nervosa. The primary difference between anorexia and bulimia is that people with the former have a body mass index well below the "normal" range, while people with the latter have a body mass index that is normal or higher than what is considered normal for that individual's height and weight. While people with anorexia or bulimia can switch between the two disorders, it is anorexia that has the highest mortality rate of any psychiatric disorder and has one of the highest suicide rates of any psychiatric disorder (Frances 2013; Maris, 2019).

Post-Traumatic Stress Disorder. Clients are diagnosed with post-traumatic stress disorder (PTSD) when they experience trauma symptoms (e.g., flashbacks or hypervigilance) that persist for over a month following a traumatic experience. Although less than 20 percent of people who experience a traumatic event will go on to develop PTSD (American Psychiatric Association, 2013), people may experience trauma symptoms without meeting full criteria for the disorder. As I have noted, trauma-related disorders are often misdiagnosed as bipolar disorders, anxiety disorders, or other mental health issues, which complicates the treatment process and can lead to further trauma or exacerbation of symptoms due to lack of appropriate treatment.

Although not everyone who experiences PTSD will experience suicidality, the disorder is nonetheless associated with increased suicide risk, especially among women. People experiencing trauma often suffer in silence, feeling isolated and alone, which likely contributes to the connection between trauma and suicide. Indeed, one of the biggest risk factors for suicidal behavior is trauma that happens early in life, including childhood neglect, childhood physical or sexual abuse, and parental death or illness (Fehling & Selby, 2021). In many situations, this is not due to a single event but to a series of events, which can lead to a "dose-response effect" in which the cumulative effect of these stressors leads to increased suicide risk (Fehling & Selby, 2021).

Personality Disorders. Of the 10 personality disorders in the *DSM*, two specific disorders are more prominent in suicidal populations: borderline and antisocial personality disorders (Maris, 2019).

Borderline personality disorder (BPD), like major depressive disorder, has suicidal ideation listed as a diagnostic criterion. BPD is marked by unstable relationships, high impulsivity, emotion dysregulation, chronic feelings of emptiness, and rage—all of which can contribute to increased suicide risk. Indeed, the risk of suicide is elevated among people with BPD, as upwards of 75 percent will attempt suicide and 10 percent will die by suicide (Black et al., 2004). BPD often co-occurs with other disorders, especially mood disorders, substance use disorders, and trauma disorders. In fact, many clinicians view BPD as a response to trauma, as most people with BPD have a trauma history beginning in childhood.

Whereas BPD is more common among females, antisocial personality disorder (ASPD) is more common among males (Frances, 2013). People with ASPD have a strong disregard for the rights of others and often engage in a variety of lawbreaking and reckless behaviors that put others (and themselves) at risk. They may also violently act out and often have contact with the criminal justice system. Interestingly, the suicide rate is elevated among those with ASPD, as they are 3.7 times more likely than the general population to attempt suicide and nine times more likely to do so if they're under the age of 30 (Maris, 2019). The aggressive and impulsive tendencies of individuals with this disorder—particularly among those who are younger and thus have less self-control—may contribute to their suicide risk.

Substance Use Disorder. Substance use disorder (SUD) is another major suicide risk factor, though as I have previously noted, it can be difficult to determine whether a person died intentionally or accidentally from a substance use overdose. Of course, people with SUD can also die by suicide using other means (e.g., shooting, hanging, or jumping), though overdose remains a common cause.

When talking about intentional versus accidental overdose, we need to take a moment to examine how deaths are recorded in the United States. Medical examiners and doctors typically determine the final cause of death, which is usually placed in one of four categories: natural, accidental, suicide, or homicide. Some states and localities add an "unknown" or "undetermined" option. This classification is often called the NASH system. As you can imagine, some deaths are difficult to classify in this system. Consider Aaron, the young man discussed in chapter 2 who died of an overdose. As I noted, we were never able to determine whether Aaron's death by drug overdose was an accident or suicide.

The NASH system and its limitations—not to mention the wide discretion and latitude that medical examiners have in labeling what type of death a person has experienced—has led to the view that suicides may be underrepresented, especially in situations where it is difficult to determine whether the death was accidental or intentional (Katz et al., 2016; Maris, 2019). This is most evident in situations involving drug overdoses, especially involving illicit substances. I have had many conversations with people struggling with SUD who did not care if they died because of their substance use. Is this "passive" suicide, if there is such a thing? I think it is a common occurrence among people with SUD—continuing to use despite knowing that continued use will be fatal. It therefore follows that a portion of the more than 100,000 annual deaths over the past few years from people using illicit substances, especially illicit fentanyl, were suicide deaths as opposed to accidental overdoses.

Of all substances, alcohol carries the highest risk of suicide, likely due to its widespread use, legality, availability, and low cost. Maris (2019) notes that in most studies, alcohol use disorder is the second most prevalent suicide risk factor, and

18 percent of people with alcohol use disorder die by suicide. This risk extends beyond alcohol, though, as people with opioid use disorder and people who inject drugs are also at high risk of suicide (Fruhbauerova & Comtois, 2019). As I argued in my book, *The Clinician's Guide to Substance Use Disorders*, most people with SUD have at least one corresponding mental health issue, with trauma, mood, and anxiety disorders being the most common (Brasler, 2022). It is therefore imperative that a SUD screening assessment be an important part of any medical or mental health service delivery, including suicide assessments. Likewise, it is very important that suicide screening and assessment be a strong part of any SUD and co-occurring disorders treatment.

One final note about mental illness and suicide. The text revision of the *DSM-5* adds diagnostic codes for suicidal behavior and non-suicidal self-injury (American Psychiatric Association, 2022). The motivation behind this was to encourage further study on suicidal behaviors outside of what are viewed as typical causes of suicidal behavior, such as depression. However, Rogers and colleagues (2019) argue that it is necessary to come up with a new diagnosis altogether so we can focus treatment on the suicidal behavior itself, as opposed to the behavior's underlying causes. Their recommended name for this diagnosis is "acute suicidal affective disturbance." We will have to wait and see if future editions of the *DSM* pursue this.

Social Isolation

Humans are social creatures. Yes, some of us are introverts and other people are shy, but for the most part, we exist within families (by blood or choice), and we involve ourselves in groups of people, whether through work, our religious life, or where we choose to live. We need other people in our lives—we need to love and be loved. We feel the need to belong, to know and be known. Our families and communities can help us during stressful times or life changes. It should then come as no surprise that when people experience social isolation following the loss of relationship and community, it can increase suicidal ideation (Knapp, 2020). In addition to diminished social support, being alone increases the risk that another person will not be available in situations when suicidal ideation leads to suicidal behaviors. Likewise, should a person attempt suicide, not having another person present to intervene or call for help increases risk. Maris (2019) notes that most suicides occur in private settings.

Hopelessness

Although we typically view hope as a future-oriented construct, hope is as much about the present as it is about the future. Hope is ultimately about our sense of purpose and place in the world. For some people, this incorporates their spiritual or religious beliefs. For others, hope is a general feeling of optimism—we admit that we can have tough days, weeks, or years, but in the end, things will work out well. A person who feels hopeless may see no purpose in their present situation and may believe that things will never get better. Death may become a more attractive option, perhaps to alleviate their hopelessness.

History of Self-Injurious Behavior or Suicidal Ideation

Self-injurious behavior includes not only cutting, but also hitting, burning, or scratching oneself or preventing wounds from healing. As I discussed in chapter 1, although conventional wisdom held that people who engaged in these behaviors were attempting suicide, once clinicians began to listen to these clients, they realized that many were telling the truth: While they were harming themselves, they had no intention or desire to die. This led to a view, which was soon adopted as conventional wisdom, that people who cut themselves were rarely (if ever) suicidal. However, as Malcolm Gladwell has demonstrated in several of his books, conventional wisdom is rarely wise and often wrong.

We currently realize that self-harming behavior can be a risk factor for suicide (Ribeiro et al., 2016). Remember that Joiner's (2007) interpersonal theory of suicide rests on the notion that people *acquire* the ability to inflict lethal self-injury. That means they reach this level by first engaging in nonlethal self-injury. It is for this reason that people who engage in self-harm are at a heightened risk of eventual suicide, with 4 percent dying by suicide within five years of beginning self-harm (Bjureberg et al., 2022). I will explore self-injurious behaviors in a later chapter.

Perceived Burdensomeness

As we age, we often rely more on younger family members to help us. Those who once parented now must be (at least partially) parented. Like many of my peers, I am experiencing my sons "leaving the nest," while also having to provide more attention to my aging father. Unfortunately, many older adults perceive this shift in caretaking roles to mean that they are a burden to their families, either because a family member has expressly stated this to them or because they inferred it from a family member's actions or indifference. Older adults may, in turn, see killing themselves as a gift to their family to not continue to be a burden to them. Our society prides itself on independence and self-reliance. When these values change or are taken away, thoughts of ending one's life may begin to appear more attractive.

In addition to older adults, other people may struggle with perceived burdensomeness that contributes to suicidality. For example, people who become injured or develop a disability that they perceive makes them a burden to others may view suicide as a means to relieve their loved ones of their "burdensomeness." While we all may struggle with belonging or believing that we are a burden to others, people who are suicidal believe this is a never-ending situation (Knapp, 2020).

Access to Lethal Means

The most common lethal means used by people who die by suicide in the US is a firearm. The use of firearms in suicide deaths in other countries is lower if that country has more stringent firearm rules. For example, in China and India, which have some of the strictest gun laws in the world, the most common form of suicide is through pesticide poisoning (Maris, 2019). In the US, it is difficult to have a substantive conversation about firearms and suicide. The issue of gun control and gun rights has become so politically inflamed that some people see talk of restricting access to firearms as an infringement of rights, while others view talking about responsible gun ownership and use as radical.

But here are the facts. In 2023, like every year before it (allowing for some minor changes in percentages), more people in the US used a firearm to kill themselves than all other forms of suicide combined. In 2023, 55 percent of people who died by suicide used a gun, while 25 percent hanged or suffocated themselves, 12.5 percent poisoned themselves, and the remaining 7.5 percent used other means (e.g., jumping, cutting, and self-immolation; AFSP, 2025). What obviously makes firearms the number one way that people kill themselves is that if a person fires a loaded gun at the right part of their body, they will likely die. Other than accessing and loading the weapon, there is little preparation required and a small margin of error that the round will not result in a lethal injury. Therefore, the presence of a firearm in a home greatly increases the risk of suicide. Bryan (2022) notes that when there are unsecured firearms in the home, the risk of suicide by children goes up exponentially, while if the gun is safely secured, suicide rates decrease by over 50 percent. As you will see in later chapters, even reducing the immediate access to firearms can decrease suicide risk.

Socioeconomic and Employment Status

Being unemployed is a suicide risk factor, as about a third of people who die by suicide are unemployed at the time of their death (Maris, 2019). In addition, as people go up the "socioeconomic ladder," suicide rates decline, meaning that people employed in nontechnical, labor-intensive positions (e.g., construction, manufacturing, or agriculture) have a higher suicide risk than those employed in middle-level service or professional and technical capacities. In fact, farmworkers have the highest rate of suicide of all occupations (Knapp, 2020). However, we need to be aware that some professional occupations have a higher suicide risk than other technical or professional jobs. A ranking by the *New Health Guide* (2015, cited by Maris, 2019) lists the following occupations (in no order) as historically having a higher suicide rate (p. 133):

- Physicians
- Dentists
- Veterinarians
- Finance workers
- Heavy-construction workers
- Lawyers
- Farm managers
- Pharmacists

We also need to pay attention to our active military service personnel, our veterans, and our first responders. Veteran suicide rates remain higher than the nonveteran population, with 6,392 veteran deaths in 2021 (US Department of

Veterans Affairs, 2023). The reasons for these higher rates are not necessarily due to deployment, since most veterans who die by suicide have never been deployed (Maris, 2019). I will examine veterans and active military personnel in a later chapter.

Chronic Medical Illness and Sleep Difficulties

Although not all medical illnesses increase suicide risk, chronic pain seems to have a greater connection with suicidal thinking, especially if attempts at ameliorating the pain have been unsuccessful. In my former practice, we used ketamine infusions to treat chronic pain, and when I completed a mental health assessment with those individuals prior to beginning treatment, I found that nearly all of them had considered suicide (although few acted on this) as a viable alternative to living in constant pain. In addition, chronic illness and pain can lead to sleep problems, which exacerbate the illness and lead to more sleep difficulties, resulting in a vicious cycle. Importantly, trouble sleeping is a strong predictor of suicidal behavior, and it remains a strong predictor even when controlling for depressive symptoms (Knapp, 2020). Insomnia is likely to contribute to suicide because poor sleep leads to fatigue as well as other difficulties in thinking through problems.

Family History of Suicide

As I noted in chapter 1, a common myth is that suicide runs in families. While there is not a "suicide" gene, there is genetic heritability in some mental health disorders that could certainly contribute to suicidal behaviors, such as mood disorders and psychotic disorders. This heritability has been documented in twin studies, which have found that the genetic basis for suicidal behavior is likely polygenic, meaning it is influenced by a combination of several genes at once—each of which contributes cumulatively to suicide risk—as opposed to a single gene (Ryan & Oquendo, 2020).

How families react to a suicide by a member, and how this suicide becomes part of the family story, also needs to be considered. In his excellent book, *People of the Lie*, M. Scott Peck (1998) relates a story from his practice in which a young man received, as a Christmas present from his parents: the shotgun his older brother had used to kill himself the previous year. Likewise, Maris (2019) notes that author Ernest Hemingway's mother gifted him the gun that his father used to kill himself. The implications of these "gifts" are clear. They suggest "Your turn" or "This is our family's story"—or, at the very least, extreme thoughtlessness.

Recent Psychiatric Hospital Discharge

One of the reasons I wrote this book was to avoid the unnecessary hospitalization of clients struggling with suicidal ideation. As you will see in the coming chapters, sometimes hospitalizing a client is the only option if they cannot remain safe outside of being closely monitored in a secure setting. Quite often, however, clients are hospitalized out of fear, even when this may not be the best option for the client. Knapp (2020) makes an excellent point about this:

> Anxious psychotherapists may, for example, adopt a "better-safe-than-sorry" approach and select the most restrictive or conservative treatment options, such as hospitalization, to reduce their own anxiety, even when a hospitalization might be clinically contraindicated. The problem is that the procedures identified as "safe" in the better-safe-than-sorry approach are not necessarily safe and may be iatrogenic. (p. 19)

Hospitalization should be an absolute last resort. One notable reason for this is that people can die by suicide while in the hospital—this most often occurs by patients strangling themselves (hanging while not suspended from the ground; Maris, 2019). More common, however, is what can happen when a client is released from the hospital, as one-third will attempt suicide within the first two weeks (Baldessarini, 2020). In fact, individuals are at highest risk for suicide either immediately following an attempt or after being discharged from the hospital following an attempt, and this risk continues for two years (Fehling & Selby, 2021). This may be more likely if the client is an adolescent or young adult. In fact, upwards of 50 percent of people who die by suicide were seen in the emergency department or admitted to a psychiatric ward sometime in the past year (Hughes et al. 2023).

Justice System Involvement

Nearly one-third of people who die by suicide have criminal justice system involvement of some sort, being either incarcerated or on probation or parole (Knapp, 2020). There are specific risk factors associated with having a criminal history that increase the risk of suicide, such as access to firearms and illicit drugs. Individuals who experience suicidal ideation while incarcerated, have a history of suicide attempts, and have a mental health disorder are at greatest risk for dying by suicide, especially if they are isolated while in jail or prison. Serving a life sentence or being convicted of a violent offense increases suicide risk as well (Zhong et al., 2021).

Aggression

Moving from suicidal ideation to suicidal behavior takes energy. For many people who are suicidal, this energy comes from aggression. In fact, Maris (2019) notes that aggression may be more likely than depression among people who die by suicide. We can see this in murder-suicide situations. A person is aggressive (in the most extreme form) toward someone else by killing them and then turns that aggression toward themselves (suicide). Maris suggests that some people feel the need to kill someone else to find a reason to kill themselves. All of this requires aggression. In addition, remember that people with ASPD have a higher risk for suicide than many other mental health disorders, and aggression is a common symptom of ASPD.

Additional Risk Factors

Additional risk factors, which may not be as clear as the ones we have examined, bear consideration. The first is sexual orientation and gender identity. In particular, members of the transgender community are at particularly heightened risk of suicidality, as up to 43 percent have attempted suicide in their lifetime (Fehling & Selby, 2021). Reasons for this include gender-based discrimination, victimization, and harassment, as well as family rejection. Beyond having an expansive gender identity, the risk for suicide is increased among the LGBTQ+ community more broadly, as research has found that students who experience same-sex attraction, orientation, or behavior are more likely to have attempted suicide during the previous year compared with their heterosexual counterparts (Hughes et al., 2023). Maris (2019) suggests that some of this increased risk among the LGBTQ+ community may be due to their sense of thwarted belongingness and perceived burdensomeness—both prominent suicide risk factors identified by Joiner.

Another risk factor currently under study is traumatic brain injury (TBI), as people with a TBI have a suicide rate three to four times greater than the general population (Torregrossa et al., 2023). This is especially the case among those who have received a TBI as a function of war, including civilians, active military, and veterans (Campbell-Stills et al., 2020). Not only do people with TBI have higher rates of suicide, but they also have higher rates of non-suicidal self-injury and all-cause mortality (Madsen et al., 2018), which underscore the difficulties of living with a TBI.

A final consideration is media reports of suicide and its impact. Whenever the media reports on the suicide death of a celebrity, there is a corresponding 13 percent increase in suicides in the subsequent time period. This number jumps to 30 percent when the media mentions the method of lethality the celebrity used (Niederkrotenthaler et al., 2020). It may be that susceptible individuals identify with the celebrity who died or may see extended media reporting as normalizing suicide as an appropriate way to deal with a problem. With the advent of social media and near-instant access to incredible amounts of information (not all of it accurate), this risk factor bears close watching.

The Swiss Cheese Model

As you have learned, while there are many risk factors that can lead to suicide, rarely, if ever, does a single risk factor result in a suicide attempt or completion. Further, it is not only the number and intensity of the risk factors that can lead to suicide, but the order and timing in which they occur and interact with one another (Bryan, 2022; Maris, 2019). Another thing we need to note is a precipitating event—something that serves as a trigger to move the person from suicidal ideation to suicidal behaviors. Precipitating events are not necessarily

Chapter 3 • Suicide Risk and Protective Factors

suicide risk factors. They can be things that happen to everyone (e.g., a job loss, a relationship ending, or financial stressors).

One way to visualize how risk factors and a precipitating event can combine to allow deleterious events is called the Swiss Cheese Model. This engineering model was developed by Dr. James Reason as a way to explain airplane crashes (Schwartz, 2019). The model holds that for a specific outcome, several factors must line up in just the right way and at the right time. If one of the factors is missing or out of sync with the others, the event cannot occur. To understand this model, visualize a slice of Swiss cheese. The holes represent problems, faults, or negative occurrences in our discussion: suicide risk factors. If you have bunch of slices of Swiss cheese and stand them up on their sides, it is likely that the holes will not line up with one another. But if we have enough holes and arrange the slices in just the right way, the holes line up, and we could pass a pencil (we can visualize the pencil as the precipitating event) through all the holes. However, if just one of the pieces of cheese is misaligned, or there are not enough holes, the outcome will not occur.

I learned about this model because I am fascinated with commercial aircraft and manned spaceflight. Being an aviation geek, I listen to several weekly podcasts on aviation, and this is where I learned about the Swiss Cheese Model. In nearly all aviation (and space) accidents, several factors coalesce to create the deadly accident. Almost never is an accident due to a single cause or action—just like suicide.

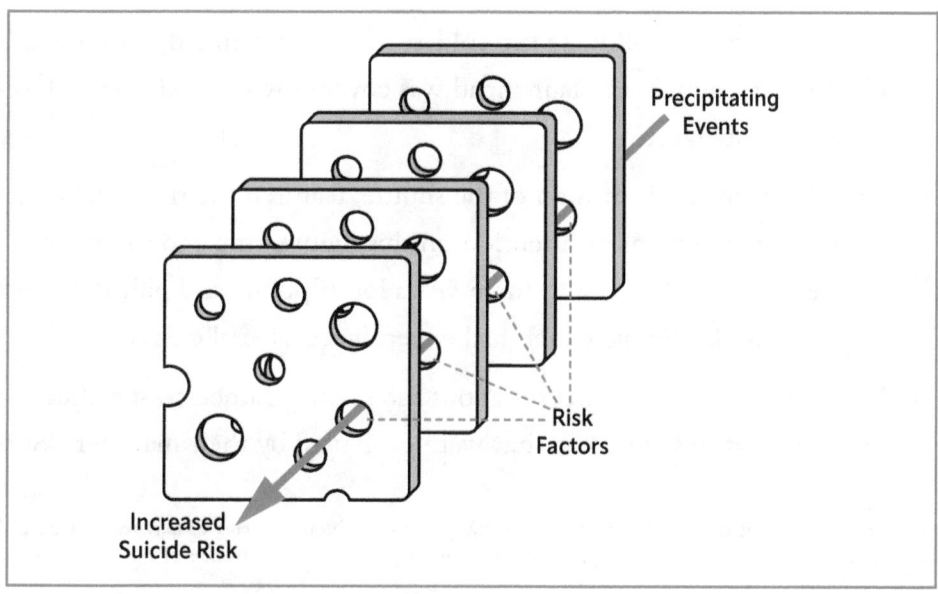

A tragic example of this is the destruction of the space shuttle *Challenger* on January 28, 1986. Like many people of my generation, I was in primary school during this event and took regular spaceflights for granted. Like most Americans, I was shocked to see the shuttle disintegrate a little more than a minute after liftoff, killing all seven astronauts. In the immediate aftermath of the incident, the focus was placed on the failure of a single part of one of the solid rocket boosters.

In the months and years that followed, we learned that this accident was more than the failure of a single, rather inexpensive, part. Rather, a series of events, many of them having nothing to do with that part (called O-rings), came together to cause the disaster. If one of these things had not happened, *when* it happened, the shuttle would likely have reached orbit. Here are some of the contributing factors:*

1. The shuttle system design itself was flawed in that it relied on solid rocket motors, which cannot be turned off once started, to provide most of the thrust for the vehicle during the first two minutes of flight. The shuttle also lacked an escape system for the crew in the event of an emergency during ascent.

2. The O-rings that held the individual sections of the solid rocket boosters together had shown partial failure (burn-through) on previous flights, but the severity of these events was dismissed by management. Furthermore, the O-rings were susceptible to failure in cold temperatures.

3. Temperatures at liftoff were the coldest ever for a manned spaceflight. The night before launch, the launchpad was covered with ice due to below-freezing temperatures.

4. This flight, the 25th mission of the shuttle, featured the first teacher in space, so there was more attention on this flight compared to previous shuttle missions. As a result, there was a lot of public and political pressure to complete this flight, which had experienced several delays.

5. Engineers had raised concerns about the flight parameters, specifically the low temperatures at launch, but were overruled by their managers. Some

---

* The information about the *Challenger* disaster is taken from the Netflix series *Challenger: The Final Flight* (2020), and Miller, R. (2022). *The space shuttle: A mission-by-mission celebration of NASA's extraordinary spaceflight program.*

engineers expected the shuttle system to explode on the launchpad and were thus somewhat relieved when the shuttle took off.

6. Upon liftoff, a slight gap developed between two of the joints, as seen in photographs, but debris within the booster soon plugged the gap. However, the shuttle experienced wind shear (a sudden change in wind direction—the highest ever recorded during a shuttle mission) as it ascended, which dislodged the plug, allowing hot gases to burn through the O-rings. This eventually led to structural failure of the external fuel tank, which exploded and destroyed the *Challenger*.

If only one of these events had not happened, it is likely that the shuttle would have achieved orbit, completed its mission, and returned its crew safely home. As Dr. Reason's model shows, each of these events had to line up to create a situation that led to disaster. If mission planners had waited a few hours to launch, allowing the temperature to rise, the O-rings would likely have not failed. If administrators had listened to engineers, perhaps the O-ring system could have been strengthened against burn-throughs (as it later was, following the disaster), and the system would not have failed. If the shuttle had not experienced wind shear, then perhaps the plugged gap would have held until solid booster separation. In addition, if there had not been political and media pressure to launch after several well-publicized delays, perhaps consideration would have been given to the engineers' concerns and the launch could have been delayed.

Let's apply Dr. Reason's model to a person at risk of suicide.

Nate is a 58-year-old male. He is married with two young adult children. Nate was diagnosed with mild major depressive disorder in his early 30s, and he takes citalopram, a selective serotonin reuptake inhibitor (SSRI) prescribed by his primary care provider. Nate drinks heavily on the weekends, usually six or more drinks on Saturdays and Sundays. He was once a distance runner, having completed several marathons, but he stopped running in his 40s and is now overweight and sedentary. Nate was recently diagnosed with hypertension and hypercholesterolemia, and he has also struggled with erectile dysfunction for the past five years. Two years ago, he was diagnosed with sleep apnea as well. He is supposed to use a CPAP, but he finds the mask uncomfortable, so he is inconsistent with his use.

Nate's father struggled with depression his entire adult life and recently died after several years of suffering from dementia. Nate's paternal grandfather died by suicide before Nate was born. Nate's mother was often overbearing and critical of Nate but not his younger brother. She is also deceased. Nate does not have a relationship with his younger brother.

Nate is married to Debbie. They met after college and have been together for nearly 30 years. Debbie works in health care, while Nate works in mid-level management for a financial company. When their children lived at home, Nate and Debbie enjoyed spending time with them, and the family took several memorable vacations together. Nate and Debbie worked hard to provide their children with a college education. Their children earned their degrees but now live in a large city halfway across the country. After their children left home, Nate and Debbie drifted apart emotionally. They have stopped being intimate and spending any quality time together, including no longer going to church.

Two of Nate's closest friends moved away from the area in the past two years. His closest friend left his wife for another woman, shocking everyone in their friendship group. Nate's other friend moved to the other side of the country to care for his aging mother. While the weekends used to be full of family events or activities with friends, Nate finds his weekends boring and unstructured. While the job he has worked for the past 25 years is also boring, it is his sole source of socialization. Debbie continues to maintain her friendships and build new ones, and often spends time with her friends, but Nate feels isolated. When Debbie invites him to activities, he often declines. Nate does not tell anyone, but for the past six months he has been feeling more hopeless, and with his children living far away, he wonders what his future will be like, or whether life is even worth living.

One Monday morning, Nate comes to his office and is surprised to see his supervisor and the head of human resources (HR) waiting for him. They usher him into an empty conference room and explain that Nate is being terminated. Nate protests that he has been with the company for 25 years and has contributed greatly to the company's success. His boss and the HR person compliment him on this and note they are offering him a "generous" severance package of half his yearly salary. They then stand up and state that he is to clean out his desk and leave the property immediately. Nate does not get a chance to say goodbye to the only people he socializes with.

Soon after, with his belongings haphazardly tossed into boxes in the backseat of his car, Nate contemplates his next move and cannot see any way forward. While the severance package will support him and Debbie for a while, they cannot subsist on her salary alone. Furthermore, Nate believes no company would hire him at his age. Nate picks up his phone and thinks about calling someone. Debbie will be busy interacting with patients at her job. He is aware that his adult children are probably headed to work, as their time zone is several hours behind Nate's. Nate feels ashamed of what has happened, and he believes he has let his family down—he will not be able to support them. Nate cannot think of any friends to call either. He is alone.

Nate drives aimlessly for several hours. The more he considers his situation, the more he feels like a burden to his family. He does not see a way out of the situation. He drives home and begins to drink. In the early afternoon, quite drunk, Nate retrieves the semiautomatic pistol he keeps in his garage. He leaves his life insurance policy on the kitchen table where Debbie will find it. Nate then walks into his backyard, goes behind his tool shed, and shoots himself through the roof of his mouth.

There are obvious risk factors associated with Nate that cannot be changed—he is male, middle-aged, and White. Nothing also can be done regarding Nate's possible genetic predisposition for depression on his paternal side. However, among Nate's other risk factors, there are many ways that the pattern that led to his suicide could have been disrupted.

1. Nate was diagnosed with mild major depressive disorder as a young man and placed on an SSRI. When was the last time the dose of his citalopram was evaluated? Nate's primary care physician prescribes his medication—has this always been the case or was Nate ever evaluated or treated by a mental health provider? Has Nate's physician suggested that he consider counseling? Has the physician regularly screened Nate for depression, alcohol use disorder, or suicide?

2. Has anyone spoken with Nate about his drinking? Does Nate realize that his drinking has become problematic? Do Nate or his family know how to access resources and support for people with alcohol use disorder? Has

Nate spoken with his primary care physician about his drinking—or was he even asked about his alcohol use?

3. Nate was recently diagnosed with high blood pressure and high cholesterol, and he has been dealing with erectile dysfunction for several years. How are these conditions being addressed medically? Has anyone spoken with Nate about how these medical conditions can also have emotional symptoms? What about possible medication side effects?

4. Nate's social circle, which was already small, has disappeared. What can Nate do to form new relationships? What hobbies or interests does he have? Could Nate and Debbie reengage with their church or find another community to be a part of?

5. Nate and Debbie have grown apart since their children successfully launched from the home. Could this be a time of relationship renewal as opposed to growing further apart? Could couples counseling (or couples coaching) be beneficial to their relationship? Even without this, could they be intentional about spending time together, perhaps traveling again?

6. Nate did not tell anyone about his increasing feelings of hopelessness and loss of purpose in his life. What if he had told this to anyone? What might they have said?

7. Nate was blindsided with his job loss, which appears to have been a significant factor leading to his death later that day. How might his former employer have handled Nate's termination in a more humane or honorable way? What about allowing him to say goodbye to the only people he interacted with? While the company provided him with a financial severance package, what about help for the mental and emotional impact of being let go from a company he had served for a quarter of a century? Does Nate have legal grounds for improper termination or potential age-discrimination lawsuits?

8. Nate felt disconnected from everyone, so he did not believe he could call anyone to talk about his job loss. He assumed his children would be on their way to their own jobs and not want to talk with him and that Debbie would be busy at work. Were these just the assumptions of

a depressed, isolated man, or were they true? Absent these connections, Nate appears to have believed that he was alone and a burden to others. Note how he made sure to leave his life insurance information where Debbie could easily find it—he had apparently hoped this act would be helpful to his family.

9. Nate had ready access to a firearm and ammunition. It does not appear to have been difficult for him to access the weapon and ammunition before shooting himself. What if it had been more difficult for Nate to access the gun, the ammunition, or both? Could more barriers to access the gun and ammo have made a difference?

10. We also need to acknowledge the precipitating factor for Nate: the sudden and unexpected loss of his job. We could argue, and I think correctly, that Nate would not have killed himself on this day had he not been fired.

One additional thing to note about Nate's actions is that he did not engage in any of the activities that most of us have been taught about people who are suicidal. He did not give away his possessions, he did not talk about suicide with anyone prior to his attempt (as far as anyone knows, this was his only suicidal action), and he did not leave a note. Nate's suicide did not appear to be planned, although the hopelessness, burdensomeness, and loneliness that drove his suicidal behaviors had been present for some time. Notice how these factors align at the same time, combining to increase suicide risk to a very high level. Removing one of these risk factors does not necessarily result in Nate not attempting (and completing) suicide but could have gone a long way to greatly decrease the likelihood of Nate's death.

Protective Factors Against Suicide

Just as there are suicide risk factors, there are things that, when present, can decrease the likelihood of a suicide attempt or death by suicide. In the same way that single risk factors rarely (if ever) lead to suicide, single protective factors rarely deter or prevent suicide, although a single protective factor can essentially cancel out the effect of several suicide risk factors (Maris, 2019). Using the Swiss Cheese

Model, we might visualize protective factors as things that "move the cheese slices" in such a way that the holes (representing various risks) will be less likely to align. Here are some of the common suicide protective factors.

Parenthood and Sense of Familial Responsibility

As previously noted, family (or lack thereof) can be a suicide risk or a protective factor. Having people around yourself is a protective factor, as nearly all people who die by suicide die alone. Having children in the home usually serves as a protective measure against suicide, as does feeling a sense of responsibility for others (such as one's family). Family members can provide a sense of purpose and support for one another. Parents, even those struggling with suicidal ideation, are often aware that harming themselves would do great damage to their children.

Religiosity and Spirituality

Having a belief in something greater than oneself, as well as having a sense of purpose, are both protective factors for many people. When someone is part of a caring, authoritative (not authoritarian) community, it decreases suicide risk overall. Spirituality can also provide reasons for living—perhaps to serve God, a higher power, or others.

My former practice was largely devoted to working with people with severe depression and PTSD, many of whom had lost connection with anything greater than themselves. Sometimes, this was a result of their struggles, while other times, their struggles were a result of not seeing anything beyond themselves. Just as we are not meant to live in isolation, we are not meant to live only for ourselves. This does not mean that we must be religious people or believe in God. What it does mean, however, is acknowledging that we are not the be-all and end-all of our existence. We can live for things outside ourselves, even if that is the betterment of humankind or healing a world harmed through neglect and abuse.

Sense of Agency

I was an angry kid growing up. It took me a while to realize that my anger was a choice in terms of how I reacted to a world that would keep moving regardless of whether I was angry or not. Before I realized this, however, I had to accept that I was not the center of the universe and that, while I had some struggles, there were plenty of people who had bigger challenges than I did. My mother, who raised my two younger brothers and me by herself, helped me to learn this when I was 15 years old. I had reached a self-destructive part of my life and thought regularly of killing myself. Mom, who was a part-time college student while working full-time and raising us, somehow sensed this. She came home early from work one day when I was home alone because she'd had a "bad feeling" at work.

That weekend, she took me to visit a young woman she was trying to help. We traveled from our working-class neighborhood to a part of Louisville, my hometown, that I had never been to before—what we called the slums. The apartment building we walked up to seemed desolate, and when the young woman, holding her newborn son, let us in, I found myself walking on cockroaches. Mom seemed to ignore this, and instead asked the young lady how she was doing and provided her with baby supplies she had gathered from people at our church. Mom also gently provided guidance and teaching for how to care for the baby. I stood around not knowing what to do and was amazed by the squalor.

I was very glad to leave that place, and I was quiet on the way home.

"Well," Mom said, "what did you see?"

"It was gross," I replied. "Why does she live like that?"

"Don't think she wants to, Paul," she replied. "And we're doing our best to help."

That was the extent of our conversation, but that outing (and several similar ones) soon changed my outlook on life. I realized there were many people struggling more than I was. I went from feeling sorry for myself to seeing that I was fortunate and I could do something.

When people realize that they have agency in their lives and that they can do things to help themselves and others, they create positive change for themselves. As clinicians, we can help clients develop this capacity to attune to the positive experiences in their lives, while simultaneously helping them bounce back from stressful experiences, which can serve as a "braking system" of sorts that protects against suicidal behaviors (Bryan, 2022). A lot of this comes through practice, both in clinical settings and in the community. In future chapters, I will look at how to help people create this change in themselves.

Social Supports

As you learned earlier in this chapter, diminished social support is a major risk factor for suicide, which explains the higher rates of suicide among older adults. As such, having a sense of belonging and being part of a community, whether it be a neighborhood, work, or faith-based community, can be a protective factor for suicide. However, it is not only humans who can provide us with social support. We also need to remember that our four-legged friends (or our winged, finned, or slithering friends) can be powerful protective factors for suicide as well. I remember several times, when working in the emergency department, I was speaking with a patient struggling with suicidal ideation and found out that their pet was a big part of them wanting to remain alive—and the reason they sought help for how they were feeling.

"If I'm gone, who's going to take care of Fluffy?" one lady said.

"Fluffy?" I asked.

"My cat!" she replied, before showing me a picture. While admiring the photos on her phone, I kept thinking, *Thank God for Fluffy*.

Resiliency

I think the concept of resiliency is misunderstood. We all experience bad things in life, while some people experience traumatic things. However, most people do not attempt to kill themselves after experiencing a bad, or even traumatic, event. Of course, this does not mean that people who respond to life stressors by considering suicide are weaker or less deserving of life. It also means that returning to baseline after a loss or other bad thing is not necessarily resilience.

For several years, I worked on a project with the Air Force's religious affairs office, where we tried to expand resilience among service men and women who were serving their fellow airmen. Pauline Boss's (2006) definition of resilience is my favorite:

> The ability to regain one's energy after adversity drains it. It is more than "bouncing back," which implies regaining the status quo; rather, it means rising above traumatic and ambiguous losses by not letting them immobilize and living well despite them. Resiliency means

flexibility, the opposite of brittleness, and movement, the opposite of paralysis. (p. 27)

If we can agree on this definition of resilience (or one similar), we must then ask ourselves, how do we foster resilience in others? If resilience can be a protective factor against suicide, how can we recognize and grow it in our clients? One way to conceptualize resilience from traumatic events is through the concept of post-traumatic growth, which is a way of *growing and learning* from traumatic events (Falke & Goldberg, 2018). Post-traumatic growth involves helping people realize that when a stressful event occurs, positive change can occur as well, such as new opportunities, deeper relationships, realized personal strengths, a deeper appreciation of life, and spiritual-existential change. I am not saying that we ignore our clients' struggles or minimize them in any way, but we can help our clients see their events in different ways, including areas for potential healing and growth.

Even when we consider protective factors, this is a book about suicide, and we need to examine suicidal ideation and consider how a person can transition from thinking about suicide to planning to kill themselves and then potentially acting on that plan. We also need to examine self-injurious behavior and its possible relationship to suicide. Those topics are the focus of the next chapter.

CHAPTER 4

Suicide Ideation to Action

Most people assume that a person's path toward a suicide attempt (or death by suicide) follows a linear path from suicidal thoughts to planning to action. While many people move from thought to action in this manner, not everyone arrives at suicidal behavior in a straightforward (and predictable) manner. Rarely in life do things move in a predictable, linear pattern. At the same time, we can learn in a linear manner, which is what we will do in this chapter where I will examine suicidal ideation, suicidal intention (including methods), and suicidal behaviors. I will also examine self-injury in the absence of suicidal intent.

Suicidal Ideation

We need to understand that thinking about suicide and acting on it are two different things. Estimates vary that between one-quarter to one-half of the US population will think about killing themselves at some point in their lives. Obviously, most people who think about killing themselves will not put action to their thoughts. At the same time, we need to take suicidal ideation seriously, and this begins by understanding the different types of suicidal ideation, as collated by Maris (2019):

1. **Situational, passive ideas of suicide.** This is likely the most common form of suicidal ideation and is usually due to specific, often situational, stressors. This type of suicidal ideation does not include any planning, and the ideation usually remits once the stressor(s) have abated.

2. **Chronic or obsessive suicidal ideation.** People with this type of ideation think constantly about killing themselves, sometimes to the exclusion of other things. Individuals with this ideation may come to view suicide as an appropriate solution to their problems. They may also find it difficult to keep suicidal thoughts out of their mind (obsessive suicidal ideation).

3. **Suicidal ideation without a plan.** When I worked in the emergency department, this was probably the most common suicidal ideation I encountered. "How are you thinking about killing yourself?" or "How would you kill yourself?" would often be answered by "I don't know." This does not mean a lack of suicidal ideation—it means the person may be ambivalent about dying or ambivalent about how they may try to kill themselves.

4. **Suicidal ideation with a nonlethal plan.** The terminology "nonlethal plan" may be a misnomer. In this context, we are talking about suicide methods that are not *immediately* fatal, such as overdosing on medications or cutting oneself, where there is usually an opportunity to intervene prior to death.

5. **Suicidal ideation with a definitive, lethal plan.** People experiencing this type of suicidal ideation have a plan to use quickly lethal methods—Maris (2019) calls these "medical certainty" methods—such as shooting themselves or falling from a high place.

Regardless of the type of suicidal ideation, any report of suicidal thought should be taken seriously. At the same time, clinicians should remain calm and listen to what the person is saying. If suicidal ideation is expressed in a clinical session, I want to gather more information, and when clients see that we are listening to them without overreacting, they are more likely to continue to engage with us.

I have heard people say that when another person says they are feeling suicidal that "they are just looking for attention." A solid clinical (human, actually) response to this would be: "Of course they're looking for attention—and now they have it! Let's see what they want to tell us."

Chapter 4 • Suicide Ideation to Action

Suicide Warning Signs

We can only become aware of suicidal ideation when clients tell us what they are thinking. Remember that many people who are suicidal do not disclose this to anyone, or when asked, they may deny any suicidal ideation. Knapp (2020) emphasizes that there is no reliable way to identify people who are falsely denying suicidal ideation. Therefore, we need to be aware of suicide warning factors in addition to the types of suicidal ideation.

Although we can differentiate risk factors (chronic or long-term characteristics) from suicide warning signs (acute, action-oriented behaviors), some things may be both risk factors and warning signs, such as mood disorders and substance use disorders. In addition, like suicide risk factors and suicidal ideation, we may not be aware of certain suicide warning signs if the person does not disclose them. Regardless, a clinician, or anyone who works with people, needs to be aware of the warning signs for suicide. Remember that these signs may appear in individuals who appear to lack suicide risk factors. We also need to remember that these are not the only warning signs. However, if our warning sign lists are too extensive, they can become unmanageable and lead to false positives where we believe a person is suicidal when they are not (Knapp, 2020). The following list of suicide warning signs is adapted from Ryan and Oquendo (2020):

1. Suicidal ideation
2. Suicide plan
3. Increasing alcohol or substance use
4. Major depressive episode, often accompanied by anxiety
5. Hopelessness
6. Agitation
7. Akathisia (a sense of inner restlessness; can also be a side effect from antipsychotic medications)
8. Withdrawing from others
9. Psychosis
10. Statements about feeling trapped

11. Talk of being a burden or hindrance to others
12. Loss of a sense of purpose for life
13. Impulsivity, especially recklessness
14. Rage or extreme anger
15. Extreme mood swings
16. Insomnia

The presence of a single suicide risk factor necessitates further inquiry from the clinician. I usually ask, "Can you tell me more [*about the warning sign observed*]?" It is very important to remain calm (or at least give the appearance of being calm) and not overreact, but at the same time, not dismiss or ignore a suicide warning sign. The presence of multiple warning signs obviously requires even more attention from the clinician.

Suicide Ideation-to-Action Theories

While we must take reports of suicidal ideation seriously, remember that most people who experience suicidal ideation will not develop a suicide plan or attempt suicide (Blanchard & Farber, 2018). However, the link between suicidal ideation and suicide attempt is supported by three ideation-to-action theories. These theories build on one another and note the transition from suicidal ideation to suicide attempt.

I discussed Joiner's (2007) interpersonal theory of suicide (IPTS) in chapter 1, which states that people work their way toward suicide because they have a desire to die, and they have acquired the ability to kill themselves. The desire to die develops because the person does not feel connected to others ("thwarted belonginess") or believes they are a burden to others ("perceived burdensomeness"). Knapp (2020) adds that while most people feel a sense of thwarted belongingness or a lack of connection with others at some points in their lives, some people believe that these feelings will always be present—thus their ability to develop a desire to die. Remember that in the IPTS model, people who attempt suicide must also work toward the capacity to kill themselves. While some of this acquired capacity may be genetic (Knapp, 2020), other people engage in incrementally more serious self-injurious behavior to habituate themselves to pain and suffering. Knapp adds that people who work in certain fields, such as medical professionals, sex workers, police officers, and correctional officers, are exposed to seeing others in pain (or experience pain themselves), which may habituate them to suffering in general.

The second ideation-to-action theory is the integrated motivational-volitional (IMV) theory by Rory O'Connor (2011), which builds on IPTS. IMV proposes three stages that a person moves through as they transition from suicidal ideation to suicidal behaviors. The first stage is the premotivational stage, during which the individual has characteristics (life events, genetics, environment) that make them vulnerable to suicidal ideation. The second stage is motivational, where the person develops suicidal ideation. This is where perceived burdensomeness and thwarted belongingness feed the emotional pain needed to move toward the third stage. The third stage is volitional—the person acts on their ideations. This is where the acquired capability for harming oneself comes into play. IMV differs from IPTS in that it focuses on defeat and entrapment as a major part of the emotional pain needed to move a person from motivational to volitional. Defeat occurs when an individual feels as though they have lost the ability to overcome their struggles, while entrapment adds the feeling that they cannot escape from this sense of hopelessness, making suicide appear as a viable (or the only) way out of the situation.

The three-step theory (3ST) of suicide by Klonsky and May (2015) is the final ideation-to-action theory. According to the theory, ideation progresses to action when "(a) the patient feels pain and hopelessness, (b) the pain is greater than the patient's sense of connectedness, and (c) the patient has acquired the capability of attempting suicide" (Knapp, 2020, p. 25). During the first step, the pain is pervasive, and as a response, the person begins to withdraw from life. Mental illness, substance use disorder, and physical pain can increase this level of pain. However, the experience of pain in and of itself cannot make someone suicidal, as they must experience a sense of hopelessness as well. In the second step, the level of pain and hopelessness overwhelm the person's sense of connection with others. The individual sees no meaning in their pain and begins to believe that others would be better off if they were dead. In the third and final step, the person acquires the capacity to kill themselves. This occurs through an ability to harm themselves and access to the means to harm themselves.

While these three ideation-to-action theories provide a framework for understanding how suicidal ideation can lead to suicidal behavior, we must remember that human behavior (or anything for that matter) does not always follow a linear trajectory. For example, there is a fourth theory of suicide known as the fluid vulnerability theory (FVT; Rudd, 2006), which maintains that the transition from suicidal ideation to suicidal behavior is not a linear process, but rather is dynamic and fluctuates across time. This matches how mental illnesses often follow a remission-to-exacerbation pattern and how various life stressors ebb and follow in an individual's life.

Suicide Intent (Planning)

Suicide intent can be seen as a move from thinking about suicide to developing a plan of action. At this point, the person is thinking about how they will kill themselves. When someone exhibits suicide intent, they have considered how to use "a particular means (e.g., suicide) to effect a result (e.g., death). Suicidal intent usually indicates that the individual understands the physical nature and consequences of the self-destructive act" (Maris, 2019, p. 26). We may also see suicide intent as a move toward the person deciding to kill themselves, even if they remain ambivalent about wanting to die. Suicide intention can transition into planning—when a person begins to put their intentions into action and may gather the things they need to die by suicide (e.g., purchase medications, a gun and ammunition, or poisons) or make other plans (e.g., locate a bridge or parking garage they could jump from).

Chapter 4 • Suicide Ideation to Action

Suicide Methods

As I mentioned in chapter 3, firearms are the number one method people in the US use to kill themselves for men and women alike, with a greater proportion of men dying by firearm compared to other methods when compared with women. The most common methods of suicide attempts and suicide deaths in the US include:

- Shooting oneself—with either a handgun or long gun (rifle or shotgun).
- Drug overdose—prescription or over-the-counter medications or illicit substances.
- Poisoning—household chemicals, usually through ingestion.
- Hanging—this is the most common method used by people who are incarcerated or hospitalized. Most people who die in this manner are not suspended from the ground, and their necks are rarely broken due to a drop. Instead, they die by strangulation.
- Suffocation—using carbon monoxide (sitting in a parked car with exhaust directed into the cab), putting a plastic bag over one's head, or inhaling chemicals within an enclosed space.
- Cutting oneself—this is difficult to do, but some people are successful in cutting themselves sufficiently to bleed to death.
- Falling—jumping from a height of more than 60 feet is nearly always fatal.
- Drowning—jumping or walking into deep water.
- Self-immolation—burning oneself to death.
- Intentional exposure to the elements—usually freezing to death.

As previously noted, most individuals select a single method with which to kill themselves. If this method is blocked or thwarted in any way, they will not automatically move to a new method (Jobes, 2023). Most people who are suicidal are ambivalent about dying and typically use the methods most easily available to them, but this feeling or desire to attempt suicide will usually pass before they think of another way to try to harm themselves (Knapp, 2020). Means safety counseling seeks to delay access to lethal means when suicide urges are high. I will examine means safety further when I discuss safety planning.

Relationship Between Method and Intent

Wanting to die is a feeling. Behaving or acting in a way that is potentially lethal is different. When dealing with people who express suicidal ideation or even engage in suicidal behavior, we often assume that the desire to die matches the behaviors that could bring about death. While this may be true sometimes, it is often not the case.

The two case studies that follow occurred within a two- or three-week period years ago. During this time, I was working full-time in emergency departments for a regional hospital company. I was based out of a small, inner-city hospital that had a moderate-sized inpatient psychiatric unit. About two-thirds of the patients I assessed were in that emergency department. But I also had to cover three other emergency departments in suburban areas and would travel to those hospitals as needed when called. The first patient, Annabelle, was seen in my main hospital, while Clara was seen at the most remote hospital I served.

Case Study: Annabelle

Annabelle had been medically cleared by the emergency department physician when I went into the room to speak with her. It had been a busy day, and I had just arrived from another hospital where I had finished a consultation. Annabelle's nurse was dealing with a medical crisis in the adjoining room, so I did not have a chance to speak with him. Also, there was limited information in the chart, as the nurse had not had time to update the chart because of the medical crisis. I decided to go ahead and begin my assessment with Annabelle because we were shorthanded, and I knew she had been waiting to speak with me.

What struck me when I first entered the room was how Annabelle appeared to have sunk into the mattress on the bed. She was in her mid-20s and wore a large flannel shirt and jeans. She had on a knit hat as well. Annabelle appeared to be underweight but not gaunt.

I introduced myself and asked if we could talk, and she consented to this.

"I haven't had a chance to talk with the doctor or your nurse, but I know that you're here for a mental health reason. The doc and nurse are dealing with a situation next door, so could you tell me what's going on?" I asked.

Annabelle barely made eye contact with me. "I just want to die," she said quietly.

"Alright," I replied. "What's going on?"

Annabelle stated that she had been living with depression for several years. She had recently had to stop attending graduate school because of her depression, and she had also lost her part-time job. Estranged from her family, Annabelle shared that she had been in an abusive relationship with a partner who had broken up with her. She felt she had no one in her life and no reason to live.

"So, I tried to kill myself," she said.

"What did you do?" I asked, feeling a little anxious, since she had not received medical attention yet.

"I took an overdose of five ibuprofen," Annabelle replied.

I was relieved for a moment, since I knew that 1,000 mg of ibuprofen was not lethal.

"Why that amount?" I asked.

"It's all I had at home, and I thought it would do the trick. But I can't even kill myself right," she replied.

"Did you take anything else?" I asked.

"No," she answered.

Throughout our conversation, Annabelle maintained a monotone voice and spoke softly. Her attitude toward living was ambivalent, she lacked supportive people in her life, and despite an attempt that was nowhere near lethal, she truly seemed to want to die. In the end, I suggested inpatient treatment, as we could not formulate a plan to keep her safe. While she was ambivalent about treatment, she consented to an inpatient psychiatric admission.

Case Study: Clara

I was typically called to the farthest hospital I served about two or three times a month. I was asked to assess Clara because she had taken a large amount of acetaminophen. Unlike the situation with Annabelle, I was able to learn more about Clara before I went into her room.

Clara, a woman in her early 20s, was sitting in a hospital bed, and the first thing I noticed was that she had two intravenous lines, one in each arm. What was unusual about this was that both lines were attached to large bags containing saline (as well as what I assumed were medications of some sort). Clara was attentive to what was happening around her. She did not appear sad or depressed.

I introduced myself and asked for permission to talk with her. Clara consented and seemed a little confused. I asked what she had taken, as I had been informed that Clara had overdosed on medication, but I was not certain what medications.

"I'm not sure," she stated. "I had a really bad headache yesterday afternoon, so I took some extra strength Tylenol. The headache didn't go away, so I kept taking Tylenol last night and today. That didn't work, so I came here."

"How many pills did you take?" I asked.

"I dunno, probably 20 to 25."

I did a quick calculation in my head. Five hundred milligrams per pill and at least 20 pills meant at least 10 grams of acetaminophen. This was a dangerous amount of medication. Acetaminophen can damage a person's liver at amounts much lower than 10 grams. That explained the two IVs running wide open—they were trying to flush the medication out. Clara must have noticed me pausing.

"What's the problem?" she asked. Turning to the IV lines on her arms, "What is all of this for?"

"Do you understand how dangerous acetaminophen can be in higher doses?"

I watched as the color drained from Clara's face.

"Oh my God! Am I going to die?" she asked, tears welling up in her eyes as her voice rose in a panic. "I don't want to die!"

I then realized that no one had asked Clara if her overdose had been intentional, and no one had told her that a mental health clinician would be coming to speak with her. Since she was asking about dying, I decided to ask the doctor to come into the room. Normally, I called the physicians and physician assistants I worked with "doc" as a sign of respect. This time, however, I stuck my head out of the room, saw the attending doctor and yelled, "Matt!" Dr. Matt was an excellent doctor and an overall good guy. He also didn't seem to mind me calling him by his first name.

"What's up?" he asked, walking toward me.

"Your patient has a question," I said as he walked into the room.

"Am I going to die?" Clara asked.

"You mean today?" Matt responded. I could have hit him.

"Yeah, today!" Clara exclaimed.

Chapter 4 • Suicide Ideation to Action

"I don't think so," said Matt, seeing the seriousness of the situation. "You took a lot of medicine that can kill you. But I think you're going to be okay now that we've got other medications rolling that can help block the effects of acetaminophen. I am going to have to medically admit you, though. The question is, why did you take so much medication?"

"I don't want to die. I want to live. I want to finish my graduate degree. I want to have a life," Clara said, dissolving into tears.

"Thanks, doc. I can take it from here," I said, as Matt reassured Clara he would check on her later.

About this time, Clara's mother entered the room, looking confused and concerned as she saw the IV lines.

"Mom, I took a lot of Tylenol for my headache and they're saying it could kill me!" cried Clara.

I introduced myself to Clara's mother and repeated what Dr. Matt had said, while explaining my role and reasons for being there. Clara asked if her mother could stay, and I said that was fine. During the interview, Clara consistently denied any suicidal ideations, any desire to die, and any previous suicide attempts. She had a supportive family and was focused on completing her education and beginning her career. Clara also had an extensive support network. Her mother concurred with what Clara stated. In the end, it appeared that what Clara had done had been foolish (it is important to read medication labels, especially over-the-counter medications), but there was no suicidal intent. To ensure the utmost safety, I recommended that a one-on-one patient aide remain with her on the medical unit and that a psychiatrist evaluate her before she was medically discharged.

At face value, based just on what (and how much) medication Annabelle and Clara took, it would make sense for Clara to be psychiatrically hospitalized while Annabelle would be discharged and treated in the community. The key in these situations is intent—what did each of them want or expect to happen when taking an overdose? Clara was looking for relief from a headache; Annabelle was looking for an exit from life. Regardless of what or how much they ingested, the focus of the assessment and subsequent action plan was on what each of them wanted and expected from taking the medications, in addition to their risk and protective factors.

Suicide Attempts and Death by Suicide

We differentiate suicide attempts from suicide deaths based on the outcome. A person who has attempted suicide has acted in such a way that death is an expected outcome, yet the death did not occur. Unfortunately, attempts can also be "successful" in that death occurs. Remember that according to Joiner's IPTS of suicide, people who are suicidal need to not just have a desire to die but must also develop the *acquired* capacity to not fear death—and they will not act on their desire to die until they achieve this capacity.

When someone attempts suicide but doesn't die, it is not uncommon for other people to not be aware. As a result, we don't have reliable data on suicide attempts, since almost 50 percent of people who attempt to kill themselves don't seek medical attention (Knapp, 2020). What is interesting is that most people who attempt suicide feel less suicidal and have a sense of emotional relief if they survive the attempt (Bryan, 2022). Many of these people may feel embarrassed that they tried to kill themselves in the first place, so they may not tell anyone about their attempt. Or they may fear being involuntarily hospitalized because of their actions.

When I ask a client if they have ever attempted suicide and they admit to a previous attempt, I ask them to tell me what happened. When I adopt a concerned and gently curious approach and do not react with fear, people usually explain what happened. I also ask if the client told others about their attempt and how other people reacted to it. As you can imagine, most family and friends express concern for their loved ones, but others do not, and this can add to future suicide risk.

I was once asked to interview a 27-year-old male (we will call him Greg) who came to the emergency department complaining of severe depression. He had been medically cleared when I was asked to speak with him. Greg stated that he had been struggling with depressive symptoms for several months, including problems with his sleep and appetite, difficulty concentrating, feeling hopeless, and being "in a fog" much of the time. He and his wife had twin 3-year-old daughters. Greg seemed eager to talk, and we quickly established a good rapport.

"You mentioned that you grew up in Florida; what was that like?" I asked.

"Pretty normal," Greg replied. "My parents split up when I was young, and I lived with my dad until I was about 14 years old. Then my mom got custody, and

Chapter 4 • Suicide Ideation to Action

I went to live with her. That was not as good as my dad since I had to move to Virginia, but it was pretty normal here, I guess."

For reasons I do not remember, I asked Greg some other questions before asking him about suicide. He denied wanting to kill himself currently, but he admitted to a previous attempt, so I asked him to explain. I was also struck by the fact that he used the word "normal" several times during his description of his upbringing and home life.

"When I was living with my mom, she kept me separate from the two kids she had with my stepfather. I slept on a concrete floor with just a blanket. I had to brush off the mouse and rat shit when I lay down at night. She'd beat me if I asked for more food, as the refrigerator was always locked. So, one day, I took an extension cord and tried to hang myself. I messed it up somehow because I wound up falling to the floor. My mom then came into the room, saw me on the floor, and said, 'You dumb shit! You can't even fucking kill yourself!'"

I was looking intently at Greg as he said all of this. I remained at a loss for words when he stopped talking.

"You know, I hadn't thought of that in a while," Greg said slowly and quietly. "That wasn't normal, was it?"

"I think you and I can agree that it was not. That was horrible."

"Yeah," said Greg. "My mom . . ." He took a breath. "Paul, do you think this could have something to do with why I am depressed?"

"I think it is certainly a good place to start," I replied.

"But why would this impact me now?"

"I honestly don't know," I said. "But I have seen situations in which people push traumatic stuff out of their minds and then it comes back later in life. It could be that now that you're a father, being a parent has brought up memories of your own parents. This could be a good place to start in counseling if you wanted to."

I referred Greg to a trusted counselor to begin his work. Greg was not the first or only person to tell me how the people who were supposed to care for them had encouraged them to kill themselves. I wonder how many people who wind up dying by suicide have made previous attempts, only for their "loved ones" to respond as Greg's mother had.

When it comes to people who die by suicide, we can only infer their ideations and intent after their death—and this information is often incomplete. The process of determining a person's possible thought process after their death is called a psychological autopsy (Maris, 2019).

Non-Suicidal Self-Injury

As I previously explained, non-suicidal self-injury is not separate from suicide attempts. Self-injurious behaviors include cutting, burning, scratching, hair-pulling, skin excoriation, and keeping wounds from healing. We need to remember that self-injurious behaviors are a suicide risk factor. However, we also need to remember that many people who engage in self-injurious behaviors have no intention or desire to die. The key to differentiating the role of self-injurious behaviors is to try to understand why the person is harming themselves.

Last year, I met a 41-year-old female client to assess her for ketamine infusion treatment in the clinic I worked in. One of the questions I asked was if she had ever been psychiatrically hospitalized, and she replied that she had been hospitalized three years prior after cutting her arms severely with broken pottery. She was adamant that while she had flown into a rage and broken a lot of things in her bedroom, she had not been suicidal at that time, and she denied any current suicidal ideation.

The client seemed to believe that this part of our conversation was over, but I needed more information. I needed to make sure that something that was a suicide attempt (even if the person felt ambiguous about their desire to die) was not being recategorized (or minimized) as a non-suicidal self-injury.

"Who called emergency services?" I asked.

"My (now) ex-husband," she replied. "I was bleedin' pretty bad, and I had to get stitched up."

"Did they ask you about suicide in the emergency department? Did they ask you anything about your self-harming behaviors?" I asked.

"They asked about suicide," she answered, "and I told them that I wasn't trying to kill myself. I think their concern was that I had a lot of healed burns and scars on my arms, legs, and chest, from where I used to put out cigarettes on myself. That's why they insisted on admitting me."

"Do you still burn yourself?"

"Oh no, I stopped it before then. I think I burned myself for a couple of years. I was feeling really bad at that time and the pain gave me something to think about. I guess you could call it a phase. Hell, I don't even smoke anymore!"

It appeared to me that my new client had stopped her self-injurious behaviors, but her willingness to endure pain over several years demonstrated what Joiner (2007) would likely categorize as her ability to acquire capacity to harm herself further. This is one of the difficulties when dealing with self-injury. Is there truly no suicidal intent? Or is this a way to "work" one's way up to lethal self-injury? What about ambivalence to both the consequences of self-injury and a suicide attempt?

There simply is no clear answer to these questions, except to make sure we assess for self-injurious behaviors during a suicide assessment. We should then not make assumptions that self-injury is really a suicide attempt or that self-injury has nothing to do with suicidal ideation or intent. Treat individuals separately—everyone's story is different anyway, but make sure you take the time to ask about self-injury.

One last word on self-injury. When I started in the clinical field in the 1990s, people who cut themselves usually did so exclusively on their wrists—usually perpendicularly across the visible veins in their wrists. This rarely led to serious injury because blood vessels were not compromised over a large portion of their arms. During the first year I worked in the emergency department, I walked into a room to see a patient, and she calmly lifted her arms and showed me the hundreds, if not thousands, of scars where she had cut herself on her forearms in the past. Sure, this was for dramatic effect, but as I told her, "You have my attention."

In recent years, people have moved from cutting themselves on their wrists, where wounds are often visible, to cutting or burning themselves in places that are hidden. Over the past few years, clients I have encountered who self-harm typically do so on their upper thighs, on their breasts or buttocks, or near their genitals. Because these wounds are hidden, I refer these clients to medical professionals for examination to ensure their wounds are healing or not infected.

Malingering Patients

Malingering involves intentionally faking physical or mental symptoms for secondary gain (American Psychiatric Association, 2013). Secondary gain usually entails admission to a hospital or program, may include economic incentives, or may be an attempt to obtain drugs. Malingering is different from factitious disorder (although the two are sometimes difficult to discern from each other), where the falsification of signs and symptoms occurs *without* secondary gain. We need to be extremely cautious when considering whether or not someone is malingering when it comes to suicidal ideation, while acknowledging some people do engage in malingering. But how can we identify it?

My rule of thumb when working in the emergency department was that even if I was certain that the patient was malingering about wanting to kill themselves, if I did not have any history on the patient, I would likely admit them. I think that this is the safest approach overall. Even in situations where I had a patient's history, and there was clear evidence of prior malingering, I tried to see the current presentation on its own merit. At the same time, I encountered a lot of people who were malingering in an attempt to get psychiatrically admitted. I happened to work with two excellent psychiatrists who understood the various reasons why people malinger and who also documented their clinical findings very well. We observed three key areas that helped us identify malingering.

The first was the context of the presentation. In other words, what was going on in the client's life that made them want to seek admission? Clients who were malingering would often try to start the interview by vehemently stating their need to be admitted, even before they explained *why* they needed to be admitted. Sometimes, they were doing so in an attempt to avoid legal proceedings or justice system involvement. As a result, there were several times that I found myself assessing clients who were looking to avoid jail time by being admitted to a psychiatric facility instead. While there are certainly situations where a person requires hospitalization, those situations must be clinical in nature and not an attempt to avoid the consequences of one's actions.

The second clue was a marked discrepancy between the individual's claimed stress or disability and the objective findings and observations of the assessment. I saw this several times when working in the emergency department. As I entered the room, I could hear the patient talking loudly on their phone and laughing. Yet when I identified myself and the reason I was there, the patient's affect immediately changed. While it is not uncommon for people to demonstrate lability in their mood and affect due to several different mental health problems, these changes are not voluntary—clients cannot simply change their affect because they want to. A major exception to this, of course, are clients who are malingering.

The third situation was usually more straightforward. We would experience a lack of cooperation from the client. I have had clients get frustrated or angry because "you keep asking me all these damn questions!" This can be accompanied by demands or threats such as "I will kill myself if you don't do this for me!" The following situation, which I faced years ago when working in the emergency department, illustrates this.

I had just entered the room to meet with a patient named George, when he immediately began demanding medication: "I just moved here about a week ago from Baltimore. I ran out of my medications four days ago. I need refills on my Suboxone, Seroquel, and Xanax. I need you to do this, or I am going to kill myself. That'll be on you if I die."

George was 38 years old, and he said this with his fists clenched while he glared at me. Before I could even introduce myself, he continued, "I've been locked up over 100 times; you can check that out. I have a doctor from Baltimore. I have his card and his personal cell number on it, and you can call him, and he can tell you that I need my meds and that I am suicidal."

"Okay," I said. "I hear you, but we have to talk so we can decide what we are going to do. That involves me asking you some questions, is that okay?"

"Sure," George replied. "No problem."

George consented to having a medical provider examine him, and he provided blood samples for medical clearance. During this time, I discovered that George had been to two other emergency departments earlier in the day. While he answered my initial questions, including information about his substance use disorder, when I began to ask how he ran out of his prescriptions, he became vague and resumed an aggressive posture. When I expressed concern about the combination of medications he was taking—adding that our medical provider would likely only provide a few days' worth of Suboxone—George became angry again.

"If you don't give me my meds, I am going to kill myself!"

I worked hard to remain calm and focused.

"If you are talking about killing yourself," I replied, "then this becomes less about your medications and more about whether we need to admit you to the psychiatric ward."

"Will I get those meds there?" George asked.

"Only if the doctor believes you need them. I can tell you, though, that benzodiazepines like Xanax are usually not prescribed to a person who is prescribed Suboxone."

"So what am I supposed to do?" George asked.

"I told you we could give you something here, and I have places you can go to tomorrow for an appointment about other services," I said.

"Fuck that!" George shouted. "I'm leaving."

He started to walk out but was stopped by the police officer in the emergency department. (We had officers present for security.)

"Do I need to detain him?" the officer asked me.

"I can leave," said George.

"He can," I said, as George walked away. "He's done the same thing in two other emergency departments today when refused what he is asking for."

I typically do not investigate whether patients who have been to previous emergency departments are "medication seeking," but George's outright hostile demeanor and demanding tone suggested malingering. An important aspect of working with clients who may be malingering is to remain calm and professional, while also having firm boundaries and setting clear expectations. My experience when doing this is that, many times, the malingering client will walk away. Of course, if there are threats of violence, those threats should be taken seriously and addressed immediately. I will discuss violent clients further in a later chapter.

Overall, being able to discern between suicidal ideation and intent (including when ideation is progressing to action)—as well as being able to identify the presence of malingering—all underscore the importance of conducting a thorough suicide screening and assessment to determine the best course of action. In the next chapter, I'll focus on the concepts of screening and assessment in more detail.

CHAPTER 5

Suicide Screening and Assessment

It is not unusual for the terms *screening* and *assessment* to be used interchangeably, but they are two separate things. A screening is used to quickly identify individuals who are potentially at risk and would benefit from further evaluation, whereas an assessment is a more in-depth evaluation used to confirm these risks and guide next steps. A thorough suicide prevention strategy must include both screening and assessment. However, as I noted earlier, patients can conceal their suicidal intentions—and this includes in written screenings or during an assessment interview. It is for this reason that experienced professionals trust their instincts and experiences, while not relying on either of these instruments alone. The best practice for suicide assessment is to utilize valid and reliable screening tools, conduct a thorough assessment, *and* utilize our interpersonal skills to try to elicit truthful responses from clients.

Making the Connection: The Importance of Set and Setting

The *setting* is the physical space in which we interact with our clients. In my work with people utilizing ketamine-assisted psychotherapy, we placed a high priority not only on the setting, but on the *set* as well. Set is short for mindset—in other words, what the client is thinking and feeling. As a clinician, my mindset is also important, especially when working with people in the "non-ordinary state of consciousness" (i.e., the ketamine experience). Clients can pick up on my attitudes and thought process, so I need to remain mindful of my "stuff" and focus on being present, open, and positive. Even when I work with clients who are not having a psychedelic experience, I must remain mindful of my attitude, my body language, and the energy I put into the conversation because this greatly influences set and setting.

While set and setting are important when using psychedelic medications, they are also important in everyday work with our clients. I think this is especially true when conducting assessments in which we delve into emotionally weighty topics such as suicide. While your mindset is something over which you have control, how can you make the setting where you interact with clients feel safe, less distracting, and less intrusive?

When I started working in the emergency department conducting psychiatric evaluations, my primary hospital was a small, overburdened facility in a poor urban area of Richmond. We had 12 rooms in our department, and room one was designated as the "psych room." Room one was abhorrent. It had dingy white tiles on the floor and walls. There were no windows, and it was lit by fluorescent tubes. The heavy door was made of solid metal, and it reminded me of the years I had visited clients in jail, as it could not be opened from inside the room. An unused (and woefully outdated) closed-circuit camera was mounted over the door, making it seem as if the room was constantly being monitored (which did wonders for patients experiencing delusions of paranoia). The room was exceptionally cold nearly year-round. Moreover, it was located next to the main door of the emergency department, and when that door opened, it did so with a loud metallic bang, causing many of my patients (and me) to jump as we sat in the room.

When I moved to a full-time position in the emergency department and built rapport with the doctors, nurses, and technicians, I pointed out all of this to them. I then suggested that we start using one of four other rooms that were away from the loud front door. These rooms had windows near the ceiling that provided natural light, and the walls were painted—not tiled. The doors were sliding, shatter-proof glass, and privacy could be maintained by pulling a curtain. The rooms also had something room one did not—a television!

The thing my teammates noticed first was that our patients experiencing psychiatric emergencies were generally more relaxed in the newer rooms. Part of this was being in a nicer, quieter space. Another aspect is that the stigma of being placed in the psych room, which looked and felt like a jail cell, was gone. Clients also enjoyed being able to watch television while they waited. After this change of setting, I noticed that clients more readily engaged with me. That meant I was able to develop rapport more quickly, allowing me to begin addressing the reasons they were in the emergency department. I also noticed that patients were less defensive and that when agitated, they could be redirected more easily. I remarked, "It's amazing how people react differently when we put them in a place that feels safe."

Even when we help create a more welcoming environment for our clients, we carry a lot of responsibility in terms of building rapport with them. That is why I wrote about needing to care for ourselves in chapter 2, so that we can manage our own emotions and respond effectively to what our clients bring us. Our mindset as providers is of paramount importance in creating a safe setting for our clients.

Screening Tools

I personally do not like to use a lot of screening tools. I have found that using as few screeners as possible—and only particularly simple, straightforward ones—is optimal for most clients. For this reason, I prioritize using a few select screening tools when working with high-risk clients, especially tools that focus on depression and suicide. While depression screening tools are not intended to screen for suicidality, they can be useful in identifying potential suicidal ideation.

Two well-used depression screening tools are the Patient Health Questionnaire-9 (PHQ-9; Kroenke et al., 1999) and the Beck Depression Inventory (BDI; Beck et al., 1961). The BDI consists of 21 questions (there are shorter versions), each of which has four statements that clients select as most appropriate for them. Each of the four statements has a value from 0 to 3. The BDI is scored by adding the values of the statements selected, with the highest score being 63 and the lowest being 0. The higher the score, the more severe the client's depression, with any score 40 and above being considered severe depression. The BDI can be completed by the client or administered by a professional.

The PHQ-9 is designed for clients to complete themselves. In many settings, the PHQ-9 has replaced the BDI as the depression screening of choice. As the name implies, there are nine questions on the PHQ-9, with each question focusing on a primary symptom of major depressive disorder and having four potential responses. Like the BDI, the responses have values of 0 to 3, and adding the responses gives a total between 0 and 27, with higher numbers representing more severe depression. Unlike the BDI, the PHQ-9 asks clients to consider how they have felt over the past two weeks, which likely provides a more accurate profile of what the client is currently thinking and feeling. The ninth question on the PHQ-9 is about suicidal ideation: "Thoughts that you would be better off dead, or of hurting yourself." Given that the PHQ-9 is designed to screen for depression, and not specifically for suicide, I would not rely on this item alone in terms of suicide screening. However, clients who endorse this item are more likely to attempt suicide than those who don't (Knapp, 2020), which makes it valuable to consider in context.

In my practice, I prefer to use the PHQ-9 in combination with a screening tool that is specific to suicide. (Incidentally, I also prefer the AUDIT-C and the DAST-10—which are screeners for alcohol and drug use—and occasionally the GAD-7, and that is it!) My preference is the Columbia-Suicide Severity Rating Scale (C-SSRS; Posner, 2007). Before I examine the C-SSRS in greater detail, I want to mention that there are other suicide screening tools that are also useful. I want to be clear that I am not advocating for one of these tools over another. I suggest you consider which tool would best meet the needs of your clientele and your setting. I also strongly suggest that you not employ multiple tools that are supposed to do the same thing, given that overuse of screening tools may dissuade clients from opening up and fully engaging with you (Moutier et al., 2021). The following chart summarizes the relevant suicide screening tools for children, adolescents, and adults as noted by Hughes and colleagues (2023).

Chapter 5 • Suicide Screening and Assessment

Measure	Age Range	Administration	# of Items
Ask Suicide-Screening Questions (ASQ)	10 to adult	Clinician or self-report	4 (5 if positive)
Risk of Suicide Questionnaire (RSQ)	8 to adult	Clinician or self-report	4
Columbia-Suicide Severity Rating Scale (C-SSRS)	11 to adult	Clinician or self-report	5–14
Scale for Suicide Ideation-Worst (SSI-W)	13 to adult	Clinician	19
Suicidal Behaviors Questionnaire-Revised (SBQ-R)	13 to 18	Self-report	4

When I had the honor of leading a team of behavioral health professionals at a federally qualified health care center, my teammates and I decided to revise and update our screening and assessment process to better meet the needs of our clients. My team divided itself into different subgroups, with each subgroup taking on a different part of our screening and assessment process. The subgroup responsible for suicide screening chose the C-SSRS due to its ease of use and the fact that we could easily incorporate it into our electronic medical record system.

The C-SSRS has demonstrated efficacy, but like any screening tool, it is only useful when the person completing the screening is being honest and the clinician interpreting the results uses those results to respond appropriately. Brown et al. (2020) note that "the psychometric evidence for the C-SSRS was mixed. History of a prior suicide attempt, as measured by the C-SSRS, provided the most parsimonious and powerful assessment for predicting future suicide attempts." (p. 1097). In the practice I just mentioned, we had our clients complete the C-SSRS during the intake process and then looked at the results with the client when we met with them. We especially focused on any answers that indicated increased suicide risk. At the same time, we would not assume an absence of risk if the client did not indicate any risk. Indeed, if a clinician believes there is concern of suicide, they should not classify a patient as low risk simply because their scores on the C-SSRS do not qualify as such (Bjureberg et al., 2022).

Despite the widespread use of suicidal screening instruments, I urge caution that you do not over-rely on them, as there is a high variation in the number of people who report suicidal ideation prior to dying by suicide. In fact, half of the people who die by suicide do not communicate their suicidal ideation prior to their deaths (Bender et al., 2019). Therefore, communicating about suicide is an important risk factor, but this communication is not always present. Bryan (2022) goes further in noting that "John Mann (2005) concluded that no studies showed that screening led to reduced suicide attempts or deaths. This was bolstered by Ivan Miller's (2017) study on emergency department suicide screenings that showed no impact on subsequent suicide attempts" (p. 69).

We also need to consider one of the myths I listed in chapter 1: Does asking a person who is not suicidal about suicide give them the idea to consider killing themselves? While this question has been the source of considerable discussion, longitudinal research has found no evidence that assessing for suicide increases risk—in fact, repeated assessments either result in no change in suicide risk or some decreases (Bender et al., 2019). Does this research suggest that screenings are useless? In my opinion, it emphasizes the practice of not relying solely on suicide screening tools. I believe the best reason to utilize screens is that in addition to identifying certain risk factors in some individuals, they create opportunities for conversation. Knapp (2020) points out that if there is a discrepancy between written and verbal responses, this creates more reasons for discussion. Even in the absence of any discrepancies, getting more information on a subject as serious as suicide is a wise decision.

Suicide Assessment

A suicide assessment is an interview between a professional and a client, which usually follows an initial screening. In high-risk environments such as emergency departments, crisis centers, and jails, assessments may be conducted regardless of what any screening results may conclude. In other settings, the suicide assessment may be abbreviated if there are few risk factors and suicide screening results indicate a low probability of suicidal thinking or behaviors. However, and I cannot emphasize this enough, if you have concerns about screening results—ask the client questions.

Chapter 5 • Suicide Screening and Assessment

In the following case study, I illustrate how to conduct a suicide assessment using questions that I have asked for years. While I put my name on the assessment, it is not something I made up on my own. Rather, it is a conglomeration of questions I have used from other assessments and have found helpful. A complete copy of the assessment is available at the end of this chapter. Feel free to use it or modify it to suit your needs. Whether you use this assessment or one of your own, it is important that you use your own words and speaking style while relying on your ability to build rapport with the person you are working with. I tend to use a conversational style, and I take minimal notes. I really want to be able to focus on what the person is saying while also paying attention to their nonverbal communication and body language. I will try to note these factors in the case study.

Case Study: Lori

Lori is a 45-year-old female who is seeking services to address PTSD and major depressive disorder. Lori is married to her second husband and has an adult daughter who is 22. Five years earlier, Lori's 15-year-old son hung himself in their home. Lori and her daughter (then 17) found him in their garage upon returning home from running errands. Lori's daughter performed CPR while Lori called emergency services, but there was nothing they could do. About four months later, Lori's husband died of the cancer he had been fighting for five years.

Lori took a few weeks off from work after her husband's death and then returned to her job as a manager at a local human-services agency. She said that people would stop by her office to offer their condolences and usually added, "You are so resilient!" While Lori admits that the following three years were filled with sadness, she "kept going because of my daughter." Lori and her daughter participated in a program at an agency that specialized in grieving families.

Two years ago, Lori married a second time, to a man she describes as "exceptionally kind and patient." Her daughter was in college at this time and doing well. About six months ago, Lori felt her depression, which she had struggled with since adolescence, suddenly worsen. Her psychiatric provider tried changing her antidepressant medications and tried adjunctive antipsychotic medications to try to help, but nothing worked. Lori found herself unable to get out of bed, she did not want to eat, she was crying all the time, and she was having consistent thoughts of wanting to die. She took time off work but found that even with this break, she could not return to the office, so she quit her job. Lori's psychiatrist suggested that Lori investigate ketamine infusions to address her depression, and Lori found our clinic via an internet search.

Lori completed our online screening process, which included (among other things) the PHQ-9 and C-SSRS. The PHQ-9 indicated severe depression, and Lori's answer to question 9 showed she was thinking every day that she wanted to be dead. Her answers on the C-SSRS indicated a high frequency of suicidal thoughts without a specific plan. Lori's substance use screening indicated no substance use.

After introducing myself and explaining how our consultation and assessment process worked, I gathered information on her presenting problems, current symptoms, and medications. I also answered questions about our practice, including the use of ketamine to treat major depression and PTSD. I then transitioned to the suicide assessment—again, this was a conversation with Lori in my office.

ME: Are you having thoughts of killing or hurting yourself?

LORI: Oh yeah, all the time. I think about dying all the time.

I tend to be direct in this question. I also have had peers who asked this as a scaling question, which I thinks works well too: "On a scale of 1 to 10, how would you rate your desire to kill yourself?"

If Lori had said that she was not thinking about dying or killing herself currently, I would ask if she had had thoughts of killing or hurting herself or wished she were dead in the past two weeks. I use two weeks as a range because most people remember how they have generally felt over the past 14 days. Some people ask about the past week or month. I think it is up to you to use what works for you. Likewise, if Lori had said that she did not want to kill herself, I could follow up with: "If you are having thoughts of hurting yourself, or have tried to hurt yourself, do you want to hurt yourself without killing yourself?" Since she did endorse having suicidal ideation, I followed up with more specific questions asking about plans and access to means.

ME: I'm sorry you're feeling like you want to die. I appreciate your honesty, and I want you to know that many of our clients struggle with these feelings, and while we take them seriously, we remain calm and do not jump to conclusions. Can you tell me what way or ways you have thought about killing yourself?

LORI: I've thought about overdosing on pills. I just want to go to sleep and not wake up.

ME: Do you have access to the drugs you would need to kill yourself?

LORI: Yeah. I mean, I have over-the-counter stuff and prescription meds.

Some people may wonder why I am "getting into the weeds" with Lori about the details of her suicidal ideation. As Maris (2019) notes, it is not enough to simply ask a client if they are having thoughts of death. You also need to get more specific by asking about any potential plans, gauging access to lethal means, and determining whether they've taken any steps to prepare to kill themselves. In addition, while you should always take suicidal ideation seriously, remember that suicidal thoughts alone do not lead to suicide (Bryan, 2022). Therefore, in Lori's case, I explain that I am taking her thoughts of suicide seriously (and hopefully demonstrate this by being calm and open to her answers), but I don't assume that she is imminently going to try to kill herself.

ME: Okay. I'm glad you haven't tried to hurt yourself. Can you tell me why you want to kill yourself?

LORI: [*exhaling slowly*] That's why I'm here.

Lori then tells me about losing her son to suicide and her first husband to cancer. Incidentally, if she had said, "I don't know" to my question about why she wanted to kill herself, that is a perfectly reasonable response. People can feel suicidal without any identifiable cause or reason.

ME: [*after a lengthy pause*] I am so sorry. How long have you been feeling suicidal?

LORI: It started about three months ago, several months after my depression started to get really bad. At first it was kind of fleeting, you know, thoughts every now and then.

ME: But then it started to happen more frequently?

LORI: Yeah. And it's not that I *wanted* to think about suicide; it just sort of happened. I miss my son so much. I want to be with him again.

She starts to cry. I remain quiet for a while, giving Lori the space she needs. Once time has passed, I continue.

ME: What has kept you from killing yourself even though you feel like killing yourself?

LORI: My daughter. She can't go through that again.

ME: I am glad she is such an important part of your life. Is it okay if I ask you some more questions about suicide? I know this is difficult, and we can always take a break.

LORI: We can keep going.

ME: Okay. Have you ever tried to kill yourself in the past?

LORI: No.

If Lori had said she had attempted suicide before, I would have followed up by asking how she attempted to kill herself. This may seem invasive, but I need to understand the attempt. I would also ask, "What happened in your life at the time to lead you to the suicide attempt, and what happened because of this attempt?"

ME: I am glad you haven't tried to hurt yourself. Have you ever been admitted to a psychiatric unit?

LORI: [*laughing through tear-filled eyes*] That depends. Are you going to lock me up?

I see this as Lori's attempts to lighten the conversation, but she is probably also curious if her honesty could result in her being admitted to a hospital.

ME: I don't plan on putting you in a hospital at this time.

LORI: [*laughing again*] No, I've never been in a hospital.

If it turned out that she had been hospitalized before, I would follow up by asking why she had been hospitalized and if she had admitted herself or if she was admitted involuntarily. Note that some clients may be unsure if they admitted themselves or were court-ordered into the hospital, as this is usually a confusing process for people experiencing a mental health crisis.

> ME: Lori, have you ever been assessed for suicide in an emergency room but not admitted to a hospital?
>
> LORI: No.
>
> ME: Do you see a psychiatrist or counselor in the community?
>
> LORI: I have a psychiatrist I see for medication management. I've been involved with Circles of Healing (a local nonprofit agency specializing in grief counseling) for years, but not recently.
>
> ME: Have you found your work with mental health professionals to be helpful? What worked and what didn't work?
>
> LORI: I like my psychiatrist a lot; she listens to me. We've tried a lot of medications, none of which seemed to be working, which is why I am here. What I like about her is that she doesn't pretend to know everything. She knew I needed more help than she could provide, so she referred me for ketamine treatment. I think that says a lot about her.
>
> ME: I agree. I don't know your doctor, but I like the fact that she tried to help you the best she could and then referred you outside of her practice. I personally cannot stand providers who act like they know everything. What about counseling?
>
> LORI: Just Circles of Healing. My daughter and I went there for years—lots of group therapy. It was good, and it helped. I went back there a couple of weeks ago and they think that what I am dealing with now is more than grief.
>
> ME: I think I agree with them. What about you?
>
> LORI: [*taking a deep breath*] Yeah. I guess so.

I would normally ask if anyone in her family has ever died by suicide, but since I already know the answer, there is no reason to ask.

ME: This may seem like a weird question, but what do you think happens to us when we die?

LORI: Wow, that's a tough one! God, I wish I knew. [*pauses*] I think there is something waiting for us after this life. God, I hope so. I really want to see my son again. Why do you ask that question?

ME I ask it as part of a suicide assessment because I want to see if the person who is thinking of taking their own life has thought beyond their own suicide to what's next.

LORI: I'm curious, what do other people say? Is it okay to ask that?

ME: That's a good question, and there's no such thing as a dumb or forbidden question here. Some people say they don't know. Some people are flummoxed because they did not expect me to ask it, so they're not sure how to respond. Others think I am trying to evangelize or convert them. (I'm doing neither.) A few have a clear idea of what lies ahead for them—and I see that more in people who seem to be determined to kill themselves.

LORI: Wow. It does get you thinking.

ME: Sure, and I'd rather people think about existential things like that, as it can be a way to continue to engage them. I just have a few more questions. How do you think the people who care about you will feel, or how will they react, if you kill yourself?

LORI: Like I said, my daughter would be devastated. My husband probably would be too, but I'm more concerned about my daughter. She misses her father so much. I miss my son more. I had five years to grieve my husband before he died of cancer. My grief for my son only came when he died, and even then, I don't know if I've ever really grieved for him.

ME: I think at least part of this is grief, but it is also very complicated, and we don't have to figure it all out now. Do you have access to a gun, knives, or medications?

Chapter 5 • Suicide Screening and Assessment

LORI: I hate guns. My husband is in law enforcement, so there are guns in the home. But he keeps them all locked and only he has access. He's offered to show me how to shoot, but I am not interested. We have kitchen knives and over-the-counter and prescription meds that all of us have access to.

ME: Okay. How would you feel if I asked your husband to secure all the knives and medications in the home for the foreseeable future?

LORI: If you think that's necessary, sure. I understand.

ME: Okay, we can discuss that when we come up with a plan to care for you. My last question is, who else knows how you feel about killing yourself?

LORI: My husband knows, and like I said, he is calm, open, and very loving. God, I bet he is having second thoughts about marrying into the shit show that is my life.

ME: He sounds like a good guy.

LORI: He is.

ME: Then he knew what he was getting into.

LORI: Yeah. My daughter may suspect how I feel, but I haven't told her. I don't want to burden her.

ME: I understand. I am glad you told your husband. I appreciate you answering my questions about this difficult topic.

LORI: Sure. No problem.

Incidentally, I did not feel the need to hospitalize Lori. While she was having intense thoughts of wanting to die and see her son again, she had many strong protective factors. She did not want her daughter to lose another family member to suicide, she had a supportive husband who was involved in her care and aware of her feelings, and she wanted to get better.

There is a balance to be struck with the ongoing use of suicide screening tools and assessments. These are not "one and done" interventions with clients. As you have seen, there is a strong temporal aspect of suicidal ideation, meaning that thoughts about suicide ebb and flow over time. Therefore, a person may have stronger thoughts one day but diminished thoughts the next day, or vice versa. While it is necessary to have ongoing monitoring of suicidal ideation, does this mean we should repeatedly conduct suicide screenings and assessments? I believe that we should, as repeatedly assessing an individual's indicators of suicide may be helpful in discovering any changes from the client's baseline, particularly changes in suicidal thinking alongside changes in mood, sleep quality, and feelings of hopelessness (Bryan, 2022).

At the same time, I am also mindful of what I noted earlier: Frequent screening and assessment can decrease reliability due to client fatigue of having to answer the same questions repeatedly. As Bryan (2022) points out, being alert for departures from a client's baseline is key to continuing assessment, as is regularly checking in on the client's emotions and thoughts. I do not think it is necessary to repeat the entire assessment but to hit key questions such as:

- "Since we last met, how have your thoughts about suicide or dying changed?"
- If there has been a change: "Why do you think this is so?"
- "Has anything changed in your living environment, or in any aspect of your life, that makes you feel more stressed, worried, depressed, or hopeless?"
- "Remind me again of some of the things that help you feel better?"

Once we complete an assessment, we need to decide our next steps. Does the client need to be hospitalized? If not, what are some of the ways we can treat the client in the community? Two additional things we need to consider when deciding on disposition: The client's mental status—specifically if they are experiencing psychotic symptoms—and the potential for violence. We'll examine these factors in the next chapter before looking at treatment disposition in the following chapter.

Sample Suicide Assessment

1. Are you having thoughts of killing or hurting yourself?
   _____
   _____
   _____

   a. Another way to ask: On a scale of 1 to 10, how would you rate your desire to kill yourself?
      _____

   b. If no, have you had thoughts of killing or hurting yourself or wished you were dead in the past two weeks?
      _____
      _____
      _____

   c. If you have thoughts of hurting yourself, or have tried to hurt yourself, do you want to hurt yourself without killing yourself?
      _____
      _____
      _____

2. In what way(s) have you thought about killing or hurting yourself?
   _____
   _____
   _____

Copyright © 2025 Paul Brasler, *The Clinician's Guide to Suicide Management*. All rights reserved.

3. Do you have access to the things you would need to kill yourself?
   _____
   _____
   _____

4. Why do you want to kill yourself?
   _____
   _____
   _____

   a. How long have you been feeling this way?
      _____
      _____
      _____

5. What has kept you from killing yourself even though you feel like killing yourself?
   _____
   _____
   _____

6. Have you ever had thoughts of killing yourself? (If the answer is no to any current or recent suicidal ideation or behaviors)
   _____
   _____
   _____

7. Have you ever tried to kill yourself (suicide attempt) in the past?
   _____
   _____
   _____

a. What did you do?
_____
_____
_____

b. What happened in your life at the time to lead you to the suicide attempt?
_____
_____
_____

c. What happened because of this attempt?
_____
_____
_____

8. Have you ever been admitted to a psychiatric unit?
_____
_____
_____

a. If yes, for what reason?
_____
_____
_____

b. Did you admit yourself or were you admitted involuntarily?
_____
_____
_____

    c. If no, have you ever been assessed for suicide in an emergency room but not admitted to a hospital?

    _____
    _____
    _____

9. Do you see a psychiatrist or counselor in the community?

_____
_____
_____

    a. Have you seen either in the past?

    _____
    _____
    _____

    b. Have you found your work with mental health professionals to be helpful?

    _____
    _____
    _____

    c. What worked?

    _____
    _____
    _____

    d. What didn't work?

    _____
    _____
    _____

10. Has anyone in your family ever died by suicide?
   _____
   _____
   _____

11. What do you think happens to us when we die?
   _____
   _____
   _____

12. How do you think the people who care about you will feel, or how will they react, if you kill yourself?
   _____
   _____
   _____

13. Do you have access to a gun, knives, or medications?
   _____
   _____
   _____

14. Who else knows how you feel?
   _____
   _____
   _____

CHAPTER 6

Additional Mental Health Emergencies

While this is a book about suicide, we need to discuss psychosis and violence, given that they present special challenges and can result in complex situations. To be clear, most people experiencing suicidal ideation are neither psychotic nor violent. Likewise, most people who struggle with psychosis are not violent, just as most people who are violent are not psychotic. But because there can be connections between these disparate factors, we need to be able to assess (and connect with appropriate treatment) people who may be experiencing psychosis and those with a potential for violence. These factors will play a large part in our decisions about how we will provide treatment.

Assessing Clients Who May Be Psychotic

Clients struggling with psychosis represent an additional challenge for practitioners, especially if the client is also struggling with suicidal ideation. I want to emphasize that just because a client is psychotic does not mean that we should assume they are automatically at high risk of suicide. Even more importantly, it is imperative that we have empathy for those living with psychosis and an understanding of the many ways that it can manifest, as well as the things that can cause psychosis.

When I worked in the emergency department, I found that I had to advocate for people with psychosis, often against medical providers who should have been more compassionate. No one *asks* to develop a psychotic disorder—yet people living with psychosis are often blamed for their condition. I also had to explain to providers that people can be diagnosed with a psychotic disorder, but this does not mean they are necessarily experiencing a psychotic episode. Several times, I was called to the emergency department of a hospital that seemed to have a particular disdain for people experiencing a mental health emergency. The providers there seemed to think that every patient who came in with a history of mental illness required an assessment from my team, regardless of their presenting problem. One telephone interaction with the staff went something like this:

NURSE: Yeah, we have a patient who needs to be seen.

ME: Okay. Can you tell me what's going on?

NURSE: The patient is schizophrenic.

ME: Alright. They *have* schizophrenia. What is going on?

NURSE: [*clearly becoming agitated*] I said they have schizophrenia.

ME: [*becoming more direct*] I understand. I am now looking at the patient list for your department [*via the electronic medical record, which I could access from my emergency department*]. It says here that the patient came in complaining of shortness of breath.

NURSE: That's right. He needed a breathing treatment. He's in his room now.

ME: What's he doing?

NURSE: Chilling. Watching TV. I'm about to order him a lunch tray.

ME: Excellent. He asked to speak with a mental health provider?

NURSE: No.

ME: Alright. Is he displaying psychotic symptoms?

NURSE: No.

ME: Then I don't see why I need to see him.

NURSE: But he has schizophrenia . . .

Me: . . . which can increase and decrease in severity. He displayed sound judgment in coming to the emergency department when he had trouble breathing. His chart says he lives in a nearby assisted-living facility. I'm going to call them, and if they report that he's been doing fine, there is no need for me to see him.

Just because a client has schizophrenia does not mean that they always need to submit to a mental health assessment. Additionally, just because a person is displaying psychotic symptoms does not mean that they have a psychotic illness. There are many medical issues that can cause psychotic symptoms that need to be ruled out. It is therefore very important for clients to receive a medical assessment, along with a mental health assessment, if they present with psychotic symptoms. Let's examine the following case study. I have included questions for you to consider as we try to figure out what is happening to this client.

Case Study: Mary

Mary was a 48-year-old Black woman who presented to the emergency department after hearing voices that had become so severe that she was contemplating suicide. The first thing I noticed about her as I entered the room was that she was wincing. This might have been understandable during a typical day in the hospital when it is often very loud, but this morning was unusually quiet. She sat on the edge of the hospital bed and looked frightened. I introduced myself and asked if I could sit down. Mary seemed relieved that someone was talking with her.

"It's so loud," she said, barely above a whisper.

"I'm sorry," I said. "What is so loud?"

"The voices," she replied.

I looked toward the door, which was slightly open to the nearly empty emergency room.

"Not there," said Mary. "There," pointing straight up with her left index finger.

I automatically looked up, even though I knew there was nothing there.

"You're hearing voices from above your head?" I asked.

"Yeah," said Mary, "they're yelling at me."

"What are they saying?"

"I can't really understand them," said Mary, "but they've been yellin' so much I can hardly sleep."

"How long has this been going on?" I asked.

"It started quietly about six weeks ago, and at first I didn't take notice," she said. "But over time, they been getting louder and louder—till they're yellin' all the time."

"Has this ever happened before?" I asked, noticing Mary wince again.

"Nope. Never," she replied. Looking at me with tears in her eyes, she asked, "Am I going crazy?"

1. What is the next thing you would do in this situation?

   _____
   _____
   _____

2. What additional information do you need?

   _____
   _____
   _____

3. How would you keep yourself and others (including Mary) safe?

   _____
   _____
   _____

Mary's vital signs were stable except for her blood pressure, which was elevated, but not to the extent that the attending doctor was immediately concerned. Her blood work did not indicate any problems, and her urinalysis was also clear. That was the extent of the medical clearance provided prior to me speaking with her, so I proceeded by conducting a mental status exam (MSE) because there was not an overt medical cause for her symptoms. An MSE is the primary method that clinicians use to try to determine a person's state of mind, including potential psychosis. An MSE assesses various areas of a client's cognitive and behavioral functioning, including appearance, attitude, behavior, speech, mood, and more. I will use Mary's case to illustrate how to use an MSE, with particular attention to the items that could suggest psychosis.

Appearance. People experiencing psychosis often have difficulties completing their activities of daily living, such as showering, grooming, dressing, and so on. A client who is disheveled is not necessarily experiencing psychosis, but the client's appearance can give us insight into their thought process. People experiencing a psychotic episode are often dressed inappropriately for the weather: They may be overdressed in the summer or underdressed in the winter. Mary was appropriately dressed for the weather and did not appear disheveled at all.

Attitude and Rapport. The client's attitude and your ability to build rapport with the client have the biggest impact on the quality of the information provided by the MSE (Brasler, 2019). Is the client cooperative, uncooperative, guarded, suspicious, or hostile? People experiencing psychosis are often guarded or fearful when interacting with others. Mary, while frightened by her symptoms and uncertain as to what she was experiencing, was nevertheless cooperative throughout the interview. She appeared to understand that I heard her and was trying to help.

Behavior. People experiencing a psychotic episode may engage in repetitive, purposeless movements such as rocking back and forth or gesturing to no one in particular. These actions can occur in people with other issues, so it is important to rule out other concerns such as an intellectual or developmental disability. Behavior can also describe how the client reacts to their environment. Are they pacing? Are they acting in an aggressive manner? My experience in working with people who are experiencing a psychotic episode is that they are often afraid, and becoming aggressive is a response to that fear.

Behavior, in the MSE, also encompasses how the client moves. How well does the client ambulate (walk)? Do they use any assistive devices to help them move, such as a wheelchair or a cane? Some people experiencing a psychotic episode shuffle their feet or have a difficult time walking normally. One of the psychiatrists I used to work with would specifically ask me if I had seen the patient I was consulting with him about walk, as he recognized shuffling as a sign of increasing psychotic symptoms in some of his patients.

Eye contact is another part of behavior. Many people experiencing a psychotic episode have difficulty maintaining eye contact. They may appear to be tracking things with their eyes when nothing is present, or they may repeatedly glance to one side. Keep in mind that some people have poor eye contact, and that does not mean they are experiencing psychosis. In addition, some ethnic groups or nationalities have cultural norms against maintaining eye contact and avoid looking directly at the person to whom they are speaking, so we need to avoid assuming that poor eye contact is a definite sign of a problem. Mary maintained eye contact during our conversation but winced a lot. When I asked her about this, she said that the voices were yelling at times, and it was painful when they were shouting.

Speech. How a person speaks can tell us a lot about their thought process. When someone is experiencing a psychotic episode, they can present differently in speech volume and content, and we can visualize this on a continuum. At one end is what is called pressured speech. People exhibiting pressured speech are often loud, and the words they use are strung together without any breaks between them—another person cannot get a word in edgewise. The flow of the conversation may make sense, or the words can be jumbled up—what is sometimes called word salad. I did not experience a client demonstrating pressured speech until I worked in the emergency department. Clients displaying pressured speech were usually experiencing a manic episode with psychotic features.

Further down the continuum is hyperverbal speech: The client is talking a lot, but another person can get a word in. The flow of the conversation and content tend to follow a logical pattern as well. We often encounter people displaying hyperverbal speech when dealing with someone who is anxious, hyperactive, or just a generally talkative person.

Following hyperverbal on the continuum is spontaneous speech—what a reasonable adult would consider to be a "normal" conversation in terms of volume and speech speed. At the other end of the spectrum is hypoverbal speech, where the client says very little and is often quiet or speaking in a whisper. This is what Mary was doing, and this is not uncommon for people experiencing psychosis. It is also common with people experiencing a depressive episode or people who are traumatized. Individuals can also be naturally shy and speak softly.

Finally, people experiencing psychosis can also be completely silent. They may ignore anyone else around them, or because of their psychosis, they may believe that nothing (or no one) around them is real. People with psychosis can also display echolalia (they repeat another person's words verbatim) or palladia (they repeat the same words repeatedly). Mary was not doing any of these. Her speech was spontaneous, and the volume of her speech was quiet, mainly because she appeared to be exhausted and very frightened.

Mood and Affect. In the MSE, mood is understood as the client's subjective report of how they are feeling. This can sometimes be inferred by the client's body language and overall demeanor, but I find it helpful to ask people how they feel. As you will see when it comes to affect, we need to determine whether a person's stated mood (what they report feeling) and their affect (what we can see) are congruent—in other words, that they match.

I asked Mary how she was feeling, and she stated she felt depressed and scared. Her affect matched her stated mood, as she sat nearly hunched over on the side of the hospital bed, trembling slightly. I typically use the client's words to describe their mood. Affect, on the other hand, can be viewed as a continuum from expansive (a lot of emotions are present and on vivid display) to euthymic (a baseline affect—"things are good for the most part"), to blunted (very little emotion), to flat (no emotional display). People experiencing a manic or hypomanic episode can display an expansive affect, and people experiencing a depressive episode often display blunted or flat affect.

Thought Process. Most of us engage in goal-directed behaviors, even when we do not realize we are doing so. Going to work and attending a meeting are goal-directed behaviors. Even sitting down to watch television or play video games is goal-directed behavior. People experiencing a psychotic episode have difficulty consistently engaging in goal-directed behaviors because their thought process is disjointed. They may start and stop projects haphazardly or even have difficulties with activities of daily living such as bathing and dressing. We can also infer this from our conversations with them, and we can visualize this on a continuum of decreasingly goal-directed actions, from circumstantial (some ability to realize goals) to tangential (completely distracted about goals) to fully disorganized thinking (Brasler, 2019). Mary appeared to display goal-directed thinking. She recognized that something was wrong and sought appropriate help by coming to the hospital.

Thought Content. Like a person's thought process, we determine a client's thought content through their speech: the main theme of what they are talking about. Thought content can include obsessions and preoccupations (e.g., being preoccupied with thoughts of dying or suicide) or delusions, which are fixed, false beliefs that are out of keeping with the client's educational, cultural, or social background. Thought content also includes the client's perceptions, such as illusions or hallucinations. Illusions are misrepresentations of things that are present (such as believing that a ceiling fan is a secret device that is spying on them), whereas hallucinations are a false sensory perception in the absence of any true external stimulus (e.g., hearing voices).

People experiencing a psychotic episode can experience hallucinations in any of our five senses, but overwhelmingly the hallucinations experienced are auditory. These hallucinations are typically one or more voices talking to or about the client. The hallucinations seem real to the client, and the voices are coming from outside their head. Mary states that she hears at least two voices, coming from above her, and that they are yelling at her. She notes that the voices began about six weeks earlier and were initially whispers she could not understand, but they have now increased in volume, intensity, and frequency. Mary was unsure if the voices were real, but she seemed relieved when I told her that I did not hear any voices except ours.

Orientation. Does the client know who they are, when they are (the day of the week and year), where they are, and what is going on? Clients who can answer these four questions correctly are said to be fully oriented, or oriented times four. The client's ability to know what is going on—or why they are presenting for services—is a key part of their being able to demonstrate competence to consent to treatment. Many people experiencing psychosis are unable to answer some or all of these basic questions. Mary was fully oriented.

Memory. Memory is assessed as either immediate, short-term, or remote. Immediate memory, which can also be used as a measure of concentration, involves recalling basic information after a few seconds' time. It is often difficult for people experiencing a psychotic episode to maintain attention and focus, so recalling items from immediate memory is difficult.

Chapter 6 • Additional Mental Health Emergencies

Short-term memory involves recalling items presented several minutes earlier. I was taught to ask clients to remember three items: a historical figure (e.g., Dr. Martin Luther King), a color (e.g., blue), and an address (e.g., 231 Elm Street); and then ask them to repeat the items after 10 to 15 minutes. Difficulty retaining this information is not uncommon among people experiencing a psychotic episode, but it can be difficult for people with mood and anxiety disorders, and for people experiencing delirium or dementia, to recall this information as well. Keep in mind that even in the absence of any of these illnesses, some people simply have a poor memory.

Finally, long-term memory involves recalling items from months or years in the past. I typically ask adults where they grew up, went to high school or college, or worked or lived when they were younger. Again, people experiencing psychosis may not remember this information or be unable to effectively communicate the information. Mary had no problems with her memory in any of these realms.

Reliability. Reliability refers to a person's ability to provide consistent information. A lack of reliability may indicate that the client is malingering, or it could be due to the disordered thinking that is common when experiencing a psychotic episode. A client's ability to provide reliable information is also part of determining their capacity to provide informed consent for treatment. Mary was consistent throughout the assessment and was deemed to be reliable.

Insight. How aware is the client of their situation? If they recognize and accept that they have a mental health problem, do they participate in treatment for their illness? A lack of insight is a primary symptom of psychosis. Clients believe that the hallucinations they are experiencing are real. They may also believe that their delusions (fixed, false beliefs) are true, and any attempt to suggest otherwise is an insult to them. Mary believed that the voices she heard were real to her, but she also understood that they were not present for other people.

Judgment. We measure judgment by determining how well a client can make decisions given their mental state. Past versions of the MSE involved asking the client: "What would you do if you were walking down the street and you found an addressed and stamped piece of mail?" The answer would be: "Put it into a mailbox." Because this question has a "correct" answer—and because I've found that many of my clients have been asked the same question many times previously—their answers are not always a true measure of their judgment. If we know the answer to a question we have been asked many times before, are we really putting any thought into our responses or just responding automatically?

I tend to examine judgment in the broader context: Why is the client seeing me? Did they exercise good judgment and seek help once they became aware of a problem? Or did someone else have to start the process to get them help? In my opinion, Mary exercised good judgment in recognizing that her problem (hearing voices) was getting progressively worse, to the point that she viewed suicide as a viable solution. However, rather than act on that thought, she brought herself to the emergency department.

Was Mary experiencing a psychotic episode? The short answer is yes, she was. But this was a complex situation that required more information. Mary was hearing voices. She told me this, and she was clearly responding to internal stimuli as she was wincing and closing her eyes when the voices became particularly loud. At the same time, her mood and affect were congruent, her speech was spontaneous, she was not displaying any delusional thinking that I could discern, she was fully oriented, and she demonstrated reliability, insight, and sound judgment.

Another key piece of evidence was that Mary had started hearing voices about six weeks earlier, and they had started as whispers and gradually progressed to shouting. Mary had not experienced hallucinations in any form prior to this. She was also 48 years old. While a person can develop a psychotic disorder such as schizophrenia at any point in adulthood, psychotic disorders usually begin in later adolescence to young adulthood. Mary did not have a history of psychosis.

Mary did have a history of major depressive disorder, including previous suicidal ideations when she was younger, but her depression had responded well to antidepressant medication. Mary also had a history of alcohol use disorder, but she had been in recovery for the past three years. The only finding from the medical exam was that her blood pressure was elevated.

My first concern was Mary's suicidal ideation. She had not developed a plan for how she might try to kill herself, and she denied having access to a firearm, but she did have access to medications and knives in her home. She also lived alone. The intensity of Mary's suicidal ideation decreased when she saw that I was taking her seriously and did not view her as "crazy." She later voiced that she did

Chapter 6 • Additional Mental Health Emergencies

not want to die at all but had viewed suicide as her only option to deal with the increasingly louder voices. Mary was willing to receive help, and it appeared that the best option was to voluntarily admit her to our behavioral health unit. She was willing to do this.

In the following chapters, I will look at ways to treat clients experiencing suicidal ideation in outpatient settings. In those situations, we are dealing with clients who are not psychotic or violent, who can consent to treatment, and who can participate in treatment on their own. Clients experiencing a psychotic episode and suicidal ideation (or behaviors) usually require inpatient psychiatric hospitalization for stabilization. If the client is unwilling or unable to consent to treatment (and psychosis generally precludes this), they likely need to be involuntarily hospitalized for their safety.

Regarding Mary, I called the on-call psychiatrist, whom I had just started working with, and explained what was happening, including my recommendation that Mary be admitted.

"What do you think is happening?" Dr. S. asked.

"I'm not sure," I replied. "If she was still drinking, I might consider alcohol-induced psychosis or alcohol withdrawal-induced psychosis, but I'm at a loss. She's too old for a first psychotic break."

"Not true," said Dr. S., "but unlikely. Have the emergency room doc get a CT (computed tomography) scan of her head. Then call me back with the results and we'll go from there."

I asked the attending physician to order this, and after some muttering about the psychiatrist "trying to practice medicine," he ordered the scan.

About 45 minutes later, I was finishing a hastily called meeting on the behavioral health ward when I ran into Dr. S. He had apparently just spoken to the emergency department physician.

"That patient you called me about," he said, "is bleeding in her brain. That is what is likely causing the hallucinations. She's going to be medically admitted."

I hurried downstairs to the emergency department, and the physician confirmed what he had told Dr. S.

"Your new psychiatrist made a good call," he said. "I should have ordered the CT in the first place because we had no record of her experiencing hallucinations. I'll remember this one."

"What's this mean?" I asked.

The doctor looked at me for a moment, then responded, "Your new doc likely just saved this lady's life. I'm bringing her blood pressure down now and she'll be admitted medically for further treatment. I think she's going to be okay. Had we admitted her to psych, it would have delayed care, and God knows what might have happened."

The emergency room doctor wasn't the only person who learned something new that day—I did too. I learned one of the many ways that people can demonstrate mental health symptoms that are caused by medical emergencies or illnesses as opposed to mental illness. I devote a chapter to this phenomenon in my book *High Risk Clients*.

Preparing for Potentially Violent Clients

Just as clients experiencing psychosis and suicidal ideation present special challenges that we need to be aware of, so do clients demonstrating violent behaviors who may also be suicidal. Clients experiencing suicidal ideation alongside psychosis, as well as clients displaying violence and suicidal ideation or behaviors, should be treated in secure, safe environments—usually in secure behavioral health units, in forensic units, or within the criminal justice system.

I want to remind you that most people experiencing suicidal ideation are a greater danger to themselves than others, just as most people experiencing psychosis are not violent. However, any person has the potential to become violent, and we need to admit this to ourselves and prepare accordingly. I do not plan on ever having a fire in my home. However, I try to make sure we have working smoke detectors, fire extinguishers, and various means of escaping. We should plan the same way when we work with people, even if we think none of our clients will ever become violent.

Hospitals and correctional institutions typically have security plans and the means to deal with potentially violent clients and visitors. However, we need to remember that plans are useless unless everyone is aware of them and knows what to do in a crisis. The only way this is possible is if the institution provides regular training and practice drills for handling potentially violent clients. Like most people

Chapter 6 • Additional Mental Health Emergencies

in my generation, I could never have imagined growing up that children in schools (and colleges) would one day be taught how to "lock down" in the event of a violent situation on campus. It pains me that my children have, at times, been afraid to go to school because they were fearful of a school shooting. One of the ways that they dealt with this fear was by having good teachers and administrators who told them (repeatedly) that this was a precaution and that it would likely not happen, but they needed to be ready just in case, just as they would practice how to handle a fire evacuation or shelter due to storms.

Having worked for a hospital system, I wish I could say with confidence that supposedly secure facilities are usually up to date on the best practices for handling violent clients, but this is not always the case. Security services may be cut when funding is tight, or some organizational leaders may not like the "look" of what they perceive as too heavy a security presence. For example, at the main hospital I served, we had several incidents of patients bringing handguns into the emergency department. We had no armed security at that time, and the administration saw no need for this or for other preventive measures. Of course, the administrative offices were far from the emergency department, and the administrators worked regular business hours, not the evening and night shifts when we were more likely to have people bring guns into the hospital. It took a high-level administrator witnessing a patient bringing a gun into the hospital—and the chief emergency medicine physician being violently assaulted by another patient—before they provided armed security and other safety measures. While this was costly to the hospital's financial bottom line, I am certain the administrators also noticed the corresponding decrease in staff turnover because staff and patients felt safer.

All of this is good for larger organizations, but what if you are a part of a small (or not-so-small) outpatient practice, or even a solo practice? What do you do when you are not only the clinical provider, but also the head of finance, the human resources officer, and the office manager all rolled into one? I have two pieces of advice. The first is to *not* assume that you will never have to deal with a violent client. Any person has the potential to become violent at any time. My second piece of advice is to think like a security person and not as a clinician. This may be difficult for you, so I encourage you to consider reaching out to your local law enforcement agency to see if they can provide some suggestions for your practice. Sometimes, just letting them know who you are and what you do can be helpful. Most police agencies are willing to have someone come out to provide a quick security assessment.

I also encourage you to examine the following items and make changes as you see fit.

1. How well lit are the parking areas and outside surroundings for your practice? How safely can you move from your office to your car? This is especially important if you provide evening appointments. Also keep in mind that the sun sets earlier from mid-fall to mid-spring, so how much visibility will there be during regular hours during the months with shorter days?

2. How do clients access your practice? Do they use the same entry as staff? Is the door kept locked during the day, and are clients admitted as they arrive?

3. If you have a waiting area, how do clients access it? Is there a staff person monitoring the waiting area (usually checking in clients, taking payments, scheduling appointments, and so on)? Is there a barrier, such as a window, separating that staff from clients? Is there a means for that staff person to call for assistance?

4. How are you as the provider notified when a client is in the waiting room, especially if there is not a staff person there? Is the access point to your office from the waiting room locked?

5. Check your office. While any item could be used as a weapon, are there things in your office that pose a greater risk, such as scissors lying on your desk or hot liquids that could be thrown (e.g., candles)? Years ago, I worked part-time in a private practice and was surprised to find that the psychologist in the office next to mine kept an ornamental knife (which was quite large and sharp) on her desk to use as a letter-opener. She was surprised when I asked if she was concerned that it could be used as a weapon. She was not concerned, but I found it interesting that she specialized in working with angry couples!

6. Do you have a way to call for help within your agency or office? How easily can you access outside help such as the police? In my practice, all

clinicians have a hidden button in their office that notifies our building's security and the police.

7. Where do you sit when providing services? You should sit so that both you and the client have access to the door. Do not sit with the client between you and the door or sit in front of the door, in case you have a client who gets upset and wants to quickly leave. Do not sit behind a desk that you could get trapped behind.

8. What about what you have on your person? Ties and scarves can be problematic because an aggressive person could choke you. Likewise, large earrings can be pulled out. Necklaces can also be used to choke a provider, so be aware of this.

9. Are weapons allowed in your practice? Do you make your policy on weapons clear when clients begin seeing you?

10. Many companies employ a run-hide-fight approach when dealing with violence. Ask yourself: Where would I run to? Where and how could I hide (e.g., what could I use to barricade the door to my office and how could I keep clear of the door if someone shoots a gun through it)? How do I fight?

I say this not to frighten you, but to encourage you to be safe. Most of us working in outpatient settings will not have to deal with violent clients, but you never know. Let's examine how we can identify potentially violent clients who may also be experiencing suicidal ideation or behavior.

Risk Factors Associated with Potential Violence

About half of all health care providers will be victims of violence in their careers (Pines et al., 2021). Pines and colleagues (2021) note that violence is most likely to occur in hospital settings, especially in the emergency department, where the injury rate can be as high as that experienced by police officers and other first responders. Viottini and colleagues (2020) add that the most common form of violence is verbal, while physical aggression is more likely to be committed by patients with cognitive limitations, mental health problems, and substance use disorders. Here are some examples of these different types of violence.

Physical	Psychological
Hitting (with fists)	Verbal abuse/cursing
Beating (with an object/weapon)	Threats
Kicking	Disrespect
Slapping	Intimidation
Stabbing	Bullying
Shooting	Harassment
Pushing	
Spitting	
Biting	

We also need to be aware of violence risk factors. This includes acknowledging that people who are suicidal often require a level of aggression to enact self-destructive behaviors. This aggression can also take the form of violence toward others. The most notable violence risk factor is anger. Visibly angry people are more likely to become violent, although we need to remember that people can be angry and not initially appear to be aggressive. It is therefore important to pay attention to clues that the client may become angry, a process often called escalation. Escalation signs can include:

1. Provocative behavior, such as prolonged staring at providers
2. Angry stated mood, or angry or hostile affect
3. Anxiety
4. Loud, aggressive, rude, or sarcastic speech
5. Tense posturing (e.g., gripping arm rails tightly or clenching fists)
6. Frequently changing body position
7. Pacing
8. Overly aggressive acts (e.g., pounding walls, throwing objects, or hitting oneself)

Later in this chapter I will discuss ways to intervene with someone who is angry or escalating.

Chapter 6 • Additional Mental Health Emergencies

A second risk factor is clients who are intoxicated on substances. Alcohol use disorder is not only the second most prevalent substance use disorder (only nicotine dependence exceeds alcohol use disorder), but alcohol intoxication on the part of clients is a primary factor in violence toward providers (Pines et al., 2021). In my experience, clients who become violent when consuming alcohol are often notably intoxicated, as demonstrated by unsteady gait, slurred words, and smelling of alcohol. When I worked in the emergency department, I was often asked to assess patients who were intoxicated and loudly stating that they wanted to kill themselves. Our solution was to keep the patients safe and medically supported, and then reassess them once they were no longer intoxicated.

We also need to be aware of clients struggling with psychiatric illnesses or symptoms. Of particular concern, in addition to psychosis, are clients struggling with neurocognitive disorders (such as dementia) or medical emergencies (such as delirium). We also need to consider clients living with cognitive or developmental disorders. In these cases, clients may not be able to verbalize their needs or understand what they are experiencing, and they may lash out violently. In these situations, violence is typically unintentional on the part of the client, but we need to try to keep ourselves safe nonetheless.

Finally, we need to consider that there are people who have no hesitation resorting to violence. As discussed in chapter 3, many of these people have ASPD, and people with this personality disorder lack empathy or concern for others. Regardless of the reasons that a person develops ASPD, they are often manipulative in trying to get their needs met. People with ASPD may resort to threats or verbal intimidation, and if their needs are not met, they may resort to violence. I will explain how to work with people who are violent, or who may become violent, at the end of this chapter.

Murder-Suicides

With the possible exception of celebrities who die by suicide, the national media typically does not report on the majority of suicide deaths. An exception is situations involving murder, followed by the suicide death of the murderer. This includes high-profile coverage of mass casualty events, such as school shootings, and situations in which a person kills their partner and occasionally other family members. While these horrific events engender a lot of attention, they are thankfully rare, comprising between 1 to 2 percent of all suicide deaths (Maris, 2019).

Maris (2019) notes that some people appear to need to kill someone else to take their own lives. In fact, he adds that approximately 80 percent of murder-suicides involve a single victim, while the remaining 20 percent involve multiple victims. It is difficult to predict when these situations might occur, just as it is difficult to predict whether a person with several risk factors will attempt suicide or, like so many people with similar risk factors, will not die by suicide. There is evidence of a higher likelihood of a history of ASPD in those who initiate a murder-suicide, but given that this is a rare occurrence, it is difficult to study.

Before you can assess a potentially violent client for suicidality or consider the disposition of a client who could be suicidal, you must maintain everyone's safety. If there is any question about your safety, I recommend notifying law enforcement. I would rather err on the side of caution than try to handle a situation that could easily spiral out of control. Thankfully, this situation is rare, but as I mentioned earlier, you need to be prepared in case this occurs.

When dealing with potentially violent clients or clients who may be experiencing psychosis, I recommend the following:

1. Start by assessing if the environment is safe. This is especially important if you are working with clients in the community (e.g., home-based services). Can you access the exits? If you are unsure, I advise proceeding with caution. Years ago, one of my clinical supervisees related a terrifying story to me. Prior to working with me, she worked for a nonprofit organization that worked with new mothers in their homes. She and a colleague made a visit to a client, and my friend noticed that the client was acting differently than she ever had before and kept glancing at a closet door in her living room. My friend later told me that she'd had a bad feeling, and she cut the session short and left with her colleague. She later contacted the client, who said that her boyfriend had been hiding in the closet, having told the client that he would kill everyone if the client said anything. My friend subsequently worked with the client to get her out of the home and to a safe place.

2. When approaching a client in crisis, maintain an open stance, with your hands visible and to your sides. This allows others to see that you do not have a weapon and that you are not approaching them in a provocative manner.

3. Take a deep breath—and repeat as necessary. Facing a potentially violent person is stressful, and it is okay to admit that.

4. If the client is already angry, remind yourself that their anger is likely not about you—this is not personal. If they are angry at you, do your best to remain calm.

5. Always know where the exits are. I remember a crisis training earlier in my career during which the trainer emphasized that there was nothing wrong with "running away with confidence."

6. If the client appears to be calming down, I offer to shake their hand, but I am also okay if they refuse to shake my hand. I introduce myself and ask what they would like to be called.

7. I offer the client the opportunity to sit down. If they sit, then I will sit too. If they remain standing, I remain standing.

8. I often ask if they would like some water to drink. Sometimes, offering support in this manner helps the client to relax. I do not offer anything hot, as hot liquids can be thrown at people. In the hospital, I would offer a meal to clients. Many times, particularly if the patient was hungry, this served to de-escalate them quickly.

9. I remain polite throughout the conversation. I also slow down the speed of my speech. In doing so, I am modeling calming behavior—just as I was doing with the slowed breathing. I also work to lower the volume of my speech. "Going low and going slow" can serve to keep everyone calmer.

10. I remain honest throughout the conversation. If I don't know the answer to a question, I say that I don't know. In the hospital, I experienced clients being told by clinicians that they would be discharged from the hospital after a short stay—even though the clinicians had no say (or idea) how long the patient might remain admitted. This led to problems on the

inpatient unit, as the patients often became angry when they were not quickly discharged, and then other staff had to deal with their aggression.

11. People may become upset or even violent because they believe that they are not being listened to. So, hear what they have to say, without interruption. Summarize what you are hearing and ask clarifying questions as needed.

12. Finally, set limits with people who are escalating or threatening violence. I do not condone threats, in any capacity or in any form, toward any of my coworkers or me. When this happens, I set firm limits but I try to do so without sounding angry or scared—even though I often *am* angry and scared. It is important that when you set limits, you do so respectfully (remember that you are a professional) and not in front of other clients. Removing an audience lessens the likelihood that the client will feel the need to escalate the situation to save face.

When I was the head of a community-based behavioral health program, one of our clients threatened one of my teammates—our nurse assistant. Our nurse could easily take care of herself, and she set appropriate limits with this particular client, at which point he cursed at her. I found out about this incident a few minutes later, having just left a leadership team meeting. I was livid. I took a deep breath and walked up to the client as he sat in the waiting room. Our interaction went something like this:

ME: Are you Mr. Smith?

MR. SMITH: Yeah.

ME: Hello, I'm Paul. Would you come with me, please?

MR. SMITH: Um, okay.

Mr. Smith followed me to a door leading out of the clinic, well away from other clients.

MR. SMITH: What are we doing?

ME: I'm walking you out.

MR. SMITH: Why?

Me: Did you threaten and curse at Michelle?

Mr. Smith: Yeah, but . . .

I held my hand up.

Me: That type of behavior is against the treatment agreement you signed. You will not be seen today. Can you come in tomorrow, and you and I will meet briefly to review our expectations?

Mr. Smith: [*standing taller than me*] What if I don't leave?

Me: I will call the police and have you charged with trespassing. You will then be banned from our clinic.

Mr. Smith: [*pause*] What time tomorrow?

Me: What works best for you?

Mr. Smith came back the next day and apologized to Michelle before he and I had a chance to meet. He and I met briefly, and he worked harder in treatment after this interaction. While it may sound like I was confident throughout this interaction, I was not. I was scared. I was angry. And I don't think straight when I'm angry and scared. But I took deep breaths, and I kept reminding myself that the interaction would not last long and that I had support from my teammates (and if necessary, from the police). This was difficult, but necessary.

Most agitated people can be easily de-escalated, including people who are concurrently expressing suicidal ideations. People who become violent because of a possible mental health problem (this is rare) should be assessed in a crisis center or emergency department. People who become violent who have control over their behaviors should be held accountable for their actions.

Duty to Protect

Before moving on to the next chapter, where I consider whether to treat a client in an outpatient setting or refer for inpatient hospitalization, we need to consider what to do when a client states that they want to harm someone else. When this occurs, most localities have laws in place that mandate that mental health providers take reasonable actions to protect the person being threatened. These laws are generally referred to as "duty to protect" or "duty to warn" laws. States have different requirements about whom clinicians or other providers need to contact, so it is important that you are aware of your legal responsibilities.

In Virginia, where I have practiced my entire career—and Virginia's statutes are like many other states' laws on this matter—I have a duty to protect a person should one of my clients make a threat to kill or harm them. Let me make a slight differentiation here. If a client states, "I am going to kill the next person who looks at me funny," I have a responsibility to further assess that individual to see if they need to be hospitalized to prevent harm to individuals in our community. However, because the client has not made a threat to a specific person (or persons), there is no one to warn (because everyone may be at risk). However, if the threat is to a specific person, I am required to make every *reasonable* effort to contact that person, advise them of the nature of the threat (including who is making the threat), and then connect them to resources that can help them remain safe.

Sometimes, it is difficult to find information about the intended "target" individual, so in those cases, I do the best I can. I have called the police to ask them to do a wellness check on an individual, only to find that the person is no longer at the address of record. A key part of the statute is that I *try* to help the individual. In disclosing information, I also must protect the individual making the threats, so I do not share medical, mental health, substance use, or any other information that is not pertinent to the situation. The following case study illustrates this process with a person who states he wants to kill someone else and then himself.

Case Study: William

"Hi, my name is Paul. What's going on?" I asked as I entered the emergency department room.

"I'm gonna kill that bitch; that's what's going on!" said William, age 57. He had been brought to the emergency department by ambulance. He was pacing in the small examination room. Police officers were outside the room.

"Okay, it seems like you're angry—what can I do to help?" I ask.

"Let me out of here; that's what you can do," responded William.

"I can't do that right now," I replied, "so let's see if we can get you what you need right now."

Chapter 6 • Additional Mental Health Emergencies

William stops pacing and looks at me. "I'm thirsty."

"I'll get you some water. Are you hungry?"

"Nope."

I got him a cup of water. "Mind telling me what is going on?" I ask.

I thought William had calmed down, but he quickly started yelling incoherently and moved toward me. I smelled alcohol on his breath as I backed toward the door.

"My damn sister threw me out on the street. I'm gonna cut that bitch's throat and then jump off the MLK bridge—you watch me, motherfucker!" he yelled.

I took a deep breath and asked, "She put you out today?"

"That's right!"

"And this came completely out of nowhere?" I asked.

"Hell yeah, it did!" said William. "I've been living there for five years, and she goes and throws me out."

"Did you all have a fight?" I asked, seeing that William was calming down.

"I guess," he replied. "She's been on my ass about my drinking. I give her money for the rent, so I don't see why what I do is any of her damn business."

"It sounds frustrating, and I can see how being asked to leave would make you angry. Let me get you some more water and some food—you can always eat it later if you want—and let's try to come up with a plan," I said, feeling confident I had been able to help William de-escalate.

I was wrong.

"Ain't no fucking need to talk, man. I'm leaving and killing that bitch!" William said as he moved toward the door.

"I can't let you do that," I replied, as the police officers stepped into view, having heard the shouting in the room. (I want to be clear that these officers, and most of the officers I work with, are not antagonistic at all. They understand that some people get upset seeing an officer, so they try to keep a low profile and let me do my job. "Less paperwork for us!" many of them say. However, when they need to step in, they do so professionally and respectfully, as these officers did.)

"Have a seat, sir," said the lead officer. William complied but was not happy about it.

After reading through my interaction with William, consider the following questions about this situation:

1. Is this a duty to protect situation? Why or why not?

   _____
   _____
   _____
   _____

2. What additional information do you need to decide how you will handle this situation beyond your interactions in the emergency room?

   _____
   _____
   _____
   _____

3. If you need to notify William's sister, how do you find her contact information? What do you communicate to her?

   _____
   _____
   _____
   _____

4. What do you do if you find yourself reacting to William?

   _____
   _____
   _____
   _____

Fortunately, William had received services from our hospital before, so we had some of his medical records. He had been diagnosed with alcohol use disorder, having been treated for alcohol withdrawal in the past. He also had a

Chapter 6 • Additional Mental Health Emergencies

diagnosis of bipolar I disorder, and he had been treated with antidepressants and mood stabilizers in the past. Given his current intoxication, I was unsure how his behaviors were impacted by alcohol and how much they were impacted by his mental health problems. We provided time and space for William to sober up, but he remained agitated and threatening his sister and himself. In the end, I started the process for an involuntary mental health admission based on his threats.

I then had to contact his sister, and William was not forthcoming with her contact information. Luckily, he had previously listed her as his emergency contact, so I was able to call her. She admitted that they had had an argument earlier in the day because she had given him notice that he had to leave her home in 30 days. (She had followed the legal requirements in doing this.) She added that while she loved her brother, his refusal to stop drinking, and subsequently damaging property, was too much for her and she felt she had given him enough chances. I told her I understood her decision and then I updated her on my reasons for calling—specifically his threats against her. William's sister seemed unfazed by this information, noting that William had made similar threats in the past. There were no weapons in the home. However, I reiterated my concerns, so we developed a plan whereby her adult sons would be present to help move William out after she obtained a restraining order and notice of eviction for him. William's sister added that the family were supportive of her, and she felt safe.

William's sister asked me what his blood alcohol level was, whether he had tested positive for other drugs, and if he had been taking his psychiatric medications. I explained that he was going to be admitted to our hospital under an involuntary commitment, and that I could not share any protected information about him. She said she understood. I assured her that one of the hospital social workers would be in touch with her prior to her brother's discharge from the hospital, to make sure she was aware of what was happening.

In situations like William's, inpatient hospitalization is likely the only viable option to protect William and his sister. Fortunately, situations like this are rare. In the next chapter, I'll discuss why psychiatric hospitalization is one option for clients experiencing suicidal ideation, but we must be very careful when considering it and see it as a last resort.

CHAPTER 7

Disposition

When working with a client who acknowledges having suicidal ideation, it is imperative that we directly address the client's suicidal thinking and behaviors. While underlying issues such as the client's trauma history or mental illness may play a part in their suicidality, we must not become sidetracked by trying to prioritize their mental health issues or trauma. Rather, we must address their suicidality first. While we can (and should) attend to these underlying concerns later (as I will discuss in chapters 8 and 9), our current job is to mitigate any imminent risk of harm and keep the client safe. Sometimes, this involves hospitalizing the client, but many times it does not. Indeed, one of the main reasons I wrote this book (and I am not the first person to advocate this) is to equip professionals to work with people who are suicidal and to avoid hospitalization as much as possible.

I want to be clear: There are situations in which psychiatric hospitalization is the only option to address suicidal behaviors or thoughts. These situations include clients who are unable or unwilling to consent to treatment outside of a secure, hospital-based setting, clients who are psychotic, and clients who present an immediate clear and present danger to themselves or others. For most of our clients, however, we need to remember that hospitalization is only a short-term solution that, at best, can buy some time but can also worsen suicidality.

Psychiatric Hospitalization

More mental health providers work in outpatient or community-based settings than in inpatient settings. It follows that most human-service providers, not only clinicians, lack an understanding of what it is like in a hospital psychiatric unit. What follows are my experiences as a clinician who provided clinical services on a 40-bed psychiatric hospital floor. To be clear, my main job was to conduct assessments in the emergency department. However, because I have a background in treating people with co-occurring disorders, I also facilitated psychoeducational groups for clients with co-occurring disorders on the inpatient unit. There were also times when I was called to the unit to assist with patients who were violent.

I want to emphasize that what follows are my impressions and experiences of being on a specific psychiatric unit at a specific time. I do not wish to infer that all psychiatric units are like this—some are likely better, while others are worse. I also want to highlight that most of the people working on the psychiatric unit in my hospital were outstanding. Despite tremendous challenges, these individuals, including patient care aides, nurses, social workers, pharmacists, and doctors (specifically the psychiatrists who came on board in my third year with the company), were exceptional people who cared about the individuals under their supervision.

What I remember striking me when I went to the psychiatric unit for the first time was seeing a dimly lit, isolated gray corridor as the elevator doors opened. I had just started working at the hospital and my supervisor wanted to show me the psychiatric unit. She produced a key and fitted it into a lock on a pair of imposing metal double doors. As the key clicked, the doors swung open, and we walked onto the unit. Despite it being the middle of the afternoon, the hallway was dimmer than the waiting area outside. Several of the overhead lights were out, while others sputtered, clearly needing to be replaced. Patients, in faded hospital gowns, wandered up and down the hall.

My supervisor explained that the behavioral health floor was divided into two units. We were currently standing in the middle of the general behavioral health unit, which was for patients who were not violent, psychotic, or overly suicidal. People struggling with depression or suicidal ideation who voluntarily admitted themselves to the hospital usually wound up on this unit. I saw patients walking

Chapter 7 • Disposition

around looking bored and sad. What I remember the most was how everything was painted gray. I kept wondering, *Whose idea was it to paint this place in the most depressing shade of gray possible?* The walls were bare, and I could see small windows in the patients' rooms through some of the open doors.

The acute unit appeared to be more crowded—there were clearly more staff members present. Whereas the patients on the general unit appeared sad and bored, many of the patients on the acute unit appeared dazed, drowsy, confused, or agitated. My supervisor explained that the acute unit was for people who had been involuntarily hospitalized and for clients who were psychotic or violent. I also noted the two seclusion rooms at the end of the unit, where patients could be physically, mechanically, or chemically restrained.

I soon found out that a cadre of psychiatrists served the patient population, but they kept strange hours, as most of them had other practices and hospitals to visit. Some of these doctors conducted patient rounds as late as 11 p.m. or as early as 6 a.m. It was not uncommon for patients to be woken up to speak with a physician, and they often saw multiple psychiatrists during their stay. Medications were changed for no reason, and clients were often discharged without any discharge plan—sometimes in the middle of the night. There did not seem to be any communication between providers, and the assessments I completed often went unread.

I also learned how traumatic the admission process to the unit was. Each client had to be strip-searched upon admission. While the personnel (generally) were caring and understanding about this and conducted the procedure with respect, I can only imagine how traumatic and humiliating that experience would be for a person with a history of sexual trauma. Yes, we needed to make sure that weapons or dangerous items were not brought onto the unit, but at what cost to the patient?

The drab, and frankly depressing, setting was improved somewhat during the third year I worked for the hospital system. A new company was brought in to enhance the hospital's delivery of mental health services, and they commenced a physical renovation of the entire unit. Gone were the gray walls, few windows, and crowded spaces. They were replaced with big windows (made of shatter-resistant glass), new lighting, artwork on the walls, and paint colors you would find in a contemporary home as opposed to industrial gray. It was an exceptional improvement and wise use of the company's investment. Patients appeared to be more relaxed overall, and the staff's morale improved.

The new company also replaced the old series of psychiatrists with two exceptional full-time psychiatrists whom I enjoyed working with immensely. They rounded at reasonable hours and included a full team of providers (nurses, social workers, and pharmacists) in their decisions. These doctors also read the assessments I had conducted! They educated patients on their diagnoses and course of treatment and treated them like fellow human beings as opposed to faceless test subjects.

However, despite improvements to the physical space and the addition of excellent physicians, there really was not much happening on the psychiatric unit for the patients. They met with their physician for 10 to 20 minutes daily and had the opportunity to attend two to four psychoeducational groups or recreational therapy groups (e.g., arts and crafts), but most of their time was spent sleeping or watching television. And while the new environment provided more room, there was no getting around that this was a locked unit, so patients were essentially stuck inside a limited space with a bunch of strangers, with little to do. It should not be surprising that many of them complained of feeling *more* depressed because of being on the unit. Many of them repeatedly asked to have more groups and counseling sessions, but the emphasis on the unit was restricted primarily to medication management.

When I asked about additional clinical services, I was told there were not enough staff to provide these services. There were two overworked social workers on the unit, but their primary task was trying to establish tenable discharge plans for the revolving cadre of patients coming in and out of the facility. Even though they wanted to provide direct clinical services to their patients, they simply had no time. The company was unwilling to add staff because it did not make financial sense to them—they would not be paid more to provide additional clinical services to their patients, so why do it? This is not unique to my hospital, as many inpatient settings focus on medication management as the primary source of treatment, with only limited psychoeducational groups available (Jobes, 2023).

Given all of this, put yourself in a patient's shoes. You've entered the hospital due to a suicide attempt, perhaps involuntarily. Like many people who display suicidal behaviors, you are experiencing ambiguity about wanting to die. Part of

Chapter 7 • Disposition

you wonders if spending time on the psychiatric unit could help you find some answers. You are therefore surprised to find yourself talking with your doctor for a few minutes a day, followed by some groups that may or may not be pertinent to your situation, all while having a lot of unstructured time with little to do. While not all hospitals are like this, many are. For example, a recent meta-analysis by Bartl and colleagues (2024) examined the experiences of patients and staff at psychiatric facilities. The following are some of the quotes the authors extracted from their interviews with patients and people whose loved ones were patients:

- "[Treatment] makes you feel worse afterwards than you did before. I'm sitting here, I'm more depressed and stressed coming out of that, and freaked out, than I was going in before." (p. 5)

- "In psychiatry, there are conditions that need a lot of improvement and especially in closed psychiatry. So when you're in there, it's really terrible that the door is closed and you're not allowed out. I wasn't allowed out for six to seven weeks and I walked up and down like a tiger in a cage, and I found it terrible and I find it terrible every time." (p. 7)

- "All she does is see a doctor once or twice a week. There's no counselor brought in [. . .] She seriously needs to talk to somebody, not for 10 minutes, how's it going, how're you feeling, are you still seeing anything? That's all she gets. She's never actually sat down with anybody and just talked about anything." (p. 29)

- "No discharge plan or anything. They didn't even explain the medications to us, how he would take it, what times to give it to him. Just said 'Bye.' They gave us a bag of medication." (p. 29)

While it may be easy for us to dismiss these observations, we need to remember that one of our primary roles as clinicians is to do what is best for our clients. Unfortunately, as Bartl and colleagues (2024) note in summarizing their findings:

> The experience of involuntary treatment and compulsory admissions is an often predominately negative, at times traumatic experience for service users and carers, not always achieving the expected therapeutic benefit. A variety of factors are reported to contribute

to this, including the use of coercive practices, too much focus on pharmaceutical treatments, lack of access to psychological and other therapies, uncaring staff attitudes, or a lack of a calm, therapeutic ward environment. (p. 36)

The Bartl article raises an important issue, especially given their focus on patients who were involuntarily admitted. What about those clients who admitted themselves voluntarily—what is their experience? Bartl and colleagues (2024) note that "Service users who undergo compulsory admission (compared to those who are admitted voluntarily) have higher rates of suicide and greater dissatisfaction with care, as well as increased risk of readmission, especially compulsory admission" (p. 2). However, a voluntary admission may not mean an absence of coercion. I have witnessed many instances of treatment that was compulsory, but technically not involuntary. In these cases, patients were told that if they did not agree to voluntary admission, they would be involuntarily committed. Of course, many of them decided to then admit themselves—having been coerced to do so. However, in doing so (at least here in Virginia), they did not have the benefit of a court review of their case within 72 hours, and they often wound up staying on the inpatient unit *longer* than those involuntarily admitted. Regardless of the outcome or reason, it is ethically wrong to coerce patients to accept treatment.

Many clients who have experienced a psychiatric hospitalization are unwilling to return to that setting and may deny or underreport their level of suicidality when speaking with clinical providers. In fact, a survey of clients who admitted to concealing their suicidal ideation said that they did so because their clinicians did not seem to understand that suicidal ideation and suicidal behaviors are different—so the clinician wound up treating them equally, usually by sending the client to a hospital (Blanchard & Farber, 2018). There are two other things we need to keep in mind about hospitalization. The first is that even when hospitalized, clients remain at risk of suicide. The second is that hospital stays are typically measured in days, so what do we do when our clients are discharged?

Patient suicide is one of the "sentinel events" (which refers to an unexpected patient safety event that results in the patient's death or injury) tracked by hospitals and their accrediting agencies. In the US, inpatient suicide is among the top five sentinel events, with risk increasing among patients who have previous suicide attempts, are using antidepressant medications, lack social support, feel hopeless, engage in substance use, and struggle with chronic pain (Turco et al., 2022). While inpatient admission can lead to a false sense of safety, suicide can nonetheless happen on psychiatric units, especially during admission and after discharge (Abbar et al., 2022).

Maris (2019) also notes that the 15-minute suicide watch checks commonly employed on behavioral health units are ineffective in preventing suicide attempts because clients can kill themselves in less than 15 minutes. Instead, supervision should include frequent observation or surveillance that does not follow a planned interval, with clients who demonstrate higher risk potentially requiring continuous observation or supervision. In addition, since hanging or strangulation is the method used in over 90 percent of suicide deaths in hospitals and correctional settings—and most of these individuals are not suspended from the ground—there are methods we can use to decrease this risk accordingly as well. This includes limiting access to anything on which a person could tie fabric or string to fashion a noose (e.g., pipes, shower curtain rods, shower heads, railings, handles, or doorknobs).

While these are all measures we can take while a patient is hospitalized, what happens when they are discharged, usually after mere days, from the hospital? This is especially crucial for us to consider given that the majority of suicides after hospitalization occur within a week of the patient's discharge (Maris, 2019). Unfortunately, many patients are not connected with appropriate or timely follow-up (or step-down) services prior to being discharged, sometimes resulting in a revolving door of leaving one hospital to go to another. I often saw clients from my hospital discharged with nowhere to go except for having been handed a bus ticket to the nearest homeless shelter.

The fact is, we are responsible for helping our clients connect with appropriate care, especially when they transition from a higher level of care. My hope is that hospitalizations would be rare, saved for the most serious and extremely high-risk situations. Except for these high-risk situations, can we effectively treat our clients' suicidal ideation in an outpatient setting? The short answer is yes, we can in most situations. But before we look at ways to treat both acute suicidality and chronic suicidal ideation, how can we keep our clients safe *and* help them in a community setting? Let's first look at what *not* to do.

Why No-Harm Contracts Are an Incredibly Bad Idea

My first social work job was as a youth counselor in a residential program for "emotionally disturbed" adolescents—young people we would now understand to be suffering from trauma-related disorders. I was hired as the program was transitioning from a pure group-process, behaviorist approach to a more strengths-based clinical approach, with an emphasis on diagnosis and mental health treatment. After working in the program for a year, I was promoted to cottage manager. During this time, I was exposed to my first client who was expressing suicidal ideations with intent and a plan. I remember talking with my supervisor on the phone, explaining what was happening.

"Have him write on a piece of paper that he promises not to kill himself," she said.

I had already begun preparations to have the young man moved to a different room for the night and for staff members to be able to observe him closely if we were advised to not send him to the hospital. I was, frankly, perplexed by what I was being told.

"I know it sounds silly," she continued, "but research shows that if people sign a no-harm contract, 95 percent of the time, they will not try to kill themselves."

I had the kid sign the contract, we maintained close observation of him, and the next day, he denied wanting to die. He finished the program successfully without any suicide attempts or self-harming behaviors.

But was my supervisor right?

The following semester of my graduate social work program included a practical applications class, and in that class, the professor discussed no-harm contracts, stating that people who signed them did not engage in suicidal behavior 85 percent of the time. I was confused—was it 95 percent or 85 percent? I later heard other numbers bandied about regarding the efficacy of no-harm contracts. I even taught others the same thing—no-harm contracts work.

Turns out we were all wrong.

We tend to accept information as truth when we hear it repeatedly. My supervisor and professor were not incompetent; they simply accepted what they had heard and passed it along to others. I have done this too, as I am sure that most of us have at some point.

The fact is, no-harm contracts not only do not work, but they can also lull professionals into a false sense of safety. For example, one study examined 650 medical records of patients who had been psychiatrically hospitalized and found that 65 percent of those who contracted for safety ended up harming themselves—in fact, those who signed no-harm contracts were five to seven times more likely to self-harm (Drew, 2001). The biggest problem with traditional no-harm contracting is an emphasis on what the patient *won't* do versus what they *will* do should they become acutely suicidal (Jobes, 2023). Unfortunately, their use continues today, despite overwhelming evidence of their uselessness (Garvey et al., 2009). In fact, up to 40 percent of clinicians still endorse these types of contracts (Rozek et al., 2023)! When I worked in the emergency department, I regularly had to deal with the local crisis team, who still used no-harm contracts.

Clinicians also need to remember that not only are no-harm or no-suicide contracts ineffective, they also do nothing to protect professionals against liability. A contract, by definition, is a legal document made between two entities who can consent to what they are agreeing to. It follows that if a person wants to kill themselves, they are likely under duress (of some form), up to and including mental illness, substance use disorder, or any of the many risk factors we have examined that could compromise their ability to make an informed decision. Please do not use these "contracts."

Safety Planning

An alternative to no-harm contracting is safety planning. This is not simply a piece of paper (although I think writing the plan down is necessary); it is a fluid and adaptable method of working *with* the client to help them remain safe. Safety plans should be individualized for each client and reviewed regularly to ensure that they meet the changing needs of the client. Here are several factors that must be present before a safety plan is considered:

1. The safety plan must be completed after a thorough suicide assessment. The responses to the suicide assessment should connect with the suicide safety plan.

2. The client must be able to participate fully in developing and implementing their safety plan. If the client is experiencing a psychotic episode or any other mental health crisis that compromises their ability to participate in a safety plan, then there is no safety plan.

3. The client must also be *willing* to participate in the safety plan. This means a willingness to include other people in their lives in their plan and a willingness to secure all lethal means that could be at their disposal. Ryan and Oquendo (2020) note that if the client is unwilling to provide contact information, then hospitalizing the client may be the safest option.

As I mentioned earlier, safety plans are more effective in reducing suicidal behavior and increasing engagement in treatment because they focus on what a client (and professional) are to *do* as opposed to what they are *not* to do, which is the sole focus of no-harm contracts. The following is a safety plan I developed over the years when I worked in emergency departments. It is not something unique—it is an amalgamation of various items I have seen over the years that I think have value in terms of helping clients remain safe. This is not a static document, as it is designed to be the foundation of a collaborative discussion with clients, so feel free to use it as is or modify it in any way. A copy of the safety plan is available at the end of the chapter. Let's look at the plan item by item. Earlier forms of this safety plan template were in my earlier books.

1. **Is the client able to participate in this safety plan?** Remember that if the client is unable or unwilling to participate in safety planning, then there can be no safety plan. It is natural that clients may be ambiguous about wanting to die, and you need to understand this without over- or underreacting. If you sense that the client is ambiguous about wanting to die, I suggest you consider the Collaborative Assessment for Management of Suicidality (CAMS), which closes out this chapter. CAMS utilizes stringent safety planning but incorporates this into active treatment to address the client's suicidal ideation. If the client cannot or will not participate in CAMS, then hospitalization should be strongly considered for client safety.

2. **Who are (at least) two people who can be a part of this safety plan? What is their relationship to the client and how can you get into contact with them?** Regardless of the setting in which you

are working with your client, if they are going home, other people need to be aware of and involved in their safety planning. If the client is unwilling to involve others, then a viable safety plan cannot be established. Professionals need to be able to speak with these individuals (or be present when the client is speaking with them) to ensure that they understand the safety plan. It is not necessary for clients (and certainly not professionals) to tell everything about the client—the focus is on the client's safety. Professionals also need to assess, to the best of their ability, the reliability and judgment of the other people involved in the safety plan.

3. **What are the warning signs or triggers that may increase the client's desire to kill themself?** Encourage your client to think about the things that could pose a risk to them, no matter how "ridiculous" it may sound. Sometimes talking about these things aloud can help clients begin the process of examining their beliefs and how they trigger their emotions and subsequent behaviors. I will examine this further in the next chapter when we discuss cognitive behavioral therapy (CBT) for suicide prevention.

4. **What are some of the coping skills the client can use when they experience those warning signs or when triggers increase their desire to kill themself?** I have found that this is a good question to foster problem-solving discussions with clients. I also strongly encourage people to think about the details of the coping skills they could use. For example, if a client lists listening to music as a coping skill, I usually ask, "What kind of music? How will you listen to it (on your computer, phone, stereo, or something else)? How do these songs or this type of music help you?" If the client lists going on a walk as a coping skill, where will they walk? Will their walking path bring them near potential methods of suicide (e.g., large parking garages or bridges they could jump off)? What if they can't go on a walk because the weather is bad—what else could they do?

5. **Once the client leaves here (office, program, or hospital emergency department), where will they be staying and for how long? Who will be with them?** Being alone is not an option, at least not early in the suicide safety planning process. If the client's home is not a safe environment, is there somewhere else they can stay temporarily?

6. **Are there firearms in the client's possession? Does the client have access to firearms where they will be staying? Who can secure any weapons available to the client, and how will these weapons be secured and stored safely away from the client?** Limiting access to firearms is nonnegotiable when creating safety plans, given that more people kill themselves with firearms than all other methods combined. This is not a Second Amendment issue or a political issue—it is a safety issue. The removal of firearms is not intended to be permanent, only as long as the client's suicidal ideation is active. Firearms should be removed from the client's access regardless of the methods of suicide they may be considering, given the high lethality of firearms.

7. **What medications is the client prescribed? How are the medications taken? What are some of the potential medication side effects? Who can secure the medications and ensure that the client takes the medication when prescribed? Who will be responsible for securing over-the-counter medications?** Most people think about medication overdoses as typically involving prescription medications, but several over-the-counter medications (e.g., acetaminophen) are lethal in higher doses.

8. **What other items will need to be secured where the client is staying?** Examples include knives and poisons (e.g., herbicides or cleaning supplies). Who will be responsible for taking care of these items?

9. **How will the next three days (an arbitrary number—feel free to establish a plan for however many days you and the client deem necessary) be scheduled or structured?** The goal is to not overwhelm the client with too many things but, at the same time, have things for the client to do to limit boredom due to unstructured time. Ideally, you should work together to select activities that the client enjoys doing with others, with an eye toward avoiding things that could trigger or stress the client. Make sure to consider alternative activities in case unforeseen circumstances arise, such as weather-related event cancellations.

10. **What is the plan for follow-up care? What services will the client receive and from whom? Have insurance and transportation issues been worked out?** I have seen hospital discharge plans for clients that included following up with providers who did not take the client's medical insurance or who were located well away from public transportation. These barriers need to be anticipated and resolved as part of the planning process.

11. **What is the local crisis center or hotline contact information? What about the 9-8-8 system? Does the client have a means to access these (and other) resources?** If necessary, rehearse accessing these resources with your client. This could include role-playing your client calling the resource.

12. **What is the plan should the client's suicidal ideation worsen, or if they display suicidal behaviors?** The safest response to this may be to call 9-1-1 or 9-8-8, but I think more planning can help with a smoother transition to a higher level of care (including inpatient psychiatric hospitalization) if needed. I have worked with patients in the emergency department on safety plans and asked them to return should their symptoms worsen. My preference was to work with the patient (and another person involved in their safety plan) to identify at least two accessible emergency departments close to where they would be staying. On several occasions, I had clients return within a day, stating that they had given the safety plan a try, but they were feeling worse and needed to consider voluntary admission for further intensive treatment.

I want to emphasize that no safety plan is foolproof or perfect. If you have any doubts about your client's safety, I suggest considering inpatient hospitalization. However, as noted in the earlier part of this chapter, we should not over-rely on hospitalization when the client's needs can be served in an outpatient setting.

One final point about safety plans. Careful, thorough, and timely documentation is the key in managing your liability in these difficult situations. Remember the adage: If you do not write it down, it never happened. I know from years of experience working in crisis settings that we clinicians are often pushed to work quickly. However, the development of a safety plan should not be rushed, even though they can be constructed quickly in some cases. Likewise, the need we have to carefully document the plan in the client's medical record is important as well. I strongly suggest that the plan be in the client's medical record by the end of your shift, or at the very least, within 24 hours.

As I mentioned at the beginning of this section, safety plans can be used with clients who are not in imminent danger of suicide and who can fully participate in developing a collaborative safety plan. But what about those clients who are not in imminent danger but may be more ambivalent about their suicidal ideation? For these clients, CAMS may be a suitable method to not only develop a sustainable safety plan but also address and decrease their suicidal ideation directly. (Note: My discussion of CAMS, alongside any other interventions in this book, such as DBT and CBT, is to provide you with an overview of best practices for addressing clients who are suicidal. It is up to you to obtain appropriate training and supervision in the use of each of these interventions.)

Collaborative Assessment for Management of Suicidality (CAMS)

I discovered CAMS during my research for this book. This approach focuses on clients who experience suicidal ideation (with or without plans) and sees inpatient hospitalization as a last resort. It has been shown to be an effective method of decreasing ideation and limiting suicidal behavior (Jobes, 2023; Jobes et al., 2017). As I read through the CAMS manual (Jobes, 2023), I often found myself in agreement with the author about the potential of harm when clients are unnecessarily hospitalized. I was also impressed by his focus on reducing suicidal ideation in clients who are acutely suicidal in a structured, time-limited setting. At the heart of CAMS is collaboration between the clinical provider and client. This is key, given that establishing strong therapeutic rapport is the cornerstone of any outpatient treatment for suicidality. Because collaboration between client and clinician is at the heart of the intervention, clients who cannot or will not collaborate with the clinician are not appropriate for CAMS.

What I enjoyed the most when learning about CAMS was the truthful, matter-of-fact approach that professionals are encouraged to employ. This includes

Chapter 7 • Disposition

becoming comfortable talking with clients who may have a strong desire to kill themselves. The professional must admit to the client (and to themselves): "Yes, you could kill yourself, and there is only so much I can do about that. I do not want you to kill yourself. I know you may see that as the only solution, and I am certain it feels that way now. I want to help you consider other ways to handle what is going on." Jobes (2023) even adds that clients could always kill themselves later, even though this is not something he wants to happen. This type of honesty with clients, along with the clinician not overreacting and not being blasé, often helps the client realize that they are being listened to. Jobes also notes, "The most important clinical question to ever ask of a patient talking about suicide: 'Is suicide your only possible solution?'" (p. 63).

Theoretically, CAMS is based on Shneidman's (1987) cubic model of suicide, which holds that the highest levels of pain ("psychache"), stress (actual and imagined), and perturbation (agitation) can intersect, with the highest level of all three of these being termed the "lethal corner" (Jobes, 2023). CAMS uses specific forms and measures to assess these constructs, starting with the Suicide Status Form (SSF), which measures psychological pain, stress, agitation, hopelessness, and self-hate on 5-point Likert scales, and then has the client rate the five domains in order of importance. While CAMS can be modified for telehealth use, it is expected that the clinician will sit next to the client while the client completes the SSF. This is my only real complaint about CAMS. I work with a lot of clients who have extremely traumatic histories. Many of these clients value their individual space and their ability to quickly get away from any real or perceived threat (which could include me). I do not see how sitting next to them would be conducive to creating a collaborative process. However, I still think that CAMS is useful, provided that the clinician does not assert their power and talk *to* the client but remains focused on a conversation that employs a lot of listening and empathy.

CAMS then moves on to asking the client to list their reasons for living and their reasons for wanting to die. CAMS also asks clients to examine their suicidal ideation in the context of themselves (what they feel internally) and in the context of their relationships (what might be driving their suicidal ideation externally—specifically relationally). The final part for the client to complete in the SSF is to rate their wish to live and their wish to die on a 0 to 8 scale. This is followed by the question: "The one thing that would help me no longer feel suicidal would be . . ." (Jobes, 2023).

Following the completion of the first part of the SSF, the clinician completes the second part, which includes a detailed analysis of suicidal ideation, planning, preparation, rehearsal, and items such as substance use, impulsivity, sleep quality, relationships with others, and additional risk factors. At this point, the clinician and client must decide whether to proceed with CAMS. This includes many elements I included in the safety planning section earlier in this chapter, including bringing other people into the plan and removing (or securing) all lethal means (especially firearms) in the client's home. If the client is unwilling to engage in this, then CAMS cannot proceed.

The next section includes treatment plan development. In the CAMS model, the primary problem to be addressed is the client's self-harm potential, with the goal being the client's safety (Jobes, 2023). CAMS also has the client identify two "drivers"—the top two things that could push the client to try to kill themselves. Clients and clinicians also complete the CAMS stabilization plan, which asks clients to list ways to reduce access to lethal means, things they can do differently to cope when experiencing a suicidal crisis, people they can ask for help or who can decrease their sense of isolation, and potential barriers and their solutions to attending treatment (Jobes, 2023). The final section of the SSF is the clinician's post-session evaluation, which includes a mental status exam, diagnostic impressions, and case notes.

The next session of CAMS is called an interim care session, and there can be anywhere from 2 to 12 (sometimes more) interim care sessions. The purpose of the interim sessions is to focus on the drivers of suicide, while also identifying "indirect drivers" (e.g., substance use, unstable housing, trauma, or mental health) that push the primary drivers (Jobes, 2023). During each interim session, the SSF is completed and reviewed for changes. CAMS is considered complete when the client rates either a 1 or 2 on the 5-point final SSF Core Assessment, the client reports that yes, they managed their thoughts and feelings in the past week, and the patient reports no regarding suicidal behavior (Jobes, 2023).

Following the resolution of the interim CAMS sessions, there is a final (dispositional) session in which the client's progress is reviewed, and the client continues to report little to no suicidal ideation. At this point, plans are made for ongoing care, including transitioning into another type of modality such as DBT. Clients are welcome to return to engage in CAMS should they find themselves feeling overwhelmed by suicidal ideation.

Jobes (2023) is clear that CAMS is specific for acute suicidal ideation and is ideally suited for outpatient settings. He is equally clear that clients must be willing to engage in the collaborative process, even if they are somewhat ambivalent at the beginning. He notes that other forms of treatment, such as CBT and DBT, are better suited for clients who are chronically suicidal. I will examine these approaches to work with chronically suicidal clients in the next chapter.

Sample Safety Plan

1. Is the client able to participate in this safety plan?
   _____
   _____
   _____
   _____

2. Who are (at least) two people who can be a part of this safety plan? What is their relationship to the client and how can you get into contact with them?
   _____
   _____
   _____
   _____

3. What are the warning signs or triggers that may increase the client's desire to kill themself?
   _____
   _____
   _____
   _____

4. What are some of the coping skills the client can use when they experience those warning signs or when triggers increase their desire to kill themself?
   _____
   _____
   _____
   _____

5. Once the client leaves here (e.g., office, program, or hospital emergency department), where will they be staying and for how long? Who will be with them?

_____
_____
_____
_____

6. Are there firearms in the client's possession? Does the client have access to firearms where they will be staying? Who can secure any weapons available to the client, and how will these weapons be secured and stored safely away from the client?

_____
_____
_____
_____

7. What medications is the client prescribed? How are the medications taken? What are some of the potential medication side effects? Who can secure the medications and ensure that the client takes the medication when prescribed? Who will be responsible for securing over-the-counter medications?

_____
_____
_____
_____

8. What other items will need to be secured where the client is staying?

_____
_____
_____
_____

9. How will the next three days (an arbitrary number—feel free to establish a plan for however many days you and the client deem necessary) be scheduled or structured?

_____
_____
_____
_____

10. What is the plan for follow-up care? What services will the client receive and from whom? Have insurance and transportation issues been worked out?

_____
_____
_____
_____

11. What is the local crisis center or hotline contact information? What about the 9-8-8 system? Does the client have a means to access these (and other) resources?

_____
_____
_____
_____

12. What is the plan should the client's suicidal ideation worsen, or if they display suicidal behaviors?

_____
_____
_____
_____

CHAPTER 8

Treatment of the Suicidal Client, Part 1

In this chapter and the following one, I will focus on treatment for clients with chronic suicidal ideation, as opposed to working with clients in crisis or at risk of imminent harm. In this chapter, you will learn about cognitive behavioral approaches, including brief CBT (BCBT) for suicide prevention. I will then examine DBT and its use with clients who engage in suicidal behaviors or self-harming behaviors.

This chapter marks a notable shift from what we have covered thus far. At this point, the client has been assessed, and initial safety concerns have been addressed. A safety plan should be in place, and the client may have benefited from the CAMS approach to treating acute suicidal ideation. The client may have been hospitalized to address immediate harm and is now back in an outpatient setting where their suicidal ideation and behaviors need to be addressed to limit the possibilities of self-harm or a return to inpatient treatment.

For many of us working with clients in this situation, the emphasis has typically been to treat the underlying mental illness (e.g., depression) or trauma, with the reasoning that in doing so, we will help the client reduce or eliminate their suicidal ideation or behaviors. This approach is called the psychiatric syndromal model, which holds that suicidal thoughts and behaviors are symptoms of a psychiatric illness. Bryan and Rudd (2018) note that even though evidence does not support this model, most providers continue to value it. The psychiatric syndromal model leads to providers treating what they perceive as the underlying mental health problems that drive suicidal thoughts but not necessarily suicidal behaviors. This evidence aligns with one of the overall purposes of this book: treating the client's suicidal ideation *directly*. While there is an obvious need to treat underlying issues, we also need to directly treat suicidal ideation and behaviors. This is especially important for clients transitioning from higher levels of care.

Three primary areas need to be addressed when helping clients transition from a higher level of care or when working with clients struggling with chronic suicidal ideation (Brasler, 2019):

1. **Emotion regulation:** Many clients with chronic suicidal ideation or suicidal behaviors see their suicidality as a coping mechanism. The primary intervention is to help clients regulate their emotions in healthy ways.

2. **Problem-solving:** Clients can view suicide as a viable solution to problems, so we must work with them to explore other options to solve their problems.

3. **Communication:** Clients may not be able to communicate their needs to others except by expressing suicidal ideation or behaviors. As professionals, we can help them develop healthier communication styles.

While CBT has some limitations, it is one of the best ways to address these primary areas.

Cognitive Behavioral Therapy

The foundation of CBT is a collaborative process between the client and clinician in which new skills are introduced, practiced in session, and then provided as homework as a bridge to the next session. During the following session, homework is reviewed, a new skill is taught, demonstrated, and rehearsed, and more opportunities are afforded to put the newly learned material into practice before the next session. Although CBT approaches do not discount an extensive psychosocial history, there is less reliance on historical information than on what is happening with the client in the present. CBT is also designed to be time-limited, as opposed to open-ended, like other forms of counseling.

At the core of CBT is the belief that how we think and feel (*cognition*) directly impacts how we act (*behave*). CBT visualizes this using the ABC model, which holds that:

- **Activating events (A)** are stressors or events that begin the process of how we think, feel, and subsequently act. Activating events are not things we do but things we experience. An example of an activating event could be receiving criticism or having conflict with a loved one. We often cannot stop or limit activating events, as they are normal parts of life.

- Activating events trigger our **beliefs (B)**, namely the things we believe about ourselves, others, and the world. If we hold negative beliefs in these areas, we will likely view the activating event in a negative light—perhaps even as an attack to which we need to respond. Much of the work in CBT is spent in this area: examining our automatic thoughts and beliefs and challenging the veracity of those thoughts and beliefs. CBT seeks to undermine these false negative beliefs and change them to more realistic thoughts.

- Our beliefs drive our emotions and behaviors, which CBT conceptualizes as **consequences (C)**. If our emotions (and behaviors) are based on false or inaccurate beliefs, we will likely act in unhealthy ways, including suicidal ideation or behaviors. This can also create additional activating events or negative beliefs that create additional emotional behaviors (consequences).

Let's use Sarah's story to see how the ABC model works. This will also help us determine ways we use CBT to help Sarah learn to question and challenge her suicidal ideation.

Case Study: Sarah

Sarah was a 41-year-old female whom I had initially seen for ketamine-assisted psychotherapy. She had a history of major depressive disorder since adolescence. Antidepressant medications had been helpful in addressing her depression but seemed to lose their effectiveness as she aged. Sarah was married and did not have any children. She led a medium-sized nonprofit agency, and she enjoyed her job and her marriage. Sarah's parents had immigrated to the United States from Thailand. Her mother was demanding, emotionally volatile, and physically abusive toward her. Sarah's mother clearly preferred Sarah's older sister and was often dismissive of Sarah. Sarah's father, while kind, was passive and deferred to his domineering spouse in everything, including parenting their daughters.

Sarah stated that she had first attempted suicide when she was an adolescent by overdosing on over-the-counter medications. Sarah's mother reacted to this by berating her and telling her how much of a disappointment she was. When Sarah was finally able to move away to attend university, she found an identity in scientific work and developed her leadership skills. However, she later realized that no matter what she accomplished, she would always be compared to her sister. When she and her husband elected not to have children, this caused further reactions from Sarah's mother. Sarah and her husband settled in Virginia, both happy in their marriage and respective careers, and far away from Sarah's family, who lived in another state.

Despite her happy marriage and fulfilling job, Sarah continued to struggle with depression, specifically low self-worth, feelings of inadequacy, and thoughts of suicide. She participated in counseling, where her therapist helped her see that her childhood experiences were abusive. Prior to working with this counselor, Sarah assumed that all children were hit a lot, deprived of food, and demeaned. She began to consider that she was not the problem and that her thoughts and feelings could be the result of her upbringing. Unfortunately, Sarah's therapist left her practice to pursue another opportunity, and Sarah decided to take a break from counseling instead of being referred to another therapist.

While Sarah was able to successfully manage her trauma and depressive symptoms for several years, her depression and negative self-talk gradually returned. She had tried several medications at this point, but none seemed to work long-term for her, and the side effects were unpleasant. She found out about ketamine infusions to treat depression from a podcast and did some research on her own. This was how she discovered our practice.

During Sarah's first two appointments with me, she shared information about her depression and trauma history, including her prior suicide attempt, but she denied experiencing suicidal ideation at the time. She then began what was to have been six ketamine infusions over a three-week period. Sarah responded moderately to the ketamine but noted that she had a difficult time "letting go to the medication." What she meant by this was that she fought to remain in control during her sessions as opposed to allowing the medication to work on its own.

Chapter 8 • Treatment of the Suicidal Client, Part 1

After her second infusion session, Sarah's older sister died unexpectedly from complications of alcohol use disorder. Sarah took a break from the infusions and traveled to her sister's home in another state to organize the funeral and take care of her sister's affairs. Sarah's sister had been separated from her husband, and her adolescent children were living with their father. Sarah and her husband had solid, caring relationships with their nieces and were supportive toward them. Sarah's parents were a part of their daughter's funeral but left most of the organizing to Sarah. At the funeral, Sarah's mother was cold and distant.

When Sarah returned from her sister's funeral several weeks later, she elected not to continue with ketamine treatment. However, because she did not have an existing counselor, she asked to continue seeing me for outpatient psychotherapy to address what she identified as depression and trauma. I agreed to work with her, noting that a big part of our initial work together would likely be devoted to grief work regarding her sister.

Our first session consisted of a lot of crying and anger about Sarah's sister's death. I was primarily supportive during this time, noting that grief takes time and that there is no wrong way to grieve except hurting oneself or someone else. I also emphasized that grief is a process and does not have a fixed series of stages, nor is it limited to a set time frame. Sarah seemed to appreciate this approach. She shared that her sister had left "a huge mess for me to clean up." Because Sarah's sister had spent the last two years of her life drinking constantly, and there was no will or legal framework established to guide others in dealing with her estate, Sarah had assumed this responsibility. I asked her why she took this on, and she responded that her father was numb from losing his daughter, while her mother expected Sarah to take care of things. Sarah's sister's ex-husband also wanted nothing to do with his ex-wife's affairs, electing to spend as much of his time and energy on his children as he could.

"He's actually become a better father than I ever imagined he could be," Sarah said toward the end of the session. "He seems to understand what his kids need, and he is just trying to be present. I didn't know he had it in him!"

"I'm glad to hear that," I responded, "since the kids need him now more than ever. But it still doesn't answer my question: Why must you take on the responsibility of your sister's estate?"

Sarah sighed. "I would like to think I am doing this so that my older niece, who is getting ready to turn 18, does not have to deal with it, and I also want to make sure the girls are as well taken care of as possible. But the fact is, my parents are refusing to do anything, so someone has to do it."

I elected not to push back on Sarah's thought process, especially since most of this session had been devoted to me holding space for Sarah to grieve as much as she needed. At the end of the session, Sarah let me know that she was returning to her sister's home over the weekend to try to get more done with settling her sister's affairs.

At the beginning of the next session, Sarah abruptly asked, "Why do people make such a big deal about staying alive?"

"As opposed to what?" I replied.

"Dying, of course."

"That's an interesting question," I responded. "What are you getting at?"

"Why do people care so much if I were to kill myself?"

I'll take a moment to illustrate Sarah's presentation as she asked this question. She was smiling, leaning slightly forward in her chair, and making clear eye contact. During my prior interactions with her, I had found Sarah to be pleasant and engaging. She had never appeared to be emotionally manipulative, and I did not believe she was trying to manipulate me this time. She was asking an honest question.

"Before you ask," Sarah said as she saw me taking a deep breath, "I am not going to kill myself today or anytime soon. At least not for another year or so. I would wrap up my affairs and then travel to Switzerland since they allow euthanasia for adults with mental illness."

"You did not talk about this previously. What is different now?" I asked.

"Well, the ketamine treatment didn't work for me. Plus, there's my sister . . ."

Sarah was quiet, so I waited for her to speak. After a minute of silence, I tried engaging her again.

"As you've mentioned, this is a huge loss, and you're feeling a lot of emotions right now, which is completely understandable and okay in every way."

Sarah was quiet for a moment. "I am so angry," she finally stated.

"You mentioned earlier that you felt rage toward your sister."

Chapter 8 • Treatment of the Suicidal Client, Part 1

"I am. I do," said Sarah. "This was avoidable. She didn't have to drink herself to death."

I was quiet, not wanting to get in her way of talking about her feelings. Sarah continued, "My husband has been in recovery since before we met. He's explained to me how alcoholism is a disease, and this is not something my sister necessarily wanted to happen."

I nodded.

"But she also had many opportunities to try recovery, and as far as I know, she never did."

I nodded again. "And now it's too late."

"Yeah," said Sarah, going quiet again. "And she stole from me."

"Please explain," I replied.

"I can't kill myself now because my sister is dead. It wouldn't be right if I died too—my parents shouldn't suffer the death of another daughter."

"So, is that one of the things keeping you alive?" I ask.

"I guess," said Sarah.

"What about your husband?"

"He's a great guy," said Sarah, "and I know he would miss me, but he'll get over it."

"You seem pretty sure," I replied. "I wonder what he'd say to that?"

"I don't know," said Sarah.

"I think you're right about that," I said, "and I wonder if you're ambivalent about living, not dying."

"Maybe you're right, but why should I live?"

"You're asking me to give you reasons to live?" I asked.

"Yeah."

"Well, that's out of my purview. That would be like me telling you what to believe or what kind of spirituality to have."

"I'm not saying that. I'm simply asking: Why choose life? What is so wrong with me wanting to kill myself?" asked Sarah.

"That is a fair question," I said, "but I want you to hear me clearly: I do not want you to kill yourself."

"I am not going to do it now," Sarah responded. "I have to put a bunch of things in order and tie up my affairs. Plus, I would want to do it medically, painlessly, and legally."

"I am glad this is not something you are considering this moment," I said, "but I would still like to create a safety plan with you before we end our session."

"I understand," Sarah replied.

"But since we still have plenty of time in the session, is there anything that has happened since we last met that is driving these thoughts of suicide? There's not always a cause for people thinking about suicide, but sometimes there is."

"Well, I just got back from my sister's house. It was a wreck, and that's just the junk in the house. Her finances are a total clusterfuck," Sarah said.

"Is that driving these thoughts of suicide?" I asked.

"That's part of it," she replied. "I mean, I'm jealous that she doesn't have to deal with the shit associated with life. I'm also angry at her for not saying goodbye—for not even trying to get sober. Then there's my parents . . ."

"What happened with them while you were there?" I asked.

"They were there at my sister's house, but not really helping. My mom just kept talking about how wonderful my sister was, how she was successful, had kids, and should not have died. My dad is just in shock. But he will never do anything to cross my mother—I'm the only one who does that."

"How do you cross your mother?" I asked.

"I don't always do it intentionally," Sarah responded. "A lot of times I simply point out what is going wrong, or I try to correct her, and she just tears my head off. We got into an argument, I forgot about what, and she said she wished I would go away too. Then she walked out." Tears welled up in Sarah's eyes.

I paused before quietly saying, "I am sorry that happened."

"It just brings up all the shit I went through when I was younger. To me, all that crap remains, and I'm just done with it. That's the main reason I just want out."

I paused before continuing. "Sarah, I think we need to work on this before we work on the depression and trauma that you first said you wanted to tackle. And by 'this' I mean your suicidal ideation—we need to address it."

"I'm not making any promises," Sarah said, "except that I am not planning on killing myself now."

Chapter 8 • Treatment of the Suicidal Client, Part 1

"That is what we'll cover when we create a safety plan for you. In terms of addressing your long-term suicidal ideation, I would like to use a cognitive behavioral approach. Could we use this as a plan to move forward?"

"I think so," Sarah replied.

We then moved to complete a safety plan that included her husband. There did not appear to be any imminent or acute risk of suicide for Sarah, so I concluded the session by introducing some of the broad concepts of CBT, which she was willing to try.

Most clients appear to like CBT's directness and its focus on tasks. However, CBT is not for every client and every situation. I personally like it for situations in which specific problems need to be addressed. Clients who are completely ambivalent about making changes or even realizing that they have a problem are usually not a good fit for CBT—for these clients I recommend using motivational interviewing. CBT is also generally not suitable, at least initially, for clients who have trouble with reality testing, such as clients who are intoxicated or may be experiencing psychosis. CBT may be less useful for clients who are extremely hypervigilant or in a constant flight-fight-freeze state due to traumatic experiences. I have also found that CBT works best with clients who can understand basic logic and cause-and-effect thinking. Sarah appeared to fit all these criteria, which was why I elected to pursue a CBT approach.

While CBT is designed to be a structured, well-planned-out approach, I must admit that I do not always follow the model dogmatically. I know some clinicians who do, and if that works for them to help their clients, I say more power to them. Many clinicians I know adapt the principles of CBT into their eclectic style, which is how I would explain what I do. I believe it is important to be authentic and adaptive to best serve the needs of clients while also maintaining fidelity to the core aspects of a given approach.

At the next session, after getting an update on how things were going for Sarah, including the usefulness of her safety plan (which we agreed to maintain), I introduced the basic concepts of CBT. I began by explaining the ABC model and how we would use it to examine and challenge the automatic thoughts that might be driving Sarah's feelings and behaviors. I suggested that we approach her suicidality first from a "what if . . .?" approach, by looking at consequences first.

I then went through the following steps to examine how she viewed suicide as a viable (and perhaps the only) solution to her problems:

1. Identify triggering situations
2. Identify the initial beliefs
3. Question the accuracy of the initial beliefs
4. Find ways to challenge automatic thoughts
5. Manage behavioral urges to act on suicidal thoughts and focus on engaging in non-self-harming behaviors

What follows in this section of the chapter is a paraphrased account of a series of discussions we had over time that illustrates each of these steps. Given Sarah's statement about killing herself in a year or so because she was tired of the pain she was living with, I started by focusing on that.

"Can we agree that death is a finite condition from which there is no coming back?" I asked.

"I believe that, yeah," Sarah responded.

"So, in a way it *is* a solution—you're no longer alive, so you don't have to deal with any of the pain you're experiencing. It's all gone."

"You're catching on!" she said. "Now I suppose you're going to have me think of all the ways that killing myself could affect others and why I shouldn't do that."

"Would that change your mind about suicide being an option?" I asked.

"Nope."

"I figured you might say that, so no, I'm not going to ask you do to that, at least not now. I just want us to agree that death is permanent and that taking your life would be the ultimate choice for you."

"I can agree with that," said Sarah.

"What I want to look at are the things that take place outside of yourself and within your mind that have led you to consider suicide as an option," I said.

Identify Triggering Situations

"Let's start by thinking about the situations in which you find yourself thinking about death or killing yourself," I said.

"Recently or in the past?" Sarah asked.

"Your call," I responded.

Chapter 8 • Treatment of the Suicidal Client, Part 1

"It seems to always be there, but sometimes I feel it stronger."

"And what times are those?"

"Well, like a few weeks ago when I was at my sister's house. I was frustrated about the mess—literally, financially, and emotionally—that she left, but it wasn't until my parents came around that I felt a ton worse," Sarah explained.

"Both your parents?" I asked.

"My mom, mainly. My father is just so sad, I wonder if he is still in shock. He tried to be helpful with some of the stuff and offered to help me deal with the finances."

"That was kind of him," I said.

"Yes, he's a kind man, but timid. He adores my mother and would never challenge her. In his mind she is always right."

"What happened when your mother showed up?" I asked.

"It was like she didn't even see me or the mess I was trying to clean up. I just wanted to disappear."

"Do you mean die?" I asked.

"Yeah."

"What about just leaving the area for a while?"

"I've done that before—it's one of the reasons I live in a different state than they do."

"So being around your mother is a trigger, for lack of a better word, for thinking about dying. And this is because of all those years of abuse, favoritism, and sheer meanness," I said.

"Yeah, that's it," Sarah replied.

"So, let's write down that being around your mother is a trigger," I said.

"Okay."

"Now, let's think about other triggers."

We began listing other things that Sarah identified as triggers. She sometimes added items to this list outside of sessions, and we would discuss them in session.

Identify the Initial Beliefs

Once we had amassed a list of triggers, with Sarah's mother at the top of the list, I asked Sarah to think about what the triggers reinforced in her and what she believed.

"You mentioned automatic thoughts before; is that the same thing as initial beliefs?" Sarah asked.

"Great question," I responded. "For our purposes, initial beliefs are the things that we hold true over time, while automatic thoughts are focused on actions we can engage in presently. Our beliefs can drive our automatic thoughts, so what I want to do first is identify (not challenge, at least not yet) the initial beliefs that make your triggers, well, triggering. This can be hard because we typically hold on to our initial beliefs for years and accept them as absolute truths."

"So, the issue at this point isn't about whether the beliefs are true—it's about trying to identify them in the first place?"

"Yes! You got it!"

"Okay," said Sarah. "I guess the first belief is that I should not be here."

"That is a belief connected to your mother?" I asked.

"Oh yeah," she replied, "it's been that way since I can remember. I was the bad one, the disappointment. I could never live up to my sister. It would have been better if I hadn't been born or at least been born a male."

"Alright, that is a lot to unpack. Let's focus on the beliefs that you should not be here, you are a disappointment, and you could not live up to your sister. Those are really intense beliefs, and you've lived with them for most of your life."

"Yeah."

Question the Accuracy of the Initial Beliefs

"But you have made several references to your love of science and how the work you do, which you love, is grounded in science. Am I remembering that correctly?" I asked.

"You are," Sarah replied.

"So, if we examine these beliefs through a scientific lens, are they true? For example, while we cannot control how your mother acts or treats you, if she believes that you are a disappointment, is that true?"

"To her it seems to be," Sarah replied.

"But is that true for you?"

"I mean, I am educated, I like my job, I love my husband . . ."

"That sounds like the opposite of a disappointment," I noted.

"Yes, but even with those things, and others, it can be really tough to go against what our parents think about us," Sarah responded.

"Totally," I said. "If this were easy, you would have already done it. And I know that our relationships with our parents have huge implications for us, so I am not trying to dumb this down. But as you become more aware of these beliefs, you can take a step back at least some of the time and ask yourself—is this true for me?"

"Well, she treats me that way, but I guess it is not true entirely. I wonder if decreasing my contact with her can be helpful. I don't think she is going to change, so what if I put space between us?"

"I think you're going in the right direction," I said. "You can't change her or how she thinks, but you can change how you think and how you relate to her."

"That will be difficult for now since I am going to have to be down there (where they live) while I settle my sister's estate and make sure my nieces are taken care of. But I can limit how much I interact with her."

"So, when you do have to interact with her, how can you set boundaries with her?" I asked.

"I've been doing that for a while—setting boundaries. But it doesn't help stop the negative comments or anything, and those build up over time and make me think I'm a piece of crap," Sarah replied.

Find Ways to Challenge Automatic Thoughts

"The way I can support you in changing these initial beliefs is by helping you recognize and challenge your automatic thoughts," I said.

"Hold on," said Sarah, "I know you already explained it, but what is the difference between initial beliefs and automatic thoughts again? It sounds confusing."

"I can see that, and it took me a while to understand it myself," I replied. "For our purposes, your beliefs are long-standing and are a response to your mother's criticism and abuse. Automatic thoughts are a reaction to these underlying beliefs but are more immediate and action oriented. We need to identify your automatic thoughts, which do not last for very long, and find ways to replace them with healthier thoughts. Make sense?"

"Yeah," said Sarah.

"Since what we are working on now is your suicidal ideation, I'd like to focus on your automatic thoughts that put forward your death as a suitable solution to your thoughts."

"Well, yeah, that's the most obvious," said Sarah.

"Okay, so how do your automatic thoughts appear?"

"They appear when I think about what you're calling my initial beliefs: that I am worthless, ugly, stupid, no good. But it is not always in relation to my mother. I could get into an argument with my husband, or have a bad day at work, or be in physical pain, and one of the first things that comes up is that I would be better off dead."

"Alright, you've just described an automatic thought," I said. "What happens next?"

"A lot of times, I'll think about killing myself for a while and then something comes up and I have to attend to that. Other times, when I am down, I go online and research ways to kill myself painlessly and legally."

"Does that make you feel better?" I asked.

"You know, sometimes it does. Sometimes, thinking about killing myself makes me feel better because I know there is a way out. However, as I mentioned, that is no longer on the table because my sister is gone. But at the same time, I still really struggle with suicidal thoughts."

"You noted that these thoughts go away?"

"Yes, usually after about 20 minutes or so," said Sarah.

"Would you say that during that time, you are more vulnerable?" I asked.

"Definitely," she replied.

"I wonder what you could do differently when those thoughts come up? Maybe something to distract yourself?"

Manage Behavioral Urges to Act on Suicidal Thoughts and Focus on Engaging in Non-Self-Harming Behaviors

"One of the things we talked about when building that safety plan was to secure anything in my home that I could use to hurt myself," said Sarah.

"Exactly," I replied, "so we're already doing that. What else could you do to not act on these automatic thoughts?"

"Well, since I go to the internet when I go to these dark places, I guess stay off my phone or computer," she said.

"I like that," I replied, "but I have found that rather than planning on *not* doing something, having a plan to *do* something works best."

"If the weather is nice, I could go outside for a walk for a few minutes. Or cuddle with my dog or make coffee."

"I like these ideas," I said, "and I like the fact that you came up with them quickly. I'd like to continue looking at other automatic thoughts that could be related to suicidal ideation and discuss ways to engage in helping, as opposed to self-harming, behaviors. This is going to take practice and monitoring. We can still talk about other things, but I want to make sure we are always checking in on this plan to see if it is working. If it doesn't work, we can always change it."

"It seems simple here," Sarah noted.

"Things usually do in an office setting," I replied, "which is why practicing outside of the session and reporting back (and changing if needed) is so important."

Sarah practiced this approach for several weeks and found it helpful. It also led to more self-discovery on her part, including her use of alcohol to numb herself. Sarah realized that her use of alcohol had become a problem, so she applied some of what she learned from the CBT model to examine her drinking habits and began to make substantive changes, which eventually led her to stop drinking.

Brief Cognitive Behavioral Therapy for Suicide Prevention

While Sarah's case study describes how to use the general themes of CBT to address chronic suicidal ideation, a more specific, highly structured method to address suicidal ideation is BCBT for suicide prevention (Bryan & Rudd, 2018).* What follows are some of the basic concepts and overall structure of this approach.

BCBT focuses on the negative thoughts and beliefs we have about ourselves, since what we tell ourselves about an event can get us "stuck," and our negative beliefs can keep us stuck (Bryan, 2022). The goal of BCBT is to disrupt these harmful thoughts and beliefs by undermining them and replacing them with helpful thoughts and beliefs.

Bryan and Rudd (2018) base BCBT on two related concepts. The first is the fluid vulnerability theory (FVT) of suicide, which holds that suicide risk contains stable factors (baseline risk factors that do not change over time) and dynamic

---

* Another excellent CBT approach for clients is *Choosing to Live: How to Defeat Suicide Through Cognitive Therapy* by Ellis and Newman (1996). This is a self-directed approach for individuals, and I would recommend it only for clients who are not engaging in suicidal behaviors and who are committed to decreasing their suicidal ideation.

characteristics (acute factors that are in flux). In many ways, this theory mirrors the stress-diathesis theory, and in both theories, higher baseline risk requires fewer dynamic factors to increase overall risk. The second concept is called the suicidal mode, which divides the risk factors into cognitive, emotional, physical, and behavioral risk factors for both the baseline and acute areas. The suicidal mode holds that with sufficient risk factors in all four areas in *both* the baseline and acute areas, all that is needed is an activating event (e.g., a fight with a loved one or financial stressors) to push the individual into suicidal behaviors.

Much of the initial work in BCBT is in helping the client to change their baseline and acute behavioral and cognitive risk factors (Bryan & Rudd, 2018). BCBT is typically delivered over 12 sessions, which include meetings at least once per week. Additional sessions can be added if needed. "BCBT is considered complete only when the patient can clearly *show* that he or she is able to effectively use skills to manage crises and prevent suicide attempts" (Bryan & Rudd, 2018, p. 71).

Bryan and Rudd (2018) divide brief CBT into three phases. The first phase includes developing a crisis response plan (like a safety plan) and means restriction counseling, also known as means safety counseling.

> Means safety counseling is based on three primary assumptions: (1) periods of acute suicidal distress are brief, (2) additional suicide attempts are unlikely if someone survives a suicidal crisis, and (3) easy access to lethal means is the strongest determinant of suicide attempt outcome (i.e., fatal versus nonfatal). (p. 143)

Once these areas have been addressed, sessions are used to address sleep quality (as not getting enough sleep is a common acute physical risk factor for suicide), as well as to provide relaxation skills training and mindfulness skills training. The final part of phase one is to work with the client to develop a "reasons for living list" (which they can add to over time) or a survival kit (a box containing meaningful items that remind the client that living can be worthwhile and that suicidal thoughts are usually fleeting).

Phase two focuses on challenging the cognitive processes that drive suicidal thinking. This includes educating the client on the ABC model. These sessions help clients challenge their automatic thoughts and plan activities to divert their thinking away from suicidal ideation. One of the tools in this phase is what the authors call coping cards, which are physical cards clients are encouraged to carry with them and read when they are struggling with automatic thoughts (Bryan & Rudd, 2018). In Bryan and Rudd's model, clients write a negative thought they are struggling with on one side of the card (e.g., "People would be better off without me"), and on the other side, they write at least two true statements (e.g., "I am important to others" and "My family and friends value me"; Bryan & Rudd, 2018, p. 223). I have also seen coping cards used with people working on recovery from substance use disorder, and they can be helpful.

The final phase of BCBT is relapse prevention and a review of what has been covered so far. If clients need to return to previous sessions for review or rehearsal, they can do so. Like general CBT, clinicians continue to assign their clients homework, practice skills in session (including role-plays), and constantly evaluate the efficiency of the approach. Once BCBT is completed, clients can determine the next steps in what they would like to work on.

Dialectical Behavioral Therapy

When I was in my master of social work graduate program, one of my professors stated that if we wound up with a client on our caseload who had borderline personality disorder (BPD), the best thing we could do would be to run away as quickly as possible. People with BPD were seen as inherently unstable and treatment resistant. Furthermore, he said that their near-constant suicidal ideation and suicide attempts made them a nightmare to work with. "Better to refer them out than to take your chances," my professor said.

Something about his cavalier tone didn't sit right with me. For starters, if we were supposed to refer people with BPD out, who could we refer them to if other therapists were seeking to also shed their caseloads of their own borderline patients? Second, did anyone ask *why* people have BPD? I had just been told by the same professor that personality disorders are not inherited or genetic (this was in the late 1990s), so what caused people to develop BPD? Recent research and clinical work have shown that BPD is typically a result of trauma, usually occurring in childhood, and that people with BPD can be effectively engaged in treatment and improve (Linehan, 2015).

The healing process for people with BPD includes learning that their disjointed emotional reactions, which often include chronic suicidal ideation, suicide attempts, and nonfatal self-injurious behaviors (among other symptoms), are a way they have learned to live with their trauma. However, treating the underlying trauma does not necessarily lead to an amelioration of their BPD. In most situations, emotional stability needs to be learned and practiced before addressing the underlying trauma. This is not very different from the approach we take with major depressive disorder, in which we first address the suicidal ideation or behaviors. While we eventually need to address the underlying depression, we must first address the suicidality.

Dialectical behavioral therapy (DBT) is an evidenced-based treatment approach that was designed to help clients learn how to manage the emotions and behaviors commonly associated with BPD (Linehan, 2015). It is based on biosocial theory, which states that clients with BPD have particular genetic vulnerabilities that make them feel emotions more intensely, and when clients with these vulnerabilities are exposed to invalidating environments, it can lead to the problematic behaviors we see in the disorder. In essence, Marsha Linehan, the creator of DBT, provided an answer to my questions in graduate school when I wondered if there was a way to not summarily dismiss people living with BPD. I am not going to go into detail about DBT here—I strongly recommend you learn more about it yourself—but instead want to focus on DBT as a treatment intervention for people living with chronic suicidal ideation.

The "dialectical" aspect of DBT is the concept that a person can hold two seemingly opposite opinions or beliefs simultaneously. It also incorporates this framework for the professionals who are engaged in the process with clients—meaning that we can also hold two disparate beliefs simultaneously. From this dialectical perspective, we can examine factors, such as a person's behaviors, from different viewpoints, with neither person being correct or incorrect (DeCou et al., 2019). One of the primary dialectics in DBT is the notion of acceptance versus change. Clients are encouraged to accept themselves as they are while also making meaningful changes to parts of their lives. They do this by acknowledging the reality of their lives, which includes painful emotions, while also working to limit unnecessary pain by limiting problematic behavior.

Chapter 8 • Treatment of the Suicidal Client, Part 1

DBT is typically delivered in outpatient settings (although it has been modified to fit a variety of settings), and clients commit to DBT for at least a year. Clients attend a weekly DBT skills group where they report on how they used the previous week's material in their lives and learn new skills. The primary areas of skills training are mindfulness, distress tolerance, emotion regulation, and interpersonal effectiveness (Linehan, 2015). Clients also meet weekly with a clinician who is proficient in DBT, although not necessarily one of the people who facilitated their skills group. Clinicians are available for emergency consultations outside of sessions, and medication prescribers may comprise part of the team as well. In addition to the skills training and individual therapy, DBT clinicians meet weekly for consultation and support (Linehan, 2015).

The efficacy of DBT in reducing the negative symptoms of BPD has been well established for adults and adolescents (Hernandez-Bustamante et al., 2023; Kothgassner et al., 2021). It has also been found to lead to a reduction in suicidal ideation and behaviors, as well as non-suicidal self-injury (DeCou et al., 2019; Kothgassner et al., 2021). While reducing suicidality is not the immediate goal of skills training—rather, it's to teach clients more general skills that they can apply to the problems in their lives—it nonetheless has this positive effect. I have seen this myself when working with many clients over the past 10 years. One long-standing client at my former clinic, who receives ketamine infusion boosters every six months or so, explained to me how participating in DBT completely stopped her suicidal behaviors and nearly eliminated her suicidal ideation. She added that the skills she learned not only helped with her emotion dysregulation and accompanying suicidal ideation, but also improved her interactions with her husband and children, leading to a more harmonious household.

In this chapter, you have learned that CBT (whether brief or traditional) and DBT are two of the more common methods of addressing suicidal ideation and behaviors in clients. As I have noted, many clinicians continue to attempt to treat the underlying issues they believe are causing or contributing to the suicidal ideation as opposed to directly addressing the suicidality itself. My hope is that I have been able to convey the necessity of treating suicidal ideation and behaviors directly. The following chapter continues this theme.

CHAPTER 9

Treatment of the Suicidal Client, Part 2

While psychotherapies such as CBT and DBT are effective in treating clients who are suicidal, they may not be sufficient for some clients (particularly those with intractable symptoms), in which case adjunctive psychopharmacological treatment may be necessary. We are currently experiencing a renaissance of sorts in which psychedelic plants and compounds are being widely investigated as effective treatment for mental health disorders, including suicide, so in this chapter, I will examine ketamine as a treatment for suicidality.

Psychopharmacology of Suicide Treatment

Most psychiatric medications treat mental illness (or more specifically their symptoms) instead of suicide directly. Although Maris (2019) states that lithium is the only mood stabilizer that has been shown to reduce suicide rates, recent analysis of this assertion is calling its veracity into question. In particular, most research regarding the efficacy of lithium has excluded studies in which no suicide deaths occurred, resulting in "missing relevant data and [making] suicide seem more common than it is" (Moncrieff & Plöderl, 2024, p. 2). If lithium were effective in limiting deaths by suicide, there should be a corresponding decrease in suicide attempts, but there is not. As previously noted, it is difficult to study suicide because it is relatively rare, and research study protocols would not be approved unless there were safety measures put in place to limit suicide deaths among people in the study; thus, it is extremely difficult to design studies that can adequately measure suicide. In fact, a randomized clinical trial on the efficacy of lithium for suicide prevention was stopped prematurely due to a lack of effect (Katz et al., 2022).

I do not think this means we can say that lithium is not effective in reducing suicide, as clearly more research is needed. Rather, these studies highlight the importance of not accepting something as "settled science," because there is no such thing! Science demands repeated questioning, analysis, and consistency over time—nothing is ever "settled." Lithium has demonstrated efficacy as a mood stabilizer, but whether it is truly effective in reducing suicide requires further study. I have had clients who took lithium to address their suicidal ideation, and they said it helped them avoid moving from ideation to action, so it worked for them. As I remind my clients all the time, I do not prescribe medications, and any changes they want to make to their medical regimen should be done in consultation with their prescribing provider.

Other than lithium, only clozapine (an antipsychotic) has demonstrated any efficacy to prevent suicide in patients with schizophrenia (Ryan & Oquendo, 2020). However, clozapine has many adverse side effects, making it an infrequently used medication for people living with schizophrenia—and a medication rarely prescribed for people who do not have schizophrenia. While there does not appear to be a psychiatric medication that can be definitively shown to prevent suicide, there may be promising options available in the realm of psychedelic medications.

Ketamine and Psychedelic-Assisted Psychotherapy

Psychedelic plants and fungi have been used by people around the world for thousands of years to address physical and mental maladies, often in the context of spiritual ceremonies and practices. The Indigenous peoples who have used these medicines, regardless of the region in which they have lived, respect these plants and mushrooms, and the misuse of them would typically warrant expulsion from the community.

Chapter 9 • Treatment of the Suicidal Client, Part 2

Our current repertoire of psychedelics includes plants, fungi, animal secretions, and synthetic compounds that mimic naturally occurring psychedelic compounds. Examples include methylenedioxymethamphetamine (MDMA, also known as ecstasy), psilocybin ("magic mushrooms"), ketamine, LSD, dimethyltryptamine (DMT, also one of the active ingredients in ayahuasca), and mescaline. To be clear, the use of these chemicals, when used in the proper context and with adequate preparation and supervision, can be therapeutic in many ways. With the exception of ketamine (and in that case, only through repeated use of high doses), a person cannot become dependent on these medications, and death by overdose is rare. Nevertheless, most of these compounds remain illegal, despite ongoing studies that demonstrate their efficacy in treating mood disorders, anxiety disorders, PTSD, and even substance use disorders. Only ketamine is approved to treat these disorders and, as of this writing, only in certain forms.

My background and experience are in substance use disorder treatment, so I was surprised when I first heard about ketamine to treat people who were suicidal in emergency departments. Actually, I was more incredulous than surprised. The doctors who shared this information with me were cavalier, and I did not take them seriously. However, about a year after I left the emergency department to head up a behavioral health unit at a clinic in Richmond, one of the doctors I used to work with, Dr. Randy, reached out to me and invited me to lunch to talk about ketamine. I always liked Dr. Randy. He is an excellent doctor and a true team player in the emergency department, and we had worked together on some difficult cases where we learned to trust and listen to each other. He had grown frustrated by his options to treat patients with severe depression in an emergency setting. In that setting, he had few options: Hospitalize the patient (which was often unnecessary but done because there was little else to do) or refer the patient to a psychiatrist who *might* prescribe a medication that *might* work but would take up to two months to be certain. Being an inquisitive person, Dr. Randy had started researching ketamine to address "treatment-resistant depression."

After he explained this to me over lunch, he asked what I thought.

"I think you're nuts," I replied.

Dr. Randy still paid for lunch and suggested that we keep in contact. I told him I was happy at my job and proud of the office-based opioid treatment program we were expanding. Still, when he opened his clinic, I went to one of his open houses, and I was intrigued by what he was doing. Dr. Randy had done a lot of work researching best practices for ketamine treatment, and he had traveled to different clinics to learn from other physicians.

Eventually, changes in top leadership occurred at the clinic where I was working, which led me to leave. Shortly after this, the COVID-19 shutdowns occurred, and I found myself working from home on a grant-funded project through Virginia Medicaid. I soon found myself missing clinical work, so I reached out to Dr. Randy. He was very interested in adding a therapist to his team, and I told him I wanted to learn more about working with psychedelics so I could connect him with a suitable candidate from the many counselors I knew in the community. After learning more about ketamine, and even though I would describe myself as a competent (not the best) therapist, I wound up working at the clinic instead.

Ketamine is a dissociative anesthetic. First marketed in the early 1960s, it was favored as an anesthetic because it did not cause a drop in blood pressure and it kept the patient's airway open—two things that must be closely monitored with other anesthesia medications. Shortly after ketamine started being used, some patients told their physicians that they felt less depressed. This eventually led to several decades of off-label use of ketamine to treat depression. Today, ketamine is viewed as a suitable treatment for depression, generalized anxiety disorder, PTSD, and other psychiatric problems. A commercial form of esketamine (Spravato) is used intranasally, and web-based providers (not all are medically based) provide ketamine lozenges. Of note, while intravenous ketamine is more effective for acute severe suicidal ideation (Abbar et al., 2022), intranasal esketamine may be more appropriate for maintenance treatment of major depressive disorder.

Dr. Randy's practice primarily uses ketamine infusions (95 percent of their clients) but also offers Spravato for clients who prefer it. Infusion treatment consists of an assessment (psychological and medical), a preparation session, six infusion sessions (which may include ketamine-assisted psychotherapy if the client wants this), followed by one or more integration sessions. Clients then return to the clinic after six weeks for a booster. Treatment beyond this depends on what the client needs, with most clients receiving booster infusions every 2 to 12 months. Randy's clinic begins with a weight-based dose, then modifies the dose based upon the client's experiences. Since they are not doing surgery, the goal is not to anesthetize the client but to place them in a mild dissociative state called the "non-ordinary state of consciousness." This is where ketamine seems to work best. Each infusion lasts 50 minutes, followed by at least a 30-minute recovery period.

We are not completely certain how ketamine works to treat depression, but it is thought to enhance the release of glutamate, which is an excitatory neurotransmitter, by blocking N-methyl-D-aspartate (NMDA) receptors (Wolfson & Hartelius, 2016). Ketamine also appears to trigger the brain's neuroplasticity to "reactivate" downregulated neuroreceptors. This molecular action appears to be part of the process that relieves depression (and other mental health disorder) symptoms. But something else is happening beyond chemical reactions—clients note a greater sense of self-awareness, connectedness to others and their environment, and huge insights into their lives. This later portion is where ketamine-assisted psychotherapy plays a big role in helping clients. Let's examine Natalie's situation to better understand this.

Case Study: Natalie

Natalie was in her late 20s, and her family reached out to me because she was due to be discharged from the hospital following a suicide attempt. I agreed to see Natalie, and I learned that she had attempted to cut her throat with a kitchen knife. She had missed severing her carotid artery or any major blood vessels, and she admitted to me that even when she cut herself, she was ambivalent about dying.

"I was just angry, scared, and hurting," she said, before adding that she had been intoxicated. Natalie said she was glad she was not dead, although she was thoroughly depressed and unsure of her next steps. This was her first suicide attempt, with one precipitating factor being the abusive relationship she'd been in with her now-ex-girlfriend, with whom she had been living. The abuse had started about a year earlier and included emotional and mental abuse (including gaslighting Natalie and separating her from people who cared about her) and, more recently, physical abuse. Following her discharge from the hospital, Natalie moved in with her mother and stepfather. She was in a doctorate program and had taken time off from her studies to focus on her health. Natalie's family was supportive, including her father and sister.

Our tasks in therapy were to establish safety around any further suicidal ideation, which we were able to do easily. We then delved into Natalie's drinking, which had been growing in intensity for several years. While Natalie did not stop drinking entirely, she greatly curtailed the frequency and amount that she drank and recognized how she used alcohol to manage her emotions. Natalie noted that her depression decreased once she was out of her abusive relationship and had decreased her drinking. She was not interested in psychiatric medication.

Further counseling revealed a childhood in which Natalie was often in her sister's shadow. Their mother had pushed both of them to excel in sports, but Natalie could never live up to her sister's athletic accomplishments. In addition, Natalie's parents had a cold, angry relationship, resulting in their divorce when Natalie was a preteen. Although Natalie wanted to address her trauma, she was not interested in pursuing eye movement desensitization and reprocessing (EMDR) because she did not think it would work for her. When I asked if she might be interested in ketamine treatment, she said she wanted to learn more about it first and, being a scientist, took it upon herself to read about the efficacy of ketamine treatment compared to other trauma-centered treatments. She liked what she saw, so she elected to have ketamine infusions, as she was especially concerned about a return of her depression and suicidal ideation.

In my former clinic, we encouraged clients to use their first infusion to simply explore the space that ketamine opened in their minds without focusing on anything specific. Natalie reported that her first session was helpful in this way. In subsequent sessions, some involving me and some with Natalie on her own, Natalie was able to examine her relationship with her ex-girlfriend and lose the emotional triggers of flight-fight-freeze that she experienced. She also noticed a decrease in her depressive symptoms. At the end of one session, however, she voiced a sense of frustration.

"Something is missing," she said. "It feels like part of me is held back by fear."

"How would you describe that part?" I asked. It was common to utilize Internal Family Systems (IFS) therapy in the ketamine setting, as the psychedelic effects of the medication allowed clients to bypass their cognitive defense mechanisms and talk with their various parts. Many clients would use this "space" to engage their inner critics (often called managers), as well as their other parts (Schwartz, 2021). IFS can certainly be successful outside psychedelic medicine, though I have been especially impressed by its impact on people experiencing ketamine treatment.

Chapter 9 • Treatment of the Suicidal Client, Part 2

"It's like a younger version of myself."

"When you were a little girl?"

"Yeah," Natalie replied, "right around the time when my folks were fighting and before the divorce."

"That was a tough time in your life. What would you like to do with it?"

"What do you mean?" she asked.

"What if you talked with your younger self? She's still in you—still a part of you. Maybe there's something you could tell her, or some type of nurturing you could provide her, that she really needed during that time but no one provided."

"I'm assuming that this is something I would do when I'm getting the ketamine," Natalie replied.

"The process is called a Gestalt approach, and it can be done with or without ketamine," I answered.

"Yeah, but you know me, and I think a lot of that therapy stuff is bullshit."

"I know," I said, "and that is the scientist in you as well as your cognitive defenses—and neither of them are negative. Given who you are, I think approaching this under ketamine would be best."

During her next infusion, Natalie talked with, held, and reassured her younger self that her parents' arguing and impending divorce were not her fault. She allowed herself to become emotional during this time, grieving that part of childhood that had been withheld from her.

Following this, Natalie worked with me in her integration sessions to synthesize what she had been working on with ketamine. She no longer felt hopeless or suicidal. She was also able to communicate what she needed from others and was able to recognize how she had often put others' needs above her own, usually to her detriment. It was amazing to watch her grow in such a relatively short time.

Ketamine, and other psychedelic compounds, may not be for everyone, and I will be the first to admit they are not always effective. However, in terms of helping clients reduce their suffering and greatly reduce, if not eliminate, their suicidal ideation, I have seen nothing else in my career that has made such a difference for so many people. I strongly encourage you to remain aware of developments in this area and learn more about psychedelic medicine and treatment.

Spirituality and Suicide

One of the recurrent themes I have noticed wherever I am practicing is the pervasive feeling of emptiness that many of my clients struggle with. They feel no purpose in life or feel that life is a complete waste of time. For some of them, this nihilism is a primary driver of their suicidal ideation. Surprisingly, this has been more common among my young adult clients, those from their late teens to early 30s. Many of these clients believe that the world is garbage, that they are somehow responsible for what is wrong in society, and that there is no point in living. They have learned this from their schools, and it has been reinforced by traditional and social media alike. For example, I remember one client who told me that when she got upset, she liked to take a 30-minute drive around the outskirts of Richmond, but even this caused her guilt.

"Driving around sounds like a good way to get your mind off of what you called your dark thoughts," I said.

"Yeah, but the problem is I'm killing the planet," she responded.

"What?"

"I'm adding carbon to the atmosphere."

I sighed, probably too loudly, before responding, "Look, you drive an extremely efficient car. It's not like you're building a coal-fired plant or anything."

It is this type of thinking—accepting blame for things we cannot help (e.g., where we were born, what our ethnicity is)—that I believe is contributing to what Jonathan Haidt (2024) calls *The Anxious Generation*, which I'll talk about more in the next chapter. When it comes to suicidal ideation, this type of thinking is further exacerbated by a lack of connection among people and a belief that life is purposeless. I believe that much of this is due to the pervasiveness of postmodern thinking in many of our educational institutions. Postmodern thinking implies that everything is deconstructed to the point that there are no absolutes. What began as a literary theory is now applied to everything and often bound with the belief that collectivism is superior to the rights of the individual. Here's an example of the fallacy of postmodernism thinking in a conversation I recently had with a young adult client.

Chapter 9 • Treatment of the Suicidal Client, Part 2

CLIENT: There are no absolutes. Everything is relative, or in shades of gray.

ME: What does that mean for you as it pertains to you wanting to kill yourself?

CLIENT: Since there is no real right or wrong, what does it matter?

ME: Maybe part of the problem is believing there is no right or wrong.

CLIENT: Well, there's not.

ME: Can we explore this a little more?

CLIENT: Sure.

ME: Since there is no right or wrong, when is it okay for an adult to sexually abuse a child?

CLIENT: Well, that's different.

ME: How? You said everything is relative and that there is no right or wrong, so are you now saying there are exceptions to that?

CLIENT: Sure, I guess.

ME: Okay, cool. So, if there are exceptions and there are some things that are good or bad or right or wrong, can we reexamine some of the thinking behind your suicidal thoughts?

As clinicians, we need to avoid pushing our beliefs, especially our spiritual or religious beliefs, on our clients. To do otherwise would be unethical and unprofessional. At the same time, spirituality can be a powerful tool in combating suicidal ideation. I believe that this takes place in two realms: service to others and a relationship with a higher power.

One of the overlooked values of 12-step programs, especially by people who are unfamiliar with them, is the emphasis on service to others. Newcomers to 12-step meetings may be asked to help set up chairs or make coffee. They may also be asked to read from a pamphlet or group literature during the meeting. The purpose of these actions is to help the individual focus outside of themselves. By helping others, even in simple ways, we take the focus off ourselves and put it toward helping others. Doing so can also help us appreciate what we have, while giving us a break from being consumed with our own struggles. Plus, let's be honest, it feels good to help other people!

Here are some of the things former and current clients have found that serve others and give them purpose:

1. Volunteer at a feeding center or food pantry.
2. Become a mentor (e.g., Big Brothers and Big Sisters).
3. Coach a sports team for children.
4. Volunteer at a pet shelter.
5. Become involved in a church, mosque, temple, or other religious organization.
6. Volunteer at a school to help tutor kids.
7. Volunteer at a nursing or rehabilitation facility.

A person's relationship with a higher power is complex and may be difficult to address in therapy, but I think it is important that we explore this with our clients, if they are open to doing so. Believing in something greater than oneself can help people find purpose in their lives—and in doing so, have more reasons to live. David DeSteno's (2021) excellent book *How God Works* illustrates how engaging in religious practices (from around the world) improves emotional and physical health. I admit that great harm has been (and continues to be) done in the name of religion, and more than a few of my clients over the years have experienced spiritual abuse. However, the benefits of engaging in a spiritual life, including religious practices, can be more positive than negative.

Another aspect of spirituality, independent of religion, is the concept of awe. Awe is the feeling of wonder or amazement that we get when we're in the presence of something that is greater than ourselves—something that transcends our normal understanding of the world. To find awe, we can look toward the eight wonders of life: moral beauty, collective effervescence, nature, music, visual design, spirituality and religion, life and death, and epiphany (Keltner, 2023). Getting out into nature, listening to a favorite artist (recorded or in concert), viewing paintings or sculptures, and seeing a play (or movie) can all feed our need to be awed. Awe opens our minds to things beyond ourselves and can remind us that we are all a part of something much larger than us. This, in turn, can help us feel connected to others and less hopeless, likely decreasing suicidal thoughts.

Case Management

Rarely in mental health treatment do we address a single issue, since clients often need help with more than one problem. Therefore, when we provide treatment to people struggling with suicidal ideation or behaviors, we must address other needs they may have as well. Since few (if any) of us have access to or knowledge of all the services that a client may require, we must be aware of all the things a person *might* need (including things they may be unaware of) and know how to connect clients to those services. This is where case management comes into play. Here are some areas where case management can help (Brasler, 2022):

- Securing housing
- Obtaining food or food vouchers
- Accessing food pantries
- Accessing clothing pantries
- Receiving medical treatment
- Receiving additional mental health services
- Obtaining health insurance
- Receiving dental care
- Finding transportation
- Obtaining childcare
- Connecting to employment services
- Enrolling in job training
- Receiving financial assistance (of any kind)
- Accessing mutual-aid or peer-recovery groups (e.g., Alcoholics Anonymous or SMART Recovery)
- Enrolling in education
- Enrolling children in school
- Obtaining immigration services
- Accessing legal aid

Helping clients make connections to these resources can potentially decrease stressors that could lead to future suicidal ideation or behaviors. For example, a client struggling with financial stressors could benefit from meeting with a financial counselor. Or, in my work with first responders, once many of them start individual counseling, they often express an interest in engaging in couples counseling with their partners. Finally, I am surprised at how many people I have seen for counseling who have not seen a primary care provider for years. In some cases, their mental health problems are connected to physical or medical problems, so I need to have places to refer these clients for primary care. It is imperative that providers be aware of services in their region and remain informed, as services frequently change. I recommend creating a database of service providers as soon as possible so you have it available when you need it.

In this chapter and the previous chapter, I have examined the ways to treat clients with chronic suicidal ideation or behaviors. In the following chapter, I will discuss how to treat children, adolescents, older adults, families, and military veterans.

CHAPTER 10

Special Populations

In this chapter, I will examine two groups of individuals who are mentioned a lot in discussions of suicide in the media (adolescents and military personnel), as well as a group that has the highest ratio of suicide deaths (older adults). There are different subgroups within these larger groups, and I will consider some of those as well. I end this chapter by looking at how to support individuals, families, and communities who are reeling from the loss of a member to suicide.

Children and Adolescents

In the preceding pages of this book, I hope I have made a clear point that suicide at any age is a tragedy that impacts a person's family and community. I believe that the suicide death of a young person is even more of a tragedy when we consider that a young life was cut short. As you saw earlier, suicide is rare overall and more likely to occur in older adults, but it is the second-highest cause of death among people aged 10 to 34, so it demands our attention. While many of the same suicide risk factors for adults can apply to adolescents too, there are some specific risk factors we need to be aware of when assessing adolescent suicide risk, which I will discuss here.

Family History

Death by suicide for people 10 and under is extremely rare. One could argue that until a child's brain develops the ability to think abstractly, around age 11, children lack a true conception of death. However, this does not eliminate suicide risk in children and young adolescents. This may be especially true in family systems where an older member has died by suicide or where a parent has died from external causes (Wasserman et al., 2021), such as a homicide or an accidental death such as a car accident. Not only does familial suicide increase the risk of childhood or adolescent suicide, but "other mechanisms may play a role in the familial transmission of suicidal behavior, such as attachment features, modeling, imitation, and social integration" (Wasserman et al., 2021, p. 7). Parent-child conflict is the most common precipitant. This does not mean that the absence of these risk factors ameliorates suicide in young people; the data simply show that the presence of these factors increases overall risk.

The methods that young people use to die by suicide are like those used by adults, with firearms accounting for nearly 44 percent of all suicide deaths, and hanging/suffocation and poisoning accounting for similar rates (43 percent; Hughes et al., 2023). While this is a lower percentage of firearm deaths than adult suicide deaths (55 percent), it is still of concern, especially when there are weapons in the home. In fact, children who have access to firearms at home have a threefold to fourfold increased risk of suicide (Hughes et al., 2022).

Demographic Factors

Male adolescents are more likely to die by suicide compared to females, and like their adult counterparts, female adolescents attempt suicide more than their male peers. Haidt (2024) notes that "the suicide rate for young adolescent girls began to rise in 2008, with a surge in 2012, after having bounced around within a limited range since the 1980s. From 2010 to 2021, the rate increased 167 percent" (p. 32). Haidt attributes this surge to the prevalence of social media among adolescents—something I will examine shortly.

In addition, as our society has become more aware of people who identify as transgender or nonbinary, we have become aware of a corresponding higher risk of suicidal behaviors in these populations. "Female to male adolescents reported the highest rate of attempted suicide (50.8 percent), followed by adolescents who identified as not exclusively male or female (41.8 percent), male to female adolescents (29.9 percent), questioning adolescents (27.9 percent), female adolescents (17.6 percent), and male adolescents (9.8 percent)" (Toomey et al., 2018, p. 1). Given the mental health challenges faced by the transgender community, these statistics are sobering. To be clear, I do not view being transgender as a mental health problem. However, the prevalence of suicidality among these populations must be acknowledged, and more importantly, clinicians need to understand this increased risk and be prepared to intervene accordingly.

Finally, regarding racial and ethnic groups, Native Americans and Alaska Natives have the highest rates of suicide, with prevalence rates that are almost double that of White people and more than double that of Black, Asian, and Latino people (Hughes et al., 2023). This follows similar patterns of adults in these ethnic groups, which underscores the importance of maintaining cultural awareness for the groups we work with.

Mental Health and Substance Use Disorders

Up to a third of children and adolescents who die by suicide have a mental health problem, with depressive disorders, anxiety disorders, disruptive behavior disorders, conduct disorder, and substance use disorders being the most common diagnoses (Wasserman et al., 2021). However, like adults, many children and adolescents do not have a diagnosed mental health issue at the time of their deaths. While this may suggest that mental health problems are not precipitating factors, I believe it highlights the lack of available treatment (or access to treatment) for young people struggling with their mental health. In addition, academic struggles can be a risk factor for suicide (Wasserman et al., 2021), which suggests that an underlying (or undiagnosed) mood or anxiety disorder, attention deficit disorder, or learning disorder could be at play. In fact, one of the primary signs I encourage parents to be aware of is a sudden drop or change in their child's grades, schoolwork completion, or school attendance, as these changes suggest underlying causes that need to be quickly addressed.

Substance use is also a risk factor for suicide, with alcohol, cannabis, and nicotine (usually in the form of vaping) being the most common substances that adolescents use. Heavy cannabis use in particular increases the risk of self-harm and overall mortality among this age group (Bahji et al., 2021). This is especially true when adolescents engage in cannabis use at a young age, use cannabis daily, and consume cannabis with a higher level of THC. Given the increasing acceptance of cannabis use in society—and to be clear, cannabis can have many benefits when used appropriately—this is another area worth monitoring.

Social Media and the Anxious Generation

The other day, I was talking with a peer who stated that today's adolescents and young adults face more stress than any generation before them. I quickly disagreed, pointing out that adolescence is a relatively new stage in human development. Until the Industrial Revolution, children moved quickly into adulthood when they were able to work or have children. Except for wealthy individuals, there were no time or resources for advanced education, let alone "finding oneself." I then pointed out that our grandparents lived during the Great Depression—not exactly a heyday of frivolity—followed by the Second World War (both of my grandfathers served in the US Army). Therefore, his assertion was questionable. My friend's point, however, about some of the unique challenges that adolescents and young adults face, has merit.

We discussed how many of our younger clients—older adolescents and young adults in their early to mid-20s—struggle with overwhelming existential anxiety. As I mentioned in chapter 9, many feel responsible for the world's ills (climate change, racial injustice, and so on) and overwhelmed by what they see as a world where only bad things happen. Much of this self-blaming attitude is fueled by external media sources, as negative headlines predominantly drive news consumption. For this reason, I regularly suggest that young clients in particular limit their social media and news intake to 10 minutes or less per day (having seen how making these changes myself greatly improved my own depression during the overlong pandemic lockdowns). I was pleasantly surprised when many of my young clients followed these suggestions, and even more pleased when they reported that they were feeling less depressed and anxious. One 22-year-old young lady exclaimed, "Recommending that I turn off my newsfeed is the single-best piece of treatment you provided for me!"

In the last chapter, I mentioned a terrific book by Jonathan Haidt (2024) called *The Anxious Generation*. I brought the book with me to read over vacation last summer, hoping to take a break from the ton of reading on suicide that I'd been doing as I wrote this book. As I devoured Haidt's book, I quickly saw connections with his extensive research, my interactions with younger clients in my practice, and the work I had been doing for this book. Haidt's premise is that social media—not the internet per se but social media sites like Instagram, TikTok, and others—have played a big role in replacing the activities that young people used to engage in that taught them how to interact with the world. He also highlights the major shortcomings of our educational systems that restrict play, along with modern parenting trends that are overcontrolling and severely limit risk-taking.

For example, Haidt notes that teenagers who use social media frequently are more likely to struggle with depression, anxiety, and other mental health concerns compared to teens who spend time socializing with one another. This is particularly impactful for females, as Haidt notes "there is a clear, consistent, and sizeable link between heavy social media use and mental illness for girls, but that relationship gets buried or minimized in studies and literature reviews that look at all digital activities for teens" (p. 146). We also hear of bullying, particularly cyberbullying, as possible precursors of suicidal behaviors in some youth (Wasserman et al., 2021), so it is incumbent that parents take an active role in their children's online life. I strongly agree with Haidt that children should not access social media without direct adult supervision until they are 16 years old.

Treatment

Since working with children and adolescents in clinical settings is different from working with adults, the following are my recommendations for doing so (Brasler, 2022). As a note, these recommendations are not just for situations involving clients experiencing suicidal thinking or behaviors—they apply to clinicians working with youth in any capacity:

1. Be respectful. This sounds obvious, but many young people often report feeling dismissed by, unheard by, or invisible to adults. See them. Listen to them.

2. Expect respect in return. It is difficult to convey our respect for others if we cannot demonstrate a respect for ourselves. Avoid power struggles, but be clear that you expect respect just as you model respect for others.

3. Be authentic. A former coworker of mine called this "practicing genuineness." What he meant was: Be yourself. As a middle-aged man, I usually don't share the same interests as the young clients I work with, nor

do I use the same slang or lingo. Were I to try to act cool, it would come off as phony, and adolescents can spot phoniness a mile away.

4. Know something about their world, and if you are not certain, ask them to explain or teach you. Demonstrating your willingness to learn can be a way to connect with adolescents. I once worked with an adolescent who was court-ordered to counseling, and he refused to say much in our sessions. When he mentioned a hip-hop artist he followed, I asked him to tell me about that artist and what attracted him to the artist. This discussion led to a broader conversation on values, including my client examining how some of his own actions did not line up with his stated beliefs and values.

5. Limit the amount of advice or "parenting" you do. This is a solid rule to practice regardless of the age of the person you're working with, but it is especially important when working with adolescents. If you feel you must provide some advice, I recommend couching what you say in an indirect way. For example: "I hear what you're saying, but would you like to know how other people your age I've worked with have solved this problem in their lives?"

6. Allow them some autonomy. Kids generally value autonomy and don't enjoy being placed in rigid "boxes" of sterile, clinical diagnoses. Make treatment a collaborative process where you aren't afraid to ask questions about their suicidal or self-harm behaviors and where you give them a voice in the decision-making process (Bellairs-Walsh et al., 2020).

7. Expect to structure the therapeutic time. Some counseling approaches have structure built into them (e.g., CBT), but you will need to have a plan for counseling when working with adolescents because they are usually unwilling to freely engage in open dialogue for a treatment hour.

While there's currently not enough data to indicate whether medication should be used for the treatment of self-harm or suicidal behaviors in kids (Bahji et al., 2021), some prescribers will nonetheless utilize lithium for its reported effects of decreasing suicidal ideation. However, psychopharmacological treatments are otherwise not recommended as a first-line treatment for pediatric suicidality.

Likewise, as with adults, inpatient psychiatric hospitalization should be reserved for adolescents who cannot maintain their safety outside of a secure setting or who lack resources to help care for them. Hughes and colleagues (2023) note that although inpatient hospitalization may provide young clients with the temporary security of a controlled environment, the costs associated with hospitalization may outweigh its benefits, especially given that 25 percent of kids are readmitted to the hospital or attempt suicide within the first six months—and 33 percent do so within one year. Instead, there is evidence that DBT and CBT can be effective interventions to treat suicidal thinking and behaviors in young people (Bahji et al., 2021), and there is even an adolescent-focused version of DBT called DBT-A. Other interventions, including CAMS, have shown promise in effective treatment as well.

Finally, the word *resilience* is often used to describe young people who have excelled in life or even survived incredibly difficult and dangerous situations. Shahram and colleagues (2021) note that resiliency is a primary suicide prevention factor, although it is unclear *how* it works as a protective factor. My experience with young people who display resilience is that there was at least one adult in their lives who believed in them unconditionally. That means one parent, teacher, coach, minister, or neighbor can make a difference in a young person's life.

Active-Duty Military Personnel, Veterans, and First Responders

Veterans constitute about 18.8 million adults in the US, while there are more than two million adults on active duty, in the reserves, or in the National Guard (US Department of Veterans Affairs, 2023). Suicide deaths among our veteran population and active military personnel have achieved increasing public attention over the past two decades, during and after sustained military operations in Afghanistan and Iraq. In fact, veteran suicide deaths have outpaced nonveteran suicide deaths substantially during recent years, with veteran suicide rates increasing by nearly 12 percent from 2020 to 2021 and suicide rates among nonveterans increasing by 4.5 percent during that same time (US Department of Veterans Affairs, 2023). "Suicide is the 13th-leading cause of death for Veterans overall, and the second-leading cause of death among Veterans under age 45-years-old. In 2021, there were 6,042 suicide deaths among Veteran men and 350 suicide deaths among Veteran women" (US Department of Veterans Affairs, 2023, p. 8).

Two significant risk factors are particularly relevant when we differentiate between veteran and active military suicides: (1) exposure to traumatic, violent events and (2) traumatic brain injury (TBI). Not only can witnessing and experiencing traumatic events be a part of military life, especially during deployment, but we also need to consider emotional trauma as a result of moral injury, which involves "the loss of trust in oneself, leaders, and systems during crisis situations as individuals may be forced to make critical decisions or allocate resources based on resource availability, rather than ethical principles or best practices" (Carson et al., 2023, p. 362). In addition, veterans can often experience TBI in the line of duty, which increases the risk of suicide fourfold (Campbell-Stills et al., 2020). As with nonveteran adults, a high percentage of veterans who die by suicide do not have a mental health or substance use disorder diagnosis (US Department of Veterans Affairs, 2023).

Like veterans, first responders—including police, fire, emergency response workers, and emergency communications personnel—often have repeated, direct exposure to traumatic events as well, including the suicide deaths of others, which puts them at higher risk of suicide. One study found that the highest proportion of suicide deaths for first responders occurs among firefighters, which may be because many localities combine fire and emergency medical services into one, so firefighters are usually the first on the scene and are exposed to the immediate traumatic event or aftermath (Vigil et al., 2021). However, even emergency services communications personnel are at heightened risk—this includes the wonderful, often overlooked people who answer 9-1-1 calls and who are exposed to significant stress as they bear witness to each caller's distress.

Finally, when trying to understand suicide among veterans, active military, and first responders, we must consider the presence and familiarity of firearms as a risk factor for these groups. When considering the number of adults in the US who died by suicide in 2021, not only did veterans use firearms more often than nonveterans (72.2 percent vs. 52 percent), but 69 percent of first responders who died by suicide used a firearm as well (Carson et al., 2023; US Department of Veterans Affairs, 2023).

Treatment

One of the largest hurdles in treating veterans, military personnel, and first responders is the social stigma against seeking mental health services in these groups. Mental toughness, often necessary to the work of these groups, can be conflated with the idea that seeking help is a sign of weakness. They may also believe that seeking help will make them "unfit" to serve or harm their career, leading many to avoid seeking help and instead suffering in silence (Horan et al., 2021). While the military has taken active steps to try to reduce these barriers to treatment—for example, by launching a $2.7 million anti-stigma campaign in 2009 known as the Real Warriors Campaign (Dingfelder, 2009)—these efforts to reduce stigma will take time.

In addition to the interventions we have examined in this text, two areas of focus have emerged that show promise in treating veterans and first responders. The first is attention to securing firearms. This includes asking personnel about how they store their weapons and access them—something I have examined with CAMS and other safety planning. Since the desire to act on suicidal thoughts often waxes and wanes, the idea is to put some time and distance between an individual and their access to a firearm. This can include using trigger locks and securing ammunition in a separate location from firearms so that any guns are locked and unloaded.

Another form of treatment is the use of peer-directed interventions, which utilize naturally occurring relationships among people who experience the same job environment to help one another during times of stress or during emergencies. I have noticed when working with veterans or first responders, members of those communities often prefer to speak with someone who "wears the uniform" as opposed to someone who lacks that experience. Peers can be useful in informal settings—where many veterans and first responders appear to seek more help—as the people they are speaking with understand their job, lifestyle, or mentality. One study noted by Horan and colleagues (2021) found that 83 percent of respondents to a veterans' crisis line reported that calling the hotline played a part in stopping them from killing themselves. Peers working with veterans are often trained in the SAVE process as a way to facilitate suicide prevention, which involves four important steps (US Department of Veterans Affairs, 2023, p. 39):

S = Signs of suicidal thinking should be recognized

A = Ask: "Are you thinking of killing yourself?"

V = Validate the Veteran's experience

E = Encourage treatment and Expedite getting help

Another option that peer support teams, or non-clinically trained people in general, can use to support first responders is the QPR Pathfinder Training program (Quinnett, 2023). QPR stands for question, persuade, and refer, and it is designed to be a primary prevention method to decrease suicide. Nonclinical staff are trained as "QPR Gatekeepers," who can intervene in situations in which they suspect a person may be at risk for suicide. Gatekeepers are trained in how to ask nonjudgmental questions about suicide, then persuade the person they are speaking with to consider options other than suicide, and finally refer the person for appropriate clinical services. One limitation of this approach, as noted by Quinnett (2023), is a lack of professionals to refer people at risk to.

With all this in mind, what can we as clinicians do when veterans, active military personnel, or first responders seek clinical help? First, unless you are a veteran or were once a first responder yourself, you must acknowledge that you have not been in that role, but you can still be of help. As with all clients, demonstrating empathy and unconditional positive regard is imperative. Sometimes, this might involve putting aside your suicide screener and taking the time to first establish a solid, trusting relationship with your client so that they feel safe enough with you to disclose their suicidality (Blanchard & Farber, 2018). When I have worked with clients in these populations, I allow space for them to share their experiences, and if I am not sure of something, I ask them to explain it. I have found that when people who serve in these important areas know that they are being listened to and seen as a person, they will typically engage in treatment, although it usually takes time to develop trust.

Chapter 10 • Special Populations

Older Adults

As I have discussed throughout this book, older adults, particularly males, have the highest suicide rate in the US (although in some years, their rates are second to that of middle-aged adults). What is also interesting in this age group is the large gap between male suicides and female suicides, especially in the 85 and older group (Shah et al., 2016), which is greater than the gap between males and females for middle-aged or young adults. Reasons for this are unclear, though statistically, the gap between men and woman who die by suicide increases as we age.

Many of the primary risk factors for suicide in this age group—which you've learned include isolation, feelings of abandonment, loss of purpose, chronic illness, and the use of methods with greater lethality—can be summarized into what is known as "Four Ds": (1) disease/disability, (2) disconnectedness, (3) depression, and (4) access to deadly means (Conwell, 2016). While depression is a risk factor for suicide among people at any age, it's important to note that the prevalence of depression actually decreases after the age of 65 (De Leo, 2022). Therefore, just as we have seen with younger people, treating depression (when it is present) does not necessarily decrease suicide rates in older adults.

In addition to the risk factors we've already explored, De Leo (2022) identifies the following warning signs that may portend suicide risk in this group:

- Begins socially isolating
- Loses interest in food
- Expresses extreme feelings of guilt and shame
- Unexpectedly visits or connects with friends or relatives, as if to say goodbye
- Appears to be stockpiling medications

De Leo points to the significance of this last item, since older adults are typically taking more medications than younger adults, giving them an available means to overdose. He also notes that in addition to the increasing isolation many older adults experience as their loved ones die, risk also increases when older adults are exposed to suicide in their social group.

Finally, we need to consider what some researchers call "silent suicide," which occurs when clients voluntarily stop eating and drinking (De Leo, 2022). A loss of appetite or desire to drink liquids is not uncommon in people nearing death due to illness, disease, or extreme old age—these are signs that the person's body is shutting down. In cases of silent suicide, however, the cessation of eating or drinking is voluntary instead of physiological.

Treatment

The same interventions that work with young and middle-aged adults experiencing suicidal ideation can work with older adults too. This includes the use of psychedelic medicine, as well psychotherapies such as CBT and DBT. However, the biggest challenge in providing treatment for older adults struggling with suicidal ideation or behaviors is the ageism that is prevalent in our society. Some of the more common statements I have heard in clinical (usually medical) settings include:

- "They're going to die soon anyway, right?"
- "Of course they're depressed—they're old!"
- "She just wants attention because she is lonely and unhappy."

This dismissive behavior, regardless of the client's age, can obviously negatively impact patient care and treatment planning, and needs to be confronted when it surfaces. Remember that "old age" is more of a social concept than a biological fact (De Leo, 2022), as many older adults live fulfilling lives with meaningful connections with others.

I was confronted with some of my own ageism when I started working with clients pursuing ketamine treatment, many of whom were older adults. Many of them were dealing with existential issues and loneliness, and having come from crisis settings, I sometimes struggled with empathy toward their situations. My initial thought was, *This is a first-world problem—I've seen people who have it really bad*. But when I stepped back and reflected on my reaction, I realized that I was being ageist, since my clients' issues were very important to them as older adults. Once I accepted this and changed how I thought, I realized how isolated many of my older adult clients were. Perhaps one of the ways we can help older adults struggling with suicidal ideation is to foster opportunities for connection and help them maintain and build communities where they can feel connected.

Another challenge for older patients is that if depression is an underlying factor in their suicidal ideation, then treating it with medication may be more difficult because of the likelihood that the client may have medical issues (and medications to treat them) that could interfere with antidepressant medication. In fact, one of the challenges of working with older adults in any capacity is that they may see several specialists, who prescribe different medications that may interact negatively with one another—and sometimes this becomes the source of mental health symptoms. For this reason, I cannot overstate the importance of having pharmacists who conduct regular medical reconciliations, especially with older patients.

Supporting Loved Ones Affected by Suicide

My father's father died of heart failure when he was in his late 70s. I was near the end of my last semester of college, and I went to St. Louis with the rest of my family for the funeral. My great-grandparents had immigrated to the US from Poland, and my grandparents were the first generation of their families born in America. They had been nonobservant Jews until my father, their second son, decided to marry a young Protestant lady (my mom) and convert to Christianity. In response, my grandparents started to attend the temple in their area and do their best to educate their grandsons on our Jewish heritage.

This was on full display when we arrived at my grandparents' home from the airport. There were people in the house all the time—and always plenty of food. I was soon told that the people present were "sitting shiva," a Jewish mourning practice. My grandmother, never one to shy away from attention, held court, and there were plenty of stories about my grandfather—an exceptionally kind, honest, and decent man—and other family members. What I remember the most about this, decades later, was the sense of community and acknowledgment of my grandfather's life and death.

In many cultures in the West, we avoid talking about death—although we have no problem with death being a large part of our entertainment in movies and television. Because we avoid talking about it, we often minimize being around people who are directly touched by death. Given the stigma associated with suicide, this is even more evident with families who have a member die by suicide. As you saw with Lori's story in chapter 5, and her struggles with her own suicidal ideation following the suicide death of her son, suicide has an indelible impact on families and communities. In fact, it is estimated that somewhere between 6 and 20 people struggle in the wake of someone's suicide—this doesn't just include family members but also friends and acquaintances (Lyra et al., 2021). This means we need to be available to families, friends, and communities impacted by death by suicide or a suicide attempt. This is not a time for judgment or insensitive platitudes—there is power in simply being present, offering a heartfelt "I am sorry," or providing a meal.

When my running buddy died by suicide in 2016, I was amazed at how the community we shared rallied around her family. The pastor conducting her funeral was direct in stating that she had killed herself. I'll paraphrase his words: "Right now this family is in a pit. They did not ask for this, and no one wanted it for them. You all might be inclined to want to reach down and pull them out of the pit. But there is a better way: Get in the pit with them! Be present, but give space when asked. Be patient and realize this will take time. And love them, because that is what communities do."

Therefore, in both our professional and personal lives, we need to make sure that families who experience a suicide death are supported emotionally, spiritually, and physically. Providing meals, helping with childcare, and being present (but not intrusively so) are important in helping families heal—and not just in the immediate aftermath, but over the long term as well.

Since clinicians are often (understandably) anxious about treating clients who are experiencing suicidal ideation, we want to make sure we are doing the right thing to not only help our clients, but to protect ourselves from legal repercussions of our client's actions. We will examine ethical considerations in the next chapter.

CHAPTER 11

Ethical and Legal Issues

Second only to the fear of a client dying by suicide is the clinician's fear of possible repercussions in those situations. *Will I be fired? Could I lose my professional license? Will I get sued?* These are legitimate questions that take on enormous weight during an already unimaginably stressful time. As I've mentioned, the fear of having to deal with this potential liability can lead professionals to avoid working with higher-risk clients, so in this chapter, I will examine risk and liability, along with client autonomy, and discuss ways that we can address these issues while providing excellent care to people in need.

A Client's Right to Self-Determination Versus Our Legal Responsibilities

Before we look at liability and autonomy, we need to have a basic understanding of ethics. Please remember that different professions may have different ethical codes, and this is important to keep in mind when you are working as part of a multidisciplinary team, where members must understand and respect one another's codes, while holding the patient's needs as sacrosanct. When I led a multidisciplinary team, I conducted an exercise where I had members of each profession summarize the code of ethics and legal requirements that they needed to follow in their respective field. This allowed the team members to better understand the guidelines that drove one another's work.

I am a licensed clinical social worker in Virginia, which means that I adhere to the National Association of Social Workers Code of Ethics. The core values of the Code of Ethics (National Association of Social Workers, 2021) are:

- Service
- Social justice
- Dignity and worth of the person
- Importance of human relationships
- Integrity
- Competence

While these values are specific, but not unique, to social work, they highlight the need for ethical considerations in all decision-making. But what happens if two or more ethical considerations come into conflict? In these situations, we need to consider a hierarchy of ethical principles (Dolgoff et al., 2005).

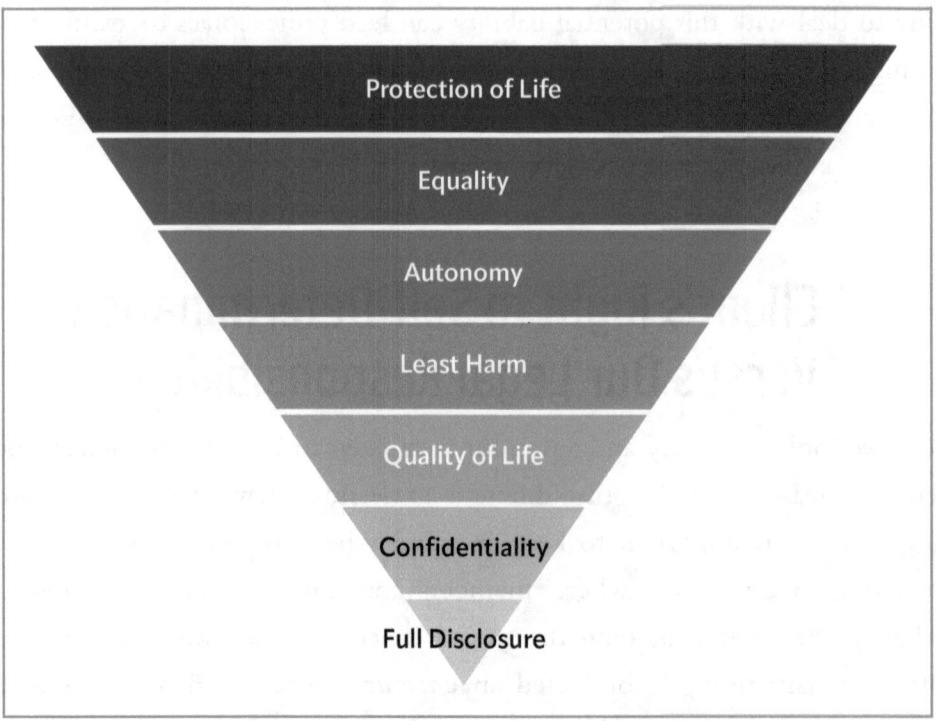

The items at the top of the figure have more value than the ones below them. For example, we have seen that a client's right to confidentiality does not mean that a clinician cannot disclose to emergency personnel when a client is a danger to themself or others (indeed some localities have laws that *mandate* that we *not* keep this information confidential). Yes, confidentiality is a necessary part of the helping relationship, but there are other factors that supersede it. While health care providers are sometimes uncertain about what information they can (and cannot) disclose to others due to the HIPAA Privacy Rule, this rule explicitly allows providers to disclose information if they believe that there is "a serious and imminent threat to the health and safety of the patient or others and the family members are in a position to lessen the threat." (Ryan & Oquendo, 2020, p. 92). Therefore, protection of life comes above all else.

At the same time, one of the primary ethical values of social work is a person's right to self-determination. But what happens when a client decides to kill themselves, or more specifically: Does a client have a *right* to kill themselves? A situation I experienced early in my time working in the emergency department illustrates this difficult situation.

"I Think We Can Agree This Is Bullshit, But We Have to Do It Anyway"

"I'm not certain what the patient in room six took, but whatever it is, he'll be fine," said Dr. Mark. "I'd like you to talk to him and figure out what's going on; I'm looking into something else he told me. Plus, as you can see, we're slammed."

Sunday nights were always busy in the emergency department. I'd only been working there for three months, yet I was still amazed at how many people waited for the end of the weekend before seeking medical treatment—sometimes for serious matters such as chest pain.

The patient in room six was Karl. He was in his mid-40s, and his housing was inconsistent. He'd recently been sleeping in his car. So far, it had been a mild autumn, but that would likely change with the coming winter. He looked sad and angry. I introduced myself and asked if I could sit, as he was sitting in the hospital bed.

"I'm pissed," Karl said.

"About what?" I responded.

"That doc. He won't tell me what I need to take to kill myself. What I took apparently won't even give me a headache."

I avoided explaining what the doctor could and could not do, and instead asked, "Why do you want to die?"

"I'm already dying," Karl responded. "Terminal cancer. I have four months or so. I'm not in pain yet, but I have no place to go. I burned bridges with my family years ago. Since I'm gonna die anyway, I want to check out now."

I was glad that Karl was willing to talk with me, so I gathered a little more information and then excused myself to speak with Dr. Mark again. A patient care technician sat in the room with Karl to ensure his safety.

"He's telling the truth," said Dr. Mark. "I pulled his records [from another hospital], and he has cancer and is likely not going to live for more than four to six months."

"Wow," I said, "is there anything we can do now?"

"There's no reason for me to medically admit him here," replied Dr. Mark. "He's sick, but his illness is chronic. He's not currently experiencing any medical symptoms. I know that sounds weird, but that's how it is. I wanted to ask you if there is a place we could send him—a medical respite program or something like that?"

"I'm not too familiar with available programs, so let me look into them," I replied.

Like many areas around the United States, central Virginia lacks services for people like Karl. I discovered that Karl was not "sick enough" to qualify for services—while he was sick, he was simply not "sick enough" to be admitted to those services, just as he was not "sick enough" to be admitted to the medical hospital. I conveyed this to Dr. Mark.

"What about hospice services?" I asked.

"I already had my intern look into that," he replied. "Karl qualifies for outpatient but not inpatient services."

"Even though he is essentially homeless?" I asked.

"Yeah."

"Okay," I said, "let me go talk with him again."

Karl was uninterested in any options available to him, which was good, since I didn't have any.

"I just want to die, right now," he said. "I am going to find a way to kill myself."

Chapter 11 • Ethical and Legal Issues

"I hear you," I said, "and I'm pretty sure I'd feel the same way in your position. The thing is, you keep talking about wanting to kill yourself, and you state that you've tried to kill yourself, so legally I'm required to do something."

"You mean put me in a psychiatric hospital?" asked Karl.

"I don't want to," I replied, "but I may have to."

"Oh, hell no!" he exclaimed. "No way."

"I agree," I quickly said. "I don't think that's where you should be, but with what you are saying, I have to do something, even if I don't want to do what I need to do."

"I don't want to go into the hospital. I won't go into the hospital voluntarily. I am not a violent person. I can take care of myself. I just want to die now."

"I hear you, Karl. And I am sorry."

"I will not go into the hospital. You'll have to commit me, I guess. That's all I have to say to you."

I walked out of the room, dejected. A hospital security guard remained in the open doorway, even though Karl had made no effort to leave the room. I was nearly oblivious to the chaos around me in the emergency room. I sat down next to Dr. Mark in the doctors' area.

"What'd he say?" the doc asked.

"He wants to kill himself, isn't willing to go into the hospital, and doesn't want anything from us."

"So, where's that leave us?" asked Dr. Mark.

I looked at the doc. He was tired and extremely busy, but I was impressed that he cared about Karl. He could have easily thrown up his hands and moved on to his other dozen or so patients.

I sighed. "We are in agreement that he is dying?"

"Yes, he is terminally ill."

"Okay. Are we also in agreement that he is suicidal?" I asked.

"He has been consistent about that throughout his stay," responded Dr. Mark.

"He is fully competent to make decisions for himself?"

"Yes, you said so yourself."

"But he is unwilling to enter the hospital to address his suicidality?"

"Correct," said the doctor.

"The law of Virginia states that with all of these factors, we have to request an assessment for an involuntary psychiatric admission," I said.

"I agree."

"Can we also agree that this is absolute bullshit that we have to do this, but we'll do it anyway or risk our respective licenses due to violating state law?" I asked.

"I agree," said Dr. Mark. "Total bullshit. I'm sorry."

Later that evening, accompanied by two sheriffs and in handcuffs, Karl was taken to another hospital as an involuntary admission. I don't know what happened to him after he was admitted.

I am not surprised that I still remember meeting Karl and my conversation with Dr. Mark. I was bothered by what I had to do, but more importantly, this was a relatively young person who had a terminal illness and limited resources, who was simply trying to exercise his right to self-determination. At the same time, I know that what I had to do was follow the laws of Virginia and follow the ethical hierarchy that puts protection of life above Karl's right to self-determination. As Knapp (2020) notes, "Even if we assume the hypothetical that the patient 'really wants to die,' according to principle-based ethics, one may temporarily override patient autonomy when it conflicts with another overarching ethical principle" (p. 31). One could argue that this is unjust for Karl, and in a way, I agree with that, but I also must follow the law, and Dr. Mark and I both had to adhere to the ethical principles of our respective fields.

A possible solution to situations such as this would be to change the laws and provide more options for people in Karl's situation. This includes defining physician-assisted suicide, decriminalizing suicide (which is still technically a crime in some localities), or both. The good thing about our system of laws is that they can be changed as society changes. It is outside the scope of this book to debate the merits of changing (or not changing) laws regarding suicide, but I know that changes can happen. Years ago, I spoke with a young man who was in jail because of possession of a relatively small amount of cannabis (this was not his first offense). We agreed that his detention was ridiculous, but he had broken the law.

"You know what I'm going to do?" he said. "I am finishing my GED, going to college, then law school, and becoming a lawyer so I can get elected and change these stupid laws."

He may have been expecting me to argue with him, but instead I replied, "You know, if you accomplish all of that, I'll likely vote for you."

He earned his GED quickly and went on to college. I don't know whether he had a part in changing some of the laws in our community, but he at least understood how things can be changed.

Managing Liability

Professionals working with people in clinical settings assume some risk by simply engaging in the work they do. However, many people who work in the counseling profession, regardless of setting, are often fearful of litigation should a client die by suicide. I saw this frequently when working in the emergency department. On many occasions, the decision to admit a client to the inpatient behavioral unit was made more from a fear of being sued if we did not admit them and they subsequently tried to harm themselves. I sometimes used that logic in my decisions, especially when I did not have a lot of information about the client.

In retrospect, I can see how this risk-avoidant approach was hardwired into me during my academic training and subsequent early years as a social worker. While weighing the risk of possible legal action is wise, it should not be the sole reason we make clinical decisions. So how do we reconcile these conflicting views?

First, we need to recognize that we do not have complete power, and therefore responsibility, over others: "Although psychotherapists must assume the responsibility to offer competent treatment, no psychotherapist can assume full responsibility for whether a person lives or dies" (Knapp, 2020, p. 20). There are exceptions to this, such as clinicians working in the legal system, with minors, and in other settings that I may be unaware of, but we must remember our limitations. The second thing we need to remember is that it is rare for clinicians to be sued when an outpatient client dies by suicide, as the courts generally recognize that clinicians are unable to control all aspects of a client's life (Knapp, 2020). This does not mean we should be cavalier and unconcerned about possible litigation, but we should not let ourselves become overanxious about it either.

In order for malpractice to be proven, the "Four Ds" of malpractice need to occur (Simon, 1992): duty, deviation from standard of care, damages, and direct harm. The first D is the *duty* of the practitioner in their role with the client. This is where informed consent at the beginning of treatment is important—how is the therapeutic relationship defined, and in the case of malpractice, how did the professional deviate from their duty toward their client? For example, if a client expresses suicidal ideation with a specific plan and intent to act on the plan, the clinician has a duty to respond in a clinically acceptable manner, up to and including hospitalizing the client involuntarily.

The second D is *deviation*, specifically, how did the practitioner deviate from accepted standards of care? Using the example from the previous paragraph, did the clinician engage in further assessment when the client's ideation became clear? Was there safety planning or another intervention utilized to minimize the risk of client self-harm? Or did the clinician utilize strategies or interventions that were not best practices?

The third D is that the client experienced *damage*, in this case injury or death. One could add that damage could also be emotional or traumatic in nature, even if physical injury or death does not occur. The fourth D is that the professional, by their action or lack of action, caused *direct* harm or injury to the client. As Knapp (2020) notes, "The best risk-management strategies avoid harming the patient (nonmaleficence), promote patient well-being (beneficence), involve patients in their treatment (respecting patient autonomy), keep promises to patients (fidelity), and treat patients fairly (justice)" (p. 177).

I recommend the following nine items when assessing how your practice can manage potential liability regarding suicide. I want to be clear that these are my suggestions. I am not an attorney, and I cannot guarantee that if you follow these suggestions you will avoid legal issues should a client die by suicide. You alone are responsible for your work. As such, it is imperative that you continue to learn about suicide and stay up to date on evidence-based practices for working with people at higher risk of suicide.

1. Know the laws, regulations, and best practices for your profession and where you practice.

While we all need to be aware of the ethical principles of our professions, each of us needs to be aware of the laws and regulations in the areas where we practice as well. Some localities have relatively straightforward laws about what professionals are required to report to authorities, while other states are vague about what is required of professionals. There are often different laws that apply to clients who are threatening suicide versus clients who are threatening violence. In my state (the Commonwealth of Virginia), if a client makes a threat of violence to another person, I am required to make a reasonable effort to not only warn the other person but to work with them to develop a means for them to remain safe. In similar situations in other states, professionals are required to notify a government agency (such as the local behavioral health authority), and that entity then works to contact the threatened individual. Regardless of the laws in place in your locality, you must be familiar with them and, obviously, follow them. Remember that ignorance of the law does not grant you immunity from being penalized for failing to follow the letter of the law.

2. Have adequate and appropriate liability insurance.

I recommend becoming informed about your agency's or practice's liability insurance, specifically the parts of it that impact you as a provider. I also recommend carrying your own liability insurance. Many medical insurance providers require empaneled clinicians to have minimal liability insurance, so make sure you have purchased enough insurance to fulfill the requirements of any insurance company you are working with.

3. Regularly review, and modify as necessary, your informed consent.

Review the informed consent with clients before beginning to work with them to ensure that they understand what the informed consent agreement states and that they are competent to provide their own consent. I also recommend that your consent agreement reflects the laws and regulations of your locale that pertain to suicide, violence, and self-injurious behaviors and what you are required to report and what may be protected information. It is best practice to have an attorney review your consent, just to be sure you have covered everything.

4. Conduct a thorough and complete assessment.

Despite knowing that suicide is a possibility in any person, an estimated 30 percent of clinicians fail to regularly ask clients about suicidal behavior (Knapp, 2020). As I made clear in chapter 5, most clinicians begin assessing for suicide by utilizing various screening tools such as the C-SSRS. Remember, though, that screening and assessment are two different processes that are often conflated.

Any suicide screening, even one that does not indicate any suicide risk, should still be followed up by verbal questions about suicidal ideation or any history of suicidal behaviors (Knapp, 2020). If a suicide screen indicates suicide risk, complete a full suicide assessment such as the one included in this book. Take your time in completing this and be aware of the client's body language and other forms of nonverbal communication during this discussion.

5. Implement a safety plan.

If there is any suicide risk, work with your client and someone close to them to develop a realistic safety plan. If the client is unable or unwilling to be a part of this plan, you may need to initiate admission to a psychiatric facility. Safety plans are more than written plans; they are guides for focusing interventions until the client's suicidal ideation has decreased. Thus, safety plans are not static—they should be revisited regularly and changed if circumstances warrant.

6. If acute suicidal risk is present, treat that before treating other things.

One of the main focuses of this book has been to dispel the idea that treating underlying trauma, anxiety, or mood disorders will automatically decrease the client's suicidal ideation. Our focus, if a patient is suicidal, should be on the suicidality itself rather than the underlying mental illness. Consider utilizing the CAMS program, or brief CBT for suicide prevention, both of which I have summarized in this text.

Chapter 11 • Ethical and Legal Issues

7. Even when suicide risk diminishes, continue to reassess regularly.

Our hope is that as we work with clients presenting with suicidal ideation, our interventions will be successful and their suicide risk will diminish. Likewise, we may have a client whose initial presentation did not indicate suicide risk, but we then notice changes in their mood or affect, or some other area of their life. In these situations, the best course of action is to reassess clients who present with major suicide risk factors, even if they deny current suicidal ideation (Knapp, 2020). Remember that it does not hurt to ask.

8. Seek supervision.

Many clinicians see supervision solely as part of their licensure process, but this is a serious mistake. Just as learning does not end when we graduate from a degree program, supervision and the quest to continually improve ourselves is the mark of a competent professional in any field. I believe that should I ever get to the point where I feel I have nothing to learn, I should quit the field. Otherwise, I will have become an incredibly dangerous professional due to arrogance.

Peer supervision can take place in structured settings (involving individual or group supervision) or can be informal. My behavioral health team devotes two hours per month, during which team members can bring challenging situations to the group and we can brainstorm potential interventions. My team also uses this time to address their own feelings of burnout and compassion fatigue and receive encouragement and reminders of how to care for themselves. In addition to making myself available for supervision as much as I can, I also encourage my teammates to seek one another out when needed for supervision.

9. Document, document, document!

Early in my career, I found myself (unwittingly) engaged in quality improvement reviews. What I soon discovered is that practitioners who otherwise engaged in excellent clinical documentation would often drop the ball when documenting crisis situations. This was especially true in situations involving clients who were suicidal. In fact, Knapp (2020) notes that clinicians working with suicidal patients often neglect (or forget) to make note of a client's suicide risk factors in their records. The well-worn adage is important to note here: *If you don't write it down, it never happened!*

What exactly should be documented? At a minimum, the following should be recorded in the client's medical record within 24 hours of client contact:

1. Suicide screening results and an indication that you have seen the results
2. Suicide risk factors and suicide assessment
3. Safety plan, including specific actions to be taken and who is responsible for these actions.
4. Treatment planning, including the utilization of CAMS or another suicide-focused treatment approach
5. Any outside contacts (method used to initiate contact, date, time, and who you contacted)
6. Ongoing monitoring of the client

Jobes (2023) cites several sources to note "it has been argued that 80–90 percent of what determines, in the mind of the attorney, whether a malpractice case should be pursued depends principally on the *quality of the written medical record*" (p. 171). See the medical record as a means to not only document the evidence-based services you have provided to your client, but also as a way to protect yourself.

I want to emphasize that following each of the previous nine steps does not make you immune to being sued. However, doing so demonstrates that you followed best practices to address your client's presenting suicidal issues.

Decision-Making Trees

I am a visual learner, and I like processes, as evidenced by my use of the Swiss Cheese Model to explain the relationships of suicide risk factors. Therefore, I've included a decision-making tree on the next page to help you conceptualize and structure your work with clients who may be suicidal.

Chapter 11 • Ethical and Legal Issues

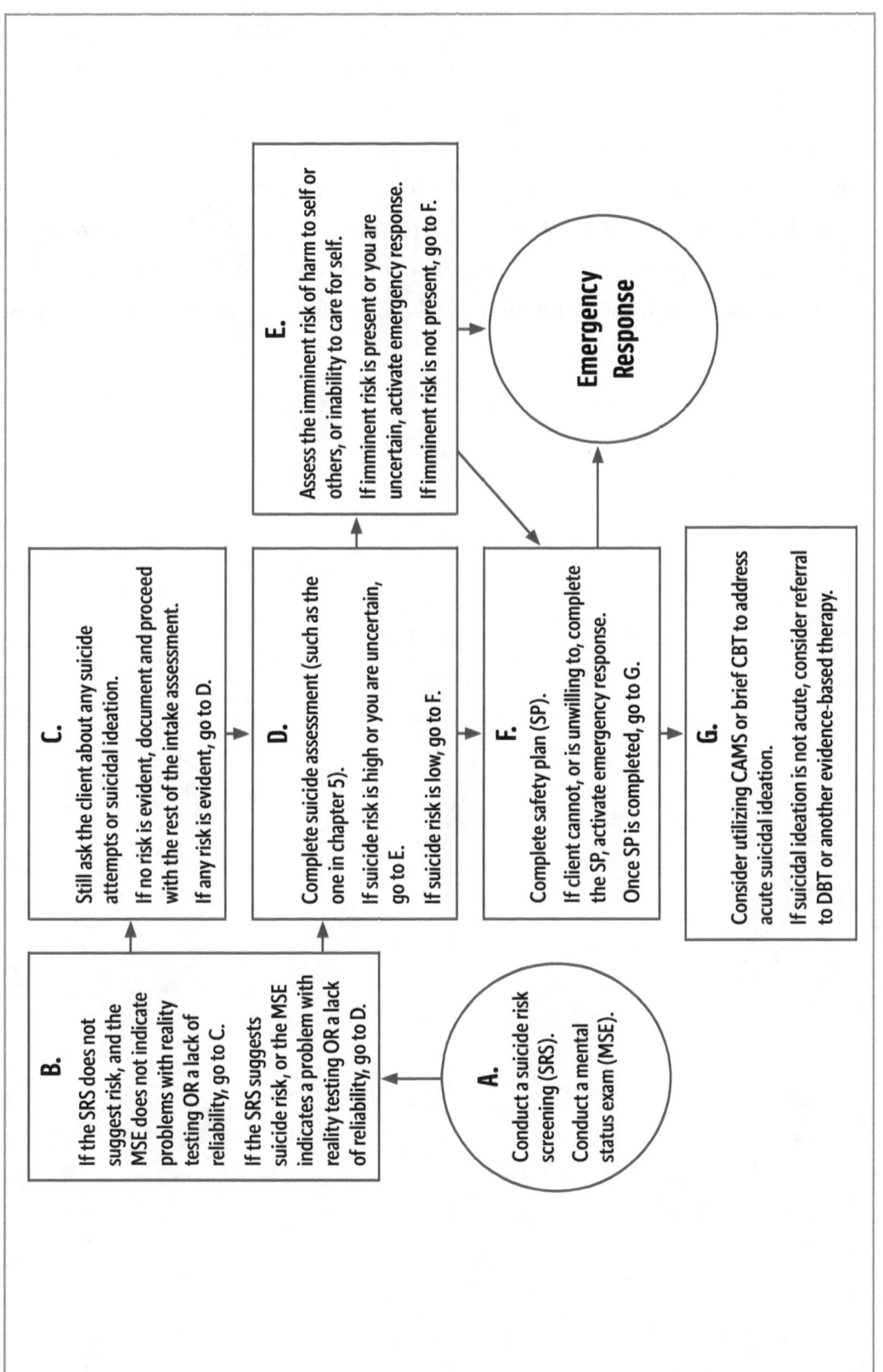

This is not meant to be used as a checklist or as a simplistic way to address (and assess) clients for suicide. There is no one-size-fits-all methodology to work with clients, so it is imperative that if you use this model to structure how you work with clients, you rely on your clinical judgment and ability to connect with individuals to make critical decisions regarding client safety.

In the final chapter of this book, we return to some of the themes introduced in the second chapter: How do we care for others and care for ourselves? This is tough work, and we must be mindful to take care of ourselves and our teammates.

CHAPTER 12

Professional Self-Care, Part 2

At the end of the day, we have done our best as professionals.

We cannot control other people, nor should we try, and we cannot predict future behaviors. At the same time, the actions of our clients, particularly those who attempt or die by suicide, can have a tremendous impact on us. Even in (most) situations where a suicide death or attempt does not occur, working with people in extreme duress who struggle whether "to be, or not to be" is immeasurably taxing to all professionals. In this final chapter, which links to chapter 2, we will come full circle in discussing how we can care for ourselves and our peers as we engage in this difficult work.

Sandford and colleagues (2021) analyzed a variety of studies, seeking to understand how a client's death by suicide impacted practitioners. Not surprisingly, they found that client suicide can have profound emotional aftereffects on a clinician, including grief, guilt, anger, sadness, and shock. In fact, one study found that 10 percent of providers experienced their own suicidal ideation following the suicide death of a client (Castelli Dransart et al., 2015). The impact of a client's death is like other traumatic events and can understandably negatively impact a provider's ability (or willingness) to continue their work. As a result, more preparation should be done to prepare clinicians for the potential suicide death of a patient.

Unfortunately, some studies have found that graduate education programs are inadequate in preparing counselors-in-training to work with people struggling with suicidal ideation, despite many of the trainees being placed in internships that put them face-to-face with clients who are suicidal *before* they have even received basic education about suicide. Perhaps even more troublesome is the fact that when graduate training programs provide this education about suicide theory and assessment, some studies have found that the training itself is often insufficient (Gibbons et al., 2009).

It is not just clinicians in training who need more support—counselors who are actively practicing need support as well. However, this does not always happen for counselors who have a client die by suicide. Sometimes, supervisors can be overly critical or insensitive to a counselor's grief in the wake of a client's suicide. Unfortunately, this can lead to feelings of shame and impact a clinician's view of themselves as competent (Wagner et al., 2020), which underscores the importance of supportive supervision that actively guides clinicians toward managing their grief and caring for themselves. In particular, Wagner and colleagues (2020) note that after a client's suicide death, the following steps can help clinicians cope: "a) facilitated debriefing, b) informal group support, c) individual counseling, d) paid leave of absence, and e) continuing education activities" (p. 251). Informal peer support may be the most helpful (Sandford et al., 2021). We clearly must do more within our professions to take care of one another when a traumatic event, such as a client's death by suicide, occurs. We also need support in situations where we have invested our time and emotional energy into a person.

Ambivalent Endings

When I worked in the emergency department, I was fortunate to get to know a lot of first responders from the various areas our hospitals served. I also got to know a lot of nurses, doctors, and technicians at the various hospitals. I was quickly struck by how many of these people would ask me how patients they had treated earlier were doing. An exchange with a paramedic might go something like this.

Tom is a paramedic who just brought a patient to the emergency department. As he is changing the linens on his gurney, he sees me and calls my name, so I walk over.

ME: Did you bring me someone today?

TOM: Not unless you can treat an 80-year-old who fell and hit their head.

Chapter 12 • Professional Self-Care, Part 2

Me: That's above my pay grade.

Tom: Mine too. I just deliver 'em to y'all. But hey, you remember that 17-year-old female I brought in last week—the one who overdosed?

Me: Yeah, I remember her.

Tom: What happened? Is she okay?

Me: Well, the good thing is, it turned out she hadn't taken very much of what she said she'd taken, so she did not have to be medically admitted. I wound up getting her a bed at the children's hospital downtown in their behavioral health program.

Tom: I'm glad she's okay. We weren't sure what she'd taken or how much. But what happens now?

Me: She's in their program until she's stabilized and then she goes home with follow-up care.

Tom: Don't you ever wonder what happens after that?

Me: I do. But I guess I haven't thought about it too much.

I had conversations like these hundreds of times over 10 years. Before long, I noticed that I was also curious about what happened to the patients I had worked with. Often, I did not know the final outcomes, but it wasn't until years later that I realized this desire to know what happened is common among people in helping professions. It wasn't until 2021, when I was giving my first training with the chaplain and chaplain assistant corps of the US Air Force in Texas, that this really stuck out to me. There were about 40 people present during my two-day training on taking care of ourselves while caring for others. This was an incredible group of dedicated, driven, and inspiring individuals. I was having the most fun I had ever had as a teacher.

About halfway through the second day, the commanding officer of the group, a colonel, pulled me aside.

"I need to talk to my team this afternoon," she said, "and I want you to be here."

"Sure, whatever you need," I replied.

"We've gotten word that the government in Afghanistan is falling, and our troops are going to be pulled out. About half of this group has served in Afghanistan on the ground, and many of them lost friends over there. They're going to have some strong feelings about this."

"Wow," I said. "Please do whatever you need to do, and I'm happy to step out."

"No," she said, "I want you to stay."

"Look," I protested, "I'm a civilian. I never chose to serve, and I don't want to intrude on your time and space."

"You won't," she said firmly. "I just need you to hold space for me and my team as we talk about this."

A week later, while on a brief vacation with my family, my wife remarked that I had returned from Texas seeming distant and distracted. I did my best to explain to her what it was like sitting in that room, trying to be as inconspicuous as possible, while the colonel did some of the most amazing work I had ever seen a caregiver provide for their peers.

The colonel started by explaining the facts. She did this without any judgment or prejudice regarding the political decisions that had been made that resulted in the situation in Afghanistan. She then asked for a show of hands of how many had served in that country—about half the group. The colonel then asked how many had known a service member who had died in Afghanistan, and most of the hands stayed in the air. Then she let them talk.

I firmly believe that our armed forces are populated by many of the best people our country can offer. Within that room were people from many different backgrounds, but they carried the same mission. During the discussion that followed, I watched as exceptional professionals put their emotions out for everyone to see. Some were angry, some sad, a few were ambivalent. Some of them wondered what the purpose had been of being in combat, away from their own families, only for the Afghan government to fall back to Taliban rule. Many of them were worried about the Afghan people they had befriended—what would happen to them as the Taliban resumed control? What also struck me during this time was how individual group members cared for others who were hurting the most. It was humbling and extremely moving to witness this. I thanked the colonel for the opportunity to be a part of it.

Less than a year later, I was again working with the Air Force, and my primary contact was Sally, who was the colonel's assistant. Sally was a master chief in the chaplain assistant corps and supervised many of her peers. Working with Sally for several years was a major highlight of my career as we collaborated on a series of resiliency retreats for chaplain assistants at a base in Florida. During our first retreat, I mentioned the Texas event the previous year. Sally remembered that, and then told me a follow-up story.

Sally was one of the people who took the news in Texas hard because she had completed two tours in Afghanistan and had interacted with a lot of the local population to try to build goodwill. She was worried about how the Taliban and their allies could hurt those people. Several months after the Taliban resumed control of Afghanistan, Sally found herself at a base in Arizona, helping to resettle refugees who had managed to escape Afghanistan.

"It was amazing," she said. "The colonel and I walked onto this plane that was bringing them to the US, and all they had were the clothes they were wearing. They were scared but relieved to have gotten out. I was able to help them begin their lives here, and Paul, I just cried. I finally saw the end of some of the work I had done. I think learning how things end is important."

Taking Sally's story into account, I remembered my earlier interactions with people in the emergency department and I began to wonder about what Sally and I started calling ambiguous endings. Turning to research, I soon found the work of Pauline Boss, which is focused on what she calls ambiguous loss.

Boss (2006) states that ambiguous loss (or endings) is about relationships. Ambiguous loss can occur when the other person is physically absent but still present in our minds, or physically present but psychologically absent—think about a spouse who is living with a partner with advanced dementia who no longer remembers them. Ambiguous loss occurs because "in cultures that value mastery, the goal is to win, not lose. Because of this strong value, there is in our culture a tendency to deny loss. Grieving is acceptable, but we should get over it and get back to work" (Boss, 2006, p. 4). She states that grieving and "reaching closure" are difficult in most losses but are nearly impossible when the loss is ambiguous because there is no official realization that the loss has occurred (e.g., a missing person).

While Boss is focused on loss as it relates to grief, I want to focus on endings—not necessarily related to objective loss. It is this experience of ambiguous endings that often haunts those of us in the helping professions. Therefore, it is important that, whenever we can, we recognize the ambiguous endings that we and our peers often experience and not dismiss them. Listen without judgment. Don't compare your losses to others. Accept that each of us wants to know "What happened?" And when the opportunity presents itself to share information (obviously appropriately and with respect to privacy concerns and client confidentiality), do so. Even learning a little about "how things turned out" can help professionals find renewed purpose in their work and decrease burnout and compassion fatigue.

How Do We Take Care of Ourselves?

My friend Cricket and I have been running buddies for over 10 years. She is full of life and spirit and never complains when she chooses to come back to me because I am running at the very back of our group. The other day she asked me, "How do you not bring your work home with you?"

Thinking for a moment, I replied, "What makes you think I don't?"

Cricket is not the first person to ask me this question, as I've been asked this question many times by supervisees and students. My old answer was to list the things I do to *not* bring what I see at work home to my family. I now realize that while there are things I can do to minimize the impact of what I see at work and how it sticks with me, inevitably, some of it will transfer to my personal life. Therefore, I accept this fact, and I encourage others to accept that we will bring some of our work home with us. But even if we bring a part of our work home, there are things we can do to ameliorate the negative impacts of our work stress.

The first thing we can do is set boundaries. As a supervisor and manager, I explain to my teammates that I expect them to work hard at work, but then go home. I encourage them to take time off whenever they need it and point out that paid time off is something they earn and should use when they see fit. At a previous position I held, several of my teammates wanted me to assign a book for the entire team to read. I responded that I would not ask them to do something outside of work, and if members of the team wanted to form a book club on their own time, then that was their business. At this same agency, when I was being oriented, I was told that I needed to take my laptop home on the weekends in case I wanted to check the electronic medical record. I responded to the head of human resources that I would not do such a thing, as it was not in my job responsibilities, and we were not an agency that kept weekend or holiday hours.

The second thing is to have a life outside of your work. Have hobbies or interests outside of your profession. I am a musician (not a very good one), a gardener, a (slow) runner, and an avid reader. I also enjoy spending time with my family and therefore spend a lot of time watching cross-country meets, basketball games, plays and musicals, and more swim meets than I care to remember. I am a husband, father, and friend *more* than I am a clinical social worker.

The third thing is to take care of all aspects of yourself. Get the sleep you need, try to eat well, and exercise. See your doctor annually and follow their advice for seeking specialist care if needed. Assess your emotional situation, and if needed, seek help for yourself. Nurture your relationships and find ways to create new relationships. If your current relationships are unhealthy, then consider doing what you can to repair them (acknowledging the other person in the relationship will need to do the same), but if the relationship cannot be repaired, then end it. Finally, care for your spiritual self. What is it you believe that is greater than yourself? What gives you purpose in the work you do and the life you live?

Finally, realize that we as professionals and helpers are not above requiring help ourselves. Be mindful of what you are thinking and feeling and recognize when you might benefit from getting help yourself. I look back on my 30-plus years of helping people as a social worker and acknowledge the times when I benefited from therapy for myself. Sometimes the help came from a psychologist, social worker, or counselor, while another time I received help from a pastoral counselor. Each of these individuals helped me address things in my life that needed to be corrected. This was sometimes difficult, painful, and demanding work. However, it not only helped me be a better social worker but, more importantly, a better husband and father.

I believe that each of us are created, unique individuals. None of us are here by accident. I also believe that each of us has a purpose in life, but we may have difficulty understanding this purpose at times. As helpers, we are purveyors of hope. We need to remind ourselves of this, especially during those times when we have to extend our hope and share it with those who lack any hope for themselves.

REFERENCES

For your convenience, purchasers can download and print selected resources from this book at pesipubs.com/managesuicide.

Abbar, M., Demattei, C., El-Hage, W., Llorca, P.-M., Samalin, L., Demaricourt, P., Gaillard, R., Courtet, P., Vaiva, G., Gorwood, P., Fabbro, P., & Jollant, F. (2022). Ketamine for the acute treatment of severe suicidal ideation: Double blind, randomized placebo controlled trial. *The British Medical Journal, 376*, Article e067194. https://doi.org/10.1136/bmj-2021-067194

Abrams, J. J., & Zipper, G. (Producers), & Leckart, S., & Junge, D. (Director). (2020). *Challenger: The final flight* [Video file]. https://www.netflix.com/title/81012137

American Foundation for Suicide Prevention. (2025). *Suicide statistics*. https://afsp.org/suicide-statistics/

American Psychiatric Association. (2013). *Diagnostic and statistical manual of mental disorders, fifth edition*. https://doi.org/10.1176/appi.books.9780890425596

American Psychiatric Association. (2022). *Diagnostic and statistical manual of mental disorders, fifth edition, text revision* (DSM-5-TR). https://doi.org/10.1176/appi.books.9780890425787

Bahji, A., Pierce, M., Wong, J., Roberge, J. N., Ortega, I., & Patten, S. (2021). Comparative efficacy and acceptability of psychotherapies for self-harm and suicidal behavior among children and adolescents: A systematic review and network meta-analysis. *JAMA Network Open, 4*(4), Article e216614. https://doi.org/10.1001/jamanetworkopen.2021.6614

Baldessarini, R. J. (2020). Epidemiology of suicide: Recent developments. *Epidemiology and Psychiatric Sciences, 29*, Article e71. https://doi.org/10.1017/S2045796019000672

Baldessarini, R. J., Tondo, L., Pinna, M., Nuñez, N., & Vázquez, G. H. (2019). Suicidal risk factors in major affective disorders. *British Journal of Psychiatry, 215*(4), 621–626. https://doi.org/10.1192/bjp.2019.167

Bartl, G., Stuart, R., Ahmed, N., Saunders, K., Loizou, S., Brady, G., Gray, H., Grundy, A., Jeynes, T., Nyikavaranda, P., Persaud, K., Raad, A., Foye, U., Simpson, A., Johnson, S., & Lloyd-Evans, B. (2024). A qualitative meta-synthesis of service users' and carers' experiences of assessment and involuntary hospital admissions under mental health legislations: A five-year update. *BMC Psychiatry, 24*, Article 476. https://doi.org/10.1186/s12888-024-05914-w

Beck, A. T., Ward, C. H., Mendelson, M., Mock, J., & Erbauch, J. (1961). *Beck Depression Inventory (BDI)* [Database record]. APA PsycTests. https://doi.org/10.1037/t00741-000

Bellairs-Walsh, I., Perry, Y., Krysinska, K., Byrne, S. J., Boland, A., Michail, M., Lamblin, M., Gibson, K. L., Lin, A., Yutong Li, T., Hetrick, S., & Robinson, J. (2020). Best practice when working with suicidal behaviour and self-harm in primary care: A qualitative exploration of young people's perspectives. *BMJ Open, 10*, Article e038855. https://doi.org/10.1136/bmjopen-2020-038855

Bender, T. W., Fitzpatrick, S., Hartmann, M., Hames, J., Bodell, L., Selby, E. A., & Joiner, T. E. (2019). Does it hurt to ask? An analysis of iatrogenic risk during suicide risk assessment. *Neurology, Psychiatry and Brian Research, 33*, 73–81. https://doi.org/10.1016/j.npbr.2019.07.005

Bjureberg, J., Dahlin, M., Carlborg, A., Edberg, H., Haglund, A., & Runeson, B. (2022). Columbia-Suicide Severity Rating Scale Screen Version: Initial screening for suicide risk in a psychiatric emergency department. *Psychological Medicine, 52*(16), 3904–3912. https://doi.org/10.1017/S0033291721000751

Black, D. W., Blum, N., Pfohl, B., & Hale, N. (2004). Suicidal behavior in borderline personality disorder: prevalence, risk factors, prediction, and prevention. *Journal of Personality Disorders, 18*(3), 226–239. https://doi.org/10.1521/pedi.18.3.226.35445

Blanchard, M., & Farber, B. A. (2018). "It is never okay to talk about suicide": Patients' reasons for concealing suicidal ideation in psychotherapy. *Psychotherapy Research, 30*(1), 124–136. https://doi.org/10.1080/10503307.2018.1543977

Boss, P. (2006). *Loss, trauma, and resilience: Therapeutic work with ambiguous loss.* W. W. Norton & Company.

Brasler, P. (2019). *High risk clients: Evidence-based assessment & clinical tools to recognize and effectively respond to mental health crises.* PESI Publishing.

Brasler, P. (2022). *The clinician's guide to substance use disorders: Practical tools for assessment, treatment & recovery.* PESI Publishing.

Brown, L. A., Boudreaux, E. D., Arias, S. A., Miller, I. W., May, A. M., Camargo, C. A., Bryan, C. J., & Armey, M. F. (2020). C-SSRS performance in emergency department patients at high risk for suicide. *Suicide and Life Threatening Behavior, 50*(6), 1097–1104. https://doi.org/10.1111/sltb.12657

Bryan, C. J. (2022). *Rethinking suicide: Why prevention fails, and how we can do better.* Oxford University Press.

Bryan, C. J., & Rudd, M. D. (2018). *Brief cognitive-behavioral therapy for suicide prevention.* Guilford Press.

Campbell-Stills, L., Stein, M. B., Liu, H., Agtarap, S., Heeringa, S. G., Nock, M. K., Ursano, R. J., & Kessler, R. C. (2020). Associations of lifetime traumatic brain injury characteristics with prospective suicide attempt among deployed US army soldiers. *Journal of Head Trauma Rehabilitation, 35*(1), 14–26. https://doi.org/10.1097/HTR.0000000000000516

Carson, L. M., Marsh, S. M., Brown, M. M., Elkins, K. L., & Tiesman, H. M. (2023). An analysis of suicides among first responders—Findings from the National Violent Death Reporting System, 2015–2017. *Journal of Safety Research, 85*, 361–370. https://doi.org/10.1016/j.jsr.2023.04.003

Castelli Dransart, D. A., Heeb, J. L., Gulfi, A., & Gutjahr, E. M. (2015). Stress reactions after a patient suicide and their relations to the profile of mental health professionals. *BMC Psychiatry, 15*, Article 265. https://doi.org/10.1186/s12888-015-0655-y

CDC National Center for Health Statistics. (2024, October 2). *Suicide and self-harm injury.* https://www.cdc.gov/nchs/fastats/suicide.htm

CDC Newsroom. (2023, August 10). Provisional suicide deaths in the United States, 2022. [Media statement]. https://www.cdc.gov/media/releases/2023/s0810-US-Suicide-Deaths-2022.html

CDC Suicide Prevention. (2025, March 26). *Suicide data and statistics.* https://www.cdc.gov/suicide/facts/data.html

References

Conwell, Y. (2016, April 22). *The four D's of suicide risk in older adults* [Video]. Washington Post. https://www.washingtonpost.com/video/national/the-four-ds-of-suicide-risk-in-older-adults/2016/04/22/012688a0-08a1-11e6-bfed-ef65dff5970d_video.html

Cureton, J. L., Clemens, E. V., Henninger, J., & Couch, C. (2021). Readiness of counselor education and supervision for suicide training: A CQR Study. *Journal of Counselor Preparation and Supervision, 14*(3), Article 1. https://research.library.kutztown.edu/cgi/viewcontent.cgi?article=1461&context=jcps

Danzer, G. S. (2019). *Therapist self-disclosure: An evidence-based guide for practitioners.* Routledge.

DeCou, C. R., Comtois, K. A., & Landes, S. J. (2019). Dialectical behavior therapy is effective for the treatment of suicidal behavior: A meta-analysis. *Behavior Therapy, 50*(1), 60–72. https://doi.org/10.1016/j.beth.2018.03.009

De Leo, D. (2022). Late-life suicide in an aging world. *Nature Aging, 2,* 7–12. https://doi.org/10.1038/s43587-021-00160-1

DeSteno, D. (2021). *How God works: The science behind the benefits of religion.* Simon & Schuster.

Dingfelder, S. F. (2009). The military's war on stigma. *Monitor on Psychology, 40*(6), 52. https://www.apa.org/monitor/2009/06/stigma-war

Dolgoff, R., Loewenberg, F. M., & Harrington, D. (2005). *Ethical decisions for social work practice* (7th ed.). Thomson Brooks/Cole.

Drew, B. L. (2001). Self-harm behavior and no-suicide contracting in psychiatric inpatient settings. *Archives of Psychiatric Nursing, 15*(3), 99–106. https://www.psychiatricnursing.org/article/S0883-9417(01)86483-9/abstract

Durkheim, E. (2007). *On suicide.* (R. Buss, Trans.). Penguin Classics. (Original work published 1897)

Ellis, T. E., & Newman, C. F. (1996). *Choosing to live: How to defeat suicide through cognitive therapy.* New Harbinger Publications.

Falke, K., & Goldberg, J. (2018). *Struggle well: Thriving in the aftermath of trauma.* Lioncrest Publishing.

Fehling, K. B., & Selby, E. A. (2021). Suicide in DSM-5: Current evidence for the proposed suicide behavior disorder and other possible improvements. *Frontiers in Psychiatry, 11,* Article 499980. https://doi.org/10.3389/fpsyt.2020.499980

Figley, C. (2002). Compassion fatigue: Psychotherapists' chronic lack of self care. *Journal of Clinical Psychology, 58*(11), 1433–1441. https://doi.org/10.1002/jclp.10090

Frances, A. (2013). *Essentials of psychiatric diagnosis: Responding to the challenge of DSM-5.* Guilford Press.

Fruhbauerova, M., & Comtois, K. A. (2019). Addiction counselors and suicide: Education and experience do not improve suicide knowledge, beliefs, or confidence in treating suicidal clients. *Journal of Substance Abuse Treatment, 106,* 29–34. https://doi.org/10.1016/j.jsat.2019.08.012

Garvey, K. A., Penn, J. V., Campbell, A. L., Esposito-Smythers, C., & Spirito, A. (2009). Contracting for safety with patients: Clinical practice and forensic implications. *Journal of the American Academy Psychiatry Law, 37*(3), 363–370. https://pubmed.ncbi.nlm.nih.gov/19767501/

Gibbons, M. M., Spurgeon, S., & Studer, J. R. (2009). Essential knowledge and skills for suicide lethality assessment. *Tennessee Counseling Association Journal, 3*(1), 3–11.

Haidt, J. (2024). *The anxious generation: How the great rewiring of childhood is causing an epidemic of mental illness.* Penguin Press.

Hernandez-Bustamante, M., Cjuno, J., Hernández, R. M., & Ponce-Meza, J. C. (2023). Efficacy of dialectical behavior therapy in the treatment of borderline personality disorder: A systematic review of randomized controlled trials. *Iran Journal of Psychiatry, 19*(1), 119–129. https://doi.org/10.18502/ijps.v19i1.14347

Horan, K. A., Marks, M., Ruiz, J., Bowers, C., & Cunningham, A. (2021). Here for my peer: The future of first responder mental health. *International Journal of Environmental Research and Public Health, 18*(21), Article 11097. https://doi.org/10.3390/ijerph182111097

Hughes, J. L., Horowitz, L. M., Ackerman, J. P., Adrian, M. C., Campo, J. V., Stulman, H. R., & Bridge, J. A. (2023). Suicide in young people: Screening, risk assessment, and intervention. *The British Medical Journal, 381*, Article e070630. https://doi.org/10.1136/bmj-2022-070630

Jobes, D. A. (2023). *Managing suicidal risk, third edition: A collaborative approach.* Guilford Press.

Jobes, D. A., Comtois, K. A., Gutierrez, P. M., Brenner, L. A., Huh, D., Chalker, S. A., Ruhe, G., Kerbrat, A. H., Atkins, D. C., Jennings, K., Crumlish, J., Corona, C. D., O'Connor, S., Hendricks, K. E., Schembari, B., Singer, B., & Crow, B. (2017). A randomized controlled trial of the collaborative assessment and management of suicidality versus enhanced care as usual with suicidal soldiers. *Psychiatry, 80*(4), 339–356. https://doi.org/10.1080/00332747.2017.1354607

Joiner, T. (2007). *Why people die by suicide.* Harvard University Press.

Katz, C., Bolton, J., & Sareen, J. (2016). The prevalence rates of suicide are likely underestimated worldwide: Why it matters. *Social Psychiatry and Psychiatric Epidemiology, 51*, 125–127. https://doi.org/10.1007/S00127-015-1158-3

Katz, I. R., Rogers, M. P., Lew, R., Thwin, S. S., Doros, G., Ahearn, E., Ostacher, M. J., DeLisi, L. E., Smith, E. G., Ringer, R. J., Ferguson, R., Hoffman, B., Kaufman, J. S., Paik, J. M., Conrad, C. H., Holmberg, E. F., Boney, T. Y., Huang, G. D., Liang, M. H., & Li+ plus Investigators. (2022). Lithium treatment in the prevention of repeat suicide-related outcomes in veterans with major depression or bipolar disorder: A randomized clinical trial. *JAMA Psychiatry, 79*(1), 24–32. https://doi.org/10.1001/jamapsychiatry.2021.3170

Keltner, D. (2023). *Awe: The new science of everyday wonder and how it can transform your life.* Penguin Press.

Klonsky, E. D., & May, A. M. (2015). The Three-Step Theory (3ST): A new theory of suicide rooted in the "ideation-to-action" framework. *International Journal of Cognitive Therapy, 8*(2), 114–129. https://doi.org/10.1521/ijct.2015.8.2.114

Knapp, S. J. (2020). *Suicide prevention: An ethically and scientifically informed approach.* American Psychological Association.

Kothgassner, O. D., Goreis, A., Robinson, K., Huscsava, M. M., Schmahl, C., & Plener, P. L. (2021). Efficacy of dialectical behavior therapy for adolescent self-harm and suicidal ideation: A systematic review and meta-analysis. *Psychological Medicine, 51*(7), 1057–1067. https://doi.org/10.1017/S0033291721001355

Kroenke, K., Spitzer, R. L., & Williams, J. B. W. (1999). *Patient Health Questionnaire-9 (PHQ-9)* [Database record]. APA PsycTests. https://doi.org/10.1037/t06165-000

Linehan, M. M. (2015). *DBT skills training manual* (2nd ed.). Guilford Press.

Lyra, R. L., McKenzie, S. K., Every-Palmer, S., & Jenkin, G. (2021). Occupational exposure to suicide: A review of research on the experiences of mental health professionals and first responders. *PLoS one, 16*(4), Article e0251038. https://doi.org/10.1371/journal.pone.0251038

References

Madsen, T., Erlangsen, A., Orlovska, S., Mofaddy, R., Nordentoft, M., & Benros, M. E. (2018). Association between traumatic brain injury and risk of suicide. *JAMA, 320*(6), 580–588. https://doi.org/10.1001/jama.2018.10211

Maris, R. W. (2019). *Suicidology: A comprehensive biopsychosocial perspective.* Guilford Press.

Mayo, D. J. (1992). What is being predicted? The definition of "suicide." In R. W. Maris, A. L. Berman, J. T. Maltsberger, & R. I. Yufit (Eds.), *Assessment and prediction of suicide* (pp. 88–101). Guilford Press.

McAdams, C. R. III, & Foster, V. A. (2000). Client suicide: Its frequency and impact on counselors. *Journal of Mental Health Counseling, 22*(2), 107–121.

Menninger, K. (1938). *Man against himself.* Harcourt Brace, Brace & World.

Michaud, L., Greenway, K. T., Corbeil, S., Bourquin, C., & Richard-Devantoy, S. (2023). Countertransference towards suicidal patients: A systematic review. *Current Psychology, 42*, 416–430. https://doi.org/10.1007/S12144-021-01424-0

Miller, R. (2022). *The space shuttle: A mission-by-mission celebration of NASA's extraordinary spaceflight program.* Artisan.

Moncrieff, J., & Plöderl, M. (2024, July 13). *Desperate measures: Ghaemi's response to our review of lithium and suicide prevention.* Mad in America. https://madinamerica.com/2024/07/desperate-measures-ghaemi-lithium/

Moutier, C. Y., Pisani, A. R., & Stahl, S. M. (2021). *Suicide prevention.* Cambridge University Press.

Mueller, A. S., Abrutyn, S., Pescosolido, B., & Diefendorf, S. (2021). The social roots of suicide: Theorizing how the external social world matters to suicide and suicide prevention. *Frontiers in Psychology, 12*, Article 621569. https://doi.org/10.3389/fpsyg.2021.621569

National Association of Social Workers. (2021). Code of Ethics of the National Association of Social Workers. https://www.socialworkers.org/About/Ethics/Code-of-Ethics/Code-of-Ethics-English

Newell, J. M., & MacNeil, G. A. (2010). Professional burnout, vicarious trauma, secondary traumatic stress, and compassion fatigue: A review of theoretical terms, risk factors, and preventive methods for clinicians and researchers. *Best Practices in Mental Health, 6*(2), 57–68.

Niederkrontenthaler, T., Braun, M., Pirkis, J., Till, B., Stack, S., Sinyor, M., Tran, U. S., Voracek, M., Cheng, Q., Arendt, F., Scherr, S., Yip, P. S. F., & Spittal, M. J. (2020). Association between suicide reporting in the media and suicide: Systematic review and meta-analysis. *British Medical Journal, 368*, Article m575. https://doi.org/10.1136/bmj.m575

Nock, M. K., Millner, A. J., Ross, E. L., Kennedy, C. J., Al-Suwaidi, M., Barak-Corren, Y., Castro, V. M., Castro-Ramirez, F., Lauricella, T., Murman, N., Petukhova, M., Bird, S. A., Reis, B., Smoller, J. W., & Kessler, R. C. (2022). Prediction of suicide attempts using clinician assessment, patient self-report, and electronic health records. *JAMA Network Open, 5*(1), Article e2144373. https://doi.org/10.1001/jamanetworkopen.2021.44373

O'Connor, R. C. (2011). Towards an integrated motivational-volitional model of suicidal behaviour. In R. C. O'Connor, S. Platt, & J. Gordon (Eds.), *International handbook of suicide prevention: Research, policy and practice* (pp. 181–198). John Wiley & Sons, Ltd. https://doi.org/10.1002/9781119998556.ch11

Olfson, M., Stroup, T. S., Huang, C., Wall, M. M., Crystal, S., & Gerhard, T. (2021). Suicide risk in Medicare patients with schizophrenia across the life span. *JAMA Psychiatry, 78*(8), 876–885. https://doi.org/10.1001/jamapsychiatry.2021.0841

Peck, M. S. (1998). *People of the lie: The hope for healing human evil.* Touchstone.

Pines, R., Giles, H., & Watson, B. (2021). Managing patient aggression in healthcare: Initial testing of a communication accommodation theory intervention. *Psychology of Language and Communication, 25*(1), 62–81. https://doi.org/10.2478/plc-2021-0004

Posner, K. (2007). *Columbia-Suicide Severity Rating Scale (C-SSRS)* [Database record]. APA PsycTests. https://doi.org/10.1037/t52667-000

Quinnett, P. G. (2023). The certified QPR Pathfinder Training Program: A description of a novel public health gatekeeper training program to mitigate suicidal ideation and suicide deaths. *Journal of Prevention, 44*, 813–824. https://doi.org/10.1007/s10935-023-00748-w

Ramchand, R., Gordon, J. A., & Pearson, J. L. (2021). Trends in suicide rates by race and ethnicity in the United States. *JAMA Network Open, 4*(5), Article e2111563. https://doi.org/10.1001/jamanetworkopen.2021.11563

Ribeiro, J. D., Franklin, J. C., Fox, K. R., Bentley, K. H., Kleiman, E. M., Chang, B. P., & Nock, M. K. (2016). Self-injurious thoughts and behaviors as risk factors for future suicide ideation, attempts, and death: A meta-analysis of longitudinal studies. *Psychological Medicine, 46*(2), 225–236. https://doi.org/10.1017/S0033291715001804

Rogers, M. L., Chu, C., & Joiner, T. (2019). The necessity, validity, and clinical utility of a new diagnostic entity: Acute suicidal affective disturbance. *Journal of Clinical Psychology, 75*(6), 999–1010. https://doi.org/10.1002/jclp.22743

Rozek, D. C., Tyler, H., Fina, B. A., Baker, S. N., Moring, J. C., Smith, N. B., Baker, J. C., Bryan, A. O., Bryan, C. J., & Dondanville, K. A. (2023). Suicide intervention practices: What is being used by mental health clinicians and mental health allies? *Archives of Suicide Research, 27*(3), 1034–1046. https://doi.org/10.1080/13811118.2022.2106923

Rudd, M. D. (2006). Fluid vulnerability theory: A cognitive approach to understanding the process of acute and chronic suicide risk. In T. E. Ellis (Ed.), *Cognition and suicide: Theory, research, and therapy* (pp. 355–368). American Psychological Association. https://psycnet.apa.org/doiLanding?doi=10.1037%2F11377-016

Ryan, E. P., & Oquendo, M. A. (2020). Suicide risk assessment and prevention: Challenges and opportunities. *Focus, 18*(2), 88–99. https://doi.org/10.1176/appi.focus.20200011

Sandford, D. M., Kirtley, O. J., Thwaites, R., & O'Connor, R. C. (2021). The impact on mental health practitioners of the death of a patient by suicide: A systematic review. *Clinical Psychology & Psychotherapy, 28*(2), 261–294. https://doi.org/10.1002/cpp.2515

Schwartz, B. (2019, July 21). *The Swiss cheese model: Designing to reduce catastrophic losses*. Engineering for Humans. https://www.engineeringforhumans.com/systems-engineering/the-swiss-cheese-model-designing-to-reduce-catastrophic-losses

Schwartz, R. C. (2021). *No bad parts: Healing trauma & restoring wholeness with the internal family systems model*. Sounds True.

Shah, A., Bhat, R., Zarate-Escudero, S., DeLeo, D., & Erlangsen, A. (2016). Suicide rates in five-year age-bands after the age of 60 years: The international landscape. *Aging & Mental Health, 20*(2), 131–138. http://dx.doi.org/10.1080/13607863.2015.1055552

Shahram, S. Z., Smith, M. L., Ben-David, S., Fedderson, M., Kemp, T. E., & Plamondon, K. (2021). Promoting "zest for life": A systematic literature review of resiliency factors to prevent youth suicide. *Journal of Research on Adolescence, 31*(1), 4–24. https://doi.org/10.1111/jora.12588

Shneidman, E. (1985). *Definition of suicide*. Wiley-Interscience.

References

Shneidman, E. S. (1987). A psychological approach to suicide. In G. R. VandenBos & B. K. Bryant (Eds.), *Cataclysms, crises, and catastrophes: Psychology in action* (pp. 147–183). American Psychological Association. https://doi.org/10.1037/11106-004

Simon, R. I. (1992). *Clinical psychiatry and the law* (2nd ed.). American Psychiatric Press, Inc.

Skovholt, T. I., & Trotter-Mathison, M. (2016). *The resilient practitioner: Burnout and compassion fatigue prevention and self-care strategies for the helping professions* (3rd ed.). Routledge.

Toomey, R. B., Syvertsen, A. K., & Shramko, M. (2018). Transgender adolescent suicide behavior. *Pediatrics, 142*(4), Article e20174218. https://doi.org/10.1542/peds.2017-4218

Torregrossa, W., Raciti, L., Rifici, C., Rizzo, G., Raciti, G., Casella, C., Naro, A., & Calabro, R. S. (2023). Behavioral and psychiatric symptoms in patients with severe traumatic brain injury: A comprehensive overview. *Biomedicines, 11*(5), Article 1449. https://doi.org/10.3390/biomedicines11051449

Turco, S., Gori, F., Papi, L., Dell'Osso, L., Carpita, B., Maiese, A., Turillazzi, E., & Di Paolo, M. (2022). Is healthcare responsibility in patients' suicide provable beyond all reasonable doubt? An analysis of preventing strategies and medical liability through a case series. *Clinical Neuropsychiatry, 19*(5), 307–313. https://doi.org/10.36131/cnfioritieditore20220506

US Department of Veterans Affairs, Office of Mental Health and Suicide Prevention. (2023). *National Veteran Suicide Prevention Annual Report.* https://www.mentalhealth.va.gov/docs/data-sheets/2023/2023-National-Veteran-Suicide-Prevention-Annual-Report-FINAL-508.pdf

Van Dernoot Lipsky, L. (2009). *Trauma stewardship: An everyday guide to caring for self while caring for others.* Berrett-Koehler Publishers, Inc.

VandenBos, G. R. (Ed.). (2013). *APA dictionary of clinical psychology.* American Psychological Association. https://doi.org/10.1037/13945-000

Vigil, N. H., Beger, S., Gochenour, K. S., Frazier, W. H., Vadeboncoeur, T. F., & Bobrow, B. J. (2021). Suicide among the EMS occupation in the United States. *Western Journal of Emergency Medicine: Integrating Emergency Care with Population Health, 22*(2), 326–332. https://doi.org/10.5811/westjem.2020.10.48742

Viottini, E., Politano, G., Fornero, G., Pavanelli, P. L., Borelli, P., Bonaudo, M., & Gianino, M. M. (2020). Determinants of aggression against all health care workers in a large-sized university hospital. *BMC Health Services Research, 20*, Article 215. https://doi.org/10.1186/s12913-020-05084-x

Wagner, N. J., Grunhaus, C. M. L., & Tuazon, V. E. (2020). Agency responses to counselor survivors of client suicide. *The Professional Counselor, 10*(2), 251–265. https://doi.org/10.15241/njw.10.2.251

Wasserman, D., Carli, V., Iosue, M., Javed, A., & Herrman, H. (2021). Suicide prevention in childhood and adolescence: A narrative review of current knowledge on risk and protective factors and effectiveness of interventions. *Asia-Pacific Psychiatry, 13*(3), Article e12452. https://doi.org/10.1111/appy.12452

Wolfson, P., & Hartelius, G. (Eds.). (2016). *The ketamine papers: Science, therapy, and transformation.* Multidisciplinary Association for Psychedelic Studies (MAPS).

Zhong, S., Senior, M., Yu, R., Perry, A., Hawton, K., Shaw, J., & Fazel, S. (2021). Risk factors for suicide in prisons: A systematic review and meta-analysis. *The Lancet Public Health, 6*(3), e164–e174. https://doi.org/10.1016/S2468-2667(20)30233-4

ACKNOWLEDGMENTS

I want to thank God for my life and the opportunities given to me.

To Claire, my beautiful wife. I'm so happy to walk through life with you. Thank you for saying yes when I first asked you out at the beginning of 2002, even though I nearly blew it.

My sons: Sam, Ben, and Eli. I am so honored and humbled to be your father.

My brothers, Kevin and Greg, for being awesome husbands and fathers (and brothers). I think Mom is smiling down on us.

To Dad: Thanks for living the adage of "in sickness and in health."

The Gibsons (Kevin, Manda, Peter, and Lucy) for your eternal friendship and our annual adventures in the mountains.

Blackhearts (RVA)—keep on running.

My late running buddy, Jill. I think it's awesome our boys run together!

All Souls Anglican Church in Richmond, especially the leadership of Danny and David.

My teammates at the Chesterfield County Employee Behavioral Health Program, Employee Medical Center, Human Resources, and our excellent first responders and human-services providers. I am honored to work with you and appreciate your dedication to serving our community.

The great staff and community members at CARITAS, who serve selflessly and humbly.

Dr. Randy and the wonderful staff (past and present) at Alchemy Wellness.

Dr. Mark Miller for his enduring friendship.

Kate Sample, Roseanne Cheng, Dr. Jenessa Jackson, and the rest of the team at PESI. Thank you all (especially Kate) for believing in my contributions throughout the years and for your belief in this project. Thank you, Dr. Jackson, for being an exceptional editor.

ABOUT THE AUTHOR

Paul Brasler, LCSW, CAIMHP, became a licensed clinical social worker in 2002. In addition to writing and teaching, Paul is the head of the Employee Behavioral Health Program for Chesterfield County, Virginia, where he and his teammates provide services to first responders and other county employees. Paul has extensive experience working with people in crisis and people living with substance use and co-occurring disorders across various settings, including adolescent residential treatment, community mental health settings, hospital emergency departments, juvenile drug court, ketamine-assisted therapy, and private practice.

Paul has been a PESI national presenter since 2016, and he has taught classes on mental health emergencies, high-risk clients, resiliency, and substance use disorders. He has written two books: *The Clinician's Guide to Substance Use Disorders* and *High Risk Clients*. Paul lives in Richmond, Virginia, with his beautiful wife, three sons (one currently away at college), a cowardly dog, and two dwarf rabbits who are quietly plotting to destroy the world.